ALBANIA

DK
ALBANIA

CONTENTS

DISCOVER 6

EXPERIENCE 60

NEED TO KNOW 186

Left: Traditional Albanian slippers
Previous pages: Rooftops of Krujë
Front cover: The scenic port of Sarandë

DISCOVER

The town and beaches of Ksamil

WELCOME TO ALBANIA

Relaxing on beautiful beaches and hiking along rugged mountain paths. Wandering through vibrant, historic cities and exploring ancient archaeological sites. Enjoying delicious local dishes and even better local drinks. Whatever your dream trip to Albania includes, this DK travel guide is the perfect companion.

1

2

3

4

1 Ancient ruins in Butrint National Park.

2 Performing folk dances in Tirana.

3 White-water rafting.

4 Historic streets of the city of Gjirokastër in Southern Albania.

Sprawled along the blue waters of the Adriatic and Ionian seas, and with epic mountain ranges farther inland, Albania packs in a huge variety for a country of its size. There are countless beautiful freshwater spots to enjoy, from the tranquil Shkodër Lake in the north to the gushing waters of the Vjosa River in the south. And, of course, there is no shortage of stellar beaches to choose from either, with the Albanian Riviera's breathtaking stretches of coast helping to make it a major emerging tourism destination.

Beyond the rural and natural, Albania's cities and towns are hubs of tradition, history and culture. Many conquerors made their way to these parts over time, leaving behind endless ancient ruins like those in Butrint and Apollonia, as well as distinctive architectural styles and cultural legacies throughout the towns and cities. These varied influences come together best in cities like Gjirokastër, a centre of food and folk traditions, full of Ottoman-style houses, and Shkodër, whose Venetian past is evident in its atmospheric old bazaar.

Albania is home to such a great variety of sights that it can be hard to know where to start. We've broken the country down into easily navigable chapters, with detailed itineraries, expert local knowledge and colourful, comprehensive maps to help you plan the perfect trip. Whether you're staying for the weekend or longer, this DK travel guide will ensure that you see the best of this spectacular country. Enjoy the book, and enjoy Albania.

REASONS TO LOVE ALBANIA

Stunning coastlines beside clear seas, pristine nature with plentiful wildlife and mountain villages where tradition thrives. There are endless reasons to love Albania, but here are some of our favourites.

1 BEAUTIFUL BEACHES

Albania's coast along the Adriatic and Ionian seas is graced with varied beaches: pebbled, sandy, backed by mountains and more. And, wherever you find yourself, the water is clear and blue.

GJIROKASTËR *2*

Crowned with a sprawling medieval castle and home to an old Ottoman bazaar, it's no wonder Gjirokastër *(p154)* has attracted poets, scholars and musicians over the centuries.

3 ALBANIAN HOSPITALITY

There's nothing quite like an Albanian welcome. It's customary for family-run guesthouses and homestays to treat guests to local delicacies and homemade treats.

BERAT 4

Known as the "City of a Thousand Windows", Berat *(p162)* showcases Albania's Ottoman heritage in its beautiful UNESCO-protected streets.

ALBANIAN ALPS 5

Jutting out between the Albanian and Montenegrin border are the jagged peaks of the Albanian Alps. Visit for quiet hiking and picturesque villages.

COFFEE CULTURE 6

Coffee culture is deeply entrenched in Albanian culture. You're never far from somewhere to enjoy a traditionally brewed *kavhe* (coffee).

CAPTIVATING CASTLES 7

A land fought over by many, Albania is littered with old fortifications. Krujë Castle *(p108)* withstood Ottoman sieges, while Porto Palermo Castle *(p140)* was later used as a defence by Ottoman Ali Pasha.

STUNNING RIVERS AND SPRINGS 8

Glacial rivers cut through Albania, like the wild Vjosa *(p166)*. Blue Eye springs *(p28)* and Komani Lake *(p98)*, meanwhile, are vivid spots of blue and green on the landscape.

9 FOLK TRADITIONS

Villages and towns all have their own set of centuries-old folk traditions. Learn more at ethnographic museums or look out for events with traditional music and singing.

10 HIKING TRAILS

Hiking routes snake their way across the best of Albania. Set off on mountainous paths like the Theth to Valbonë trail *(p92)* or seaside routes like the Southern Coastal Trail *(p40)*.

UNDERGROUND HISTORIES 11

Concrete bunkers dotting the landscape are a legacy of Albania's communist past. Step inside one of the underground structures, like Bunk'Art *(p66)* in Tirana, to learn more.

BUTRINT 12

The stellar ancient ruins of Butrint *(p116)* are well preserved. Come face to face with thousands of years of power struggles, invasions and innovation among its remains.

EXPLORE ALBANIA

This guide divides Albania into four colour-coded sightseeing areas: Tirana, Northern Albania, the Albanian Riviera and Southern Albania, as shown on this map. Find out more about each area on the following pages.

MONTENEGRO
Gropat e Selcës
Podgorica
Theth
Koplik
Skhodër Lake
Boric I Math
Shkodër
Komani Lake
Ulcinj
Shëngjin
Lezhë
Rubik
Milot
Laç
Kep i Rodonit
Krujë
Fushë-Krujë
Vorë
Kamez
Shijak
TIRANA
p62
Durrës
Adriatic Sea
Kavaja
Rrogozhinë
Peqin
Divjakë
Karavasta Bay
Lushnja
THE ALBANIAN RIVIERA
p112
Fier
Roskovec
Patos
Novosele
Ballsh
Selenicë
Vlorë
Cape Gjuhëza
Dukat Bay
Orikum
Dukat
Dhërmi
Himarë
Qeparo

LOCATOR MAP

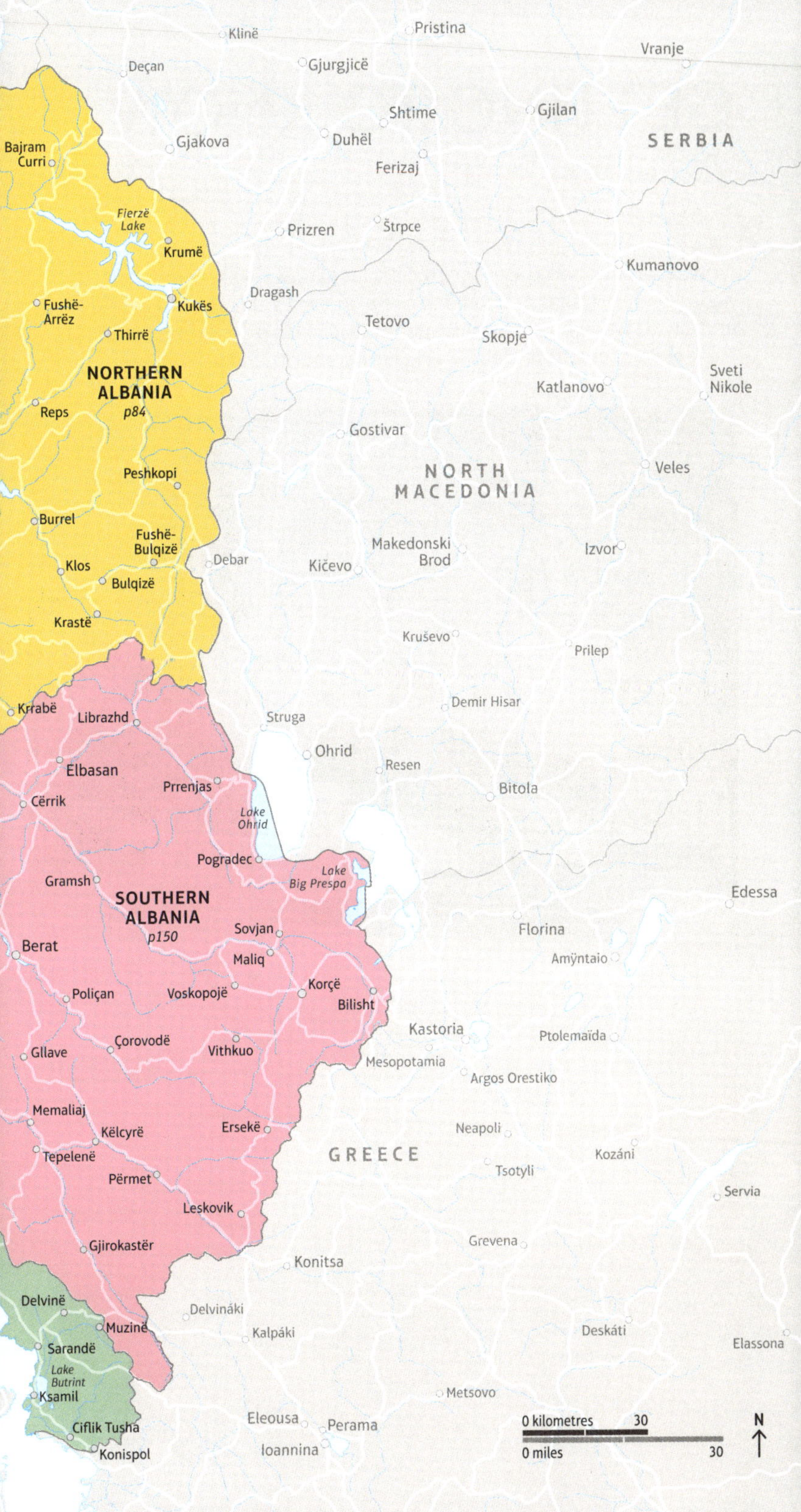

Klinë
Pristina
Deçan
Gjurgjicë
Vranje
Shtime
Gjilan
Bajram Curri
Gjakova
Duhël
SERBIA
Ferizaj
Fierzë Lake
Prizren
Štrpce
Krumë
Kumanovo
Dragash
Kukës
Fushë-Arrëz
Tetovo
Skopje
Thirrë
NORTHERN ALBANIA
p84
Sveti Nikole
Katlanovo
Reps
Gostivar
NORTH MACEDONIA
Veles
Peshkopi
Burrel
Fushë-Bulqizë
Makedonski Brod
Izvor
Debar
Kičevo
Klos
Bulqizë
Krastë
Kruševo
Prilep
Demir Hisar
Krrabë
Librazhd
Struga
Ohrid
Elbasan
Resen
Prrenjas
Bitola
Cërrik
Lake Ohrid
Pogradec
Lake Big Prespa
Gramsh
SOUTHERN ALBANIA
p150
Edessa
Sovjan
Florina
Berat
Maliq
Amÿntaio
Korçë
Poliçan
Voskopojë
Bilisht
Kastoria
Çorovodë
Ptolemaïda
Vithkuo
Gllave
Mesopotamia
Argos Orestiko
Memaliaj
Neapoli
Ersekë
Kёlcyrë
GREECE
Kozáni
Tepelenë
Tsotyli
Përmet
Servia
Leskovik
Gjirokastër
Grevena
Konitsa
Delvinë
Delvináki
Muzinë
Kalpáki
Deskáti
Elassona
Sarandë
Lake Butrint
Ksamil
Metsovo
Eleousa
Ciflik Tusha
Perama
0 kilometres 30
Konispol
Ioannina
0 miles 30
N

GETTING TO KNOW ALBANIA

Albania has no shortage of spectacular landscapes. Its long coast passes not one but two seas, it's home to one of Europe's oldest and deepest lakes, and it has sweeping mountain ranges along much of its inland borders. Most of its population, meanwhile, lives in and around the capital, Tirana.

PAGE 62

TIRANA

Tirana, Albania's busy capital, is a vibrant city. Its ever-changing skyline reflects its storied past, with modern skyscrapers and structures appearing alongside landmarks like Et'hem Bey Mosque, and plenty of communist-era monuments, brightened by bold street art and contemporary installations. Aside from sights, Tirana has a thriving social scene: expect lively coffee shops, traditional restaurants and buzzing public squares. It's a place where modern Albanian culture thrives, offering countless spots to explore the energy of a city that's always on the move.

Best for

Museums, galleries, coffee culture, street art

Home to

Bunk'Art, Dajti Mountain, Skanderbeg Square

Experience

Bunk'Art 1, a huge underground complex and museum, before taking the nearby cable car up to the top of Dajti Mountain

PAGE 84

NORTHERN ALBANIA

Deep wilderness makes up most of Albania's north. It's home to jagged mountain peaks, glacial valleys and deep blue lakes, with quiet mountain villages nestled in between. There's little human activity in the national parks of Theth and Valbonë, save for the odd shepherd moving their flock from the craggy mountainside in search of mountain meadows. In the foothills of the Accursed Mountains, lakes offer pleasure cruises, while towns with preserved Ottoman streets are home to ethnographic museums, pavement cafés and bazaars where traditional mountain wares are sold.

Best for

Picturesque villages, hiking trails, folk traditions

Home to

Shkodër, Theth National Park, Valbonë National Park, Komani Lake, Bovilla Lake

Experience

Hiking through the untamed parkland between Valbonë and Theth villages, passing meadows, slate-grey peaks tipped with snow and a glacial river

→

PAGE 112

THE ALBANIAN RIVIERA

Sprawling from the picturesque town of Ksamil to the thriving port city of Durrës, the Albanian Riviera is the country's most famous stretch of coastline. There's no shortage of pristine beaches here, where tourists and locals unwind at beach bars and beside relaxing waters. Ancient ruins and historic fortifications, left behind by former conquerors and empires, dot the land between the famous shores. The twisting coastal road, meanwhile, winds between red-roofed villages, where traditional Albanian restaurants and folk culture centres await.

Best for

Beaches, buzzing bars, scenic coastal drives

Home to

Butrint National Park, Ksamil, Sarandë, Durrës, Vlorë, Llogara National Park

Experience

Exploring Butrint National Park, once an ancient Greek then Roman hub of trade and culture

PAGE 150

SOUTHERN ALBANIA

Southern Albania is the country's unofficial centre of tradition and heritage. From Roman ruins to Ottoman streets, there are countless UNESCO-listed neighbourhoods and sights to explore. Both Gjirokastër and Berat are home to preserved 15th-century architecture and sprawling castle complexes, dating back to the days of Ottoman sieges and feudal lords. Between the charming cities and towns lies a verdant landscape, filled with hillside vineyards, mountainous hiking trails and, winding across it all, the Vjosa, Europe's last wild river.

Best for

Historic towns, folk music and traditions, wild nature

Home to

Gjirokastër, Berat, Vjosa Wild River National Park, Korçë

Experience

Wandering the preserved Ottoman streets of Gjirokastër's Old Town

1

2

3

4

1 Ascending the Pyramid of Tirana.

2 Cable cars on the leafy Dajti Mountain.

3 Flaky slices of *byrek*, a popular breakfast choice.

4 The Pazari i Ri market.

Albania has a huge variety of things to see and do, and its small size means that you can make your way around the country with relative ease. These itineraries will help you make the most of your visit.

2 DAYS

in Tirana

Day 1

Morning Kick-start your tour of Albania's capital city with a distinctly local dish: a flaky, savoury *byrek*. At hole-in-the-wall Byrektore Albani *(Rruga Shyqyri Bërxolli)*, choose from a selection of *byrek* with cheese, spinach or tomato. When you're ready, make your way to Skanderbeg Square *(p72)* to see the statue of the 15th-century military figure Gjergj Kastrioti, better known as Skanderbeg, before heading to the National Historical Museum *(p73)*. Spend time exploring the collection, which spans centuries of history, then stop by the Et'hem Bey Mosque *(p72)*, also on the square.

Afternoon Pause for lunch at one of the upmarket restaurants in Tirana Castle *(p77)*. Once a fortress built for the Roman Emperor Justinian, this castle has been transformed into a hub of fine-dining restaurants and souvenir shops. From here, it's a short walk to the Pyramid of Tirana *(p78)*, which has stunning views over the skyline from its top. Back down to earth, make your way to the nearby Bunk'Art 2 *(p68)*. This underground bunker was a hideout for key members of the communist regime; now it's been converted into a museum space that tells the story of the former secret police.

Evening Peruse the stalls of the bustling Pazari i Ri market *(p74)*, where folk sell everything from local produce to military paraphernalia and souvenirs. The market is also surrounded by alfresco coffee shops and bars, perfect for a pre-dinner drink. Afterwards, enjoy a traditional Albanian dining experience at the atmospheric Oda Garden Restaurant *(www.odagardenrestaurant.com)*. See off the day in the nostalgic Kometiti Bar *(Rruga Papa Gjon Pali II)*, where the selection of raki is second to none.

Day 2

Morning Today begins beyond the city centre. Head to the main bus station outside the Opera House and catch the Blue Line towards Bunk'Art 1 *(p66)*. This disused sprawling bunker complex, carved into the mountainside, today houses a museum. It showcases the preserved rooms to which the highest up of the former Communist Party would have fled in the event of a nuclear attack.

Afternoon Take the bus to the Dajti cable-car stop, where visitors can catch a ride up the Dajti Mountain *(p70)*. At the top, there are panoramic views of Tirana as well as many opportunities for outdoor activities like mini golf, horse riding and hiking. Enjoy a late lunch at Balkonie Restaurant *(www.dajtiekspres.com/facilities/restaurant-ballkoni-dajtit)*, before heading back down to the centre.

Evening Take a stroll around the Grand Park of Tirana *(p79)* before dinner. Indulge in some local fine dining at Mullixhiu Restaurant *(www.mullixhiu.al)*, located near the park. Here, chef Bledar Kola *(p42)* champions fresh, local produce from the surrounding Tirana County countryside in his exquisite dishes.

1

2

3

4

1 The UNESCO-listed ruins at Butrint.

2 The clock tower of Gjirokastër Castle.

3 Bënjë thermal springs.

4 Berat's Ottoman buildings.

3 DAYS

on the UNESCO Trail

Day 1

Morning Over the next three days, you'll take a road trip to Albania's three cultural UNESCO World Heritage Sites – Berat, Gjirokastër and Butrint – as well as a number of other historical highlights. The trip starts in the city of Elbasan, about 40 km (25 miles) southeast of Tirana. Here, you'll find the crumbling fortifications of the 15th-century Elbasan Castle *(p176)*, plus a fine selection of coffee shops and bakeries ideal for a pick-me-up post-castle tour.

Afternoon On your way from Elbasan to Berat, the first of your UNESCO stops, break at the peaceful parkland of Bysheku and then at Çobo Winery *(p174)*, which is set in rolling hills at the foot of Mount Tomorr; its dry red, made from the local Sheshi i Zi grape, is a standout. Once you've reached Berat *(p162)*, take a walk around the city's Mangalem district, known for its restored Ottoman-era buildings, and spend some time in Berat's National Ethnographic Museum.

Evening Come evening, wander the preserved streets of the Gorica neighbourhood, where ancient Orthodox churches sit between old stone houses. This is the perfect spot for dinner at one of Berat's traditional restaurants before retiring for the night.

Day 2

Morning Spend the morning exploring more of Berat, beginning with mighty Berat Castle. Overlooking the city, it dates back to the 4th century BCE, and its crenulated walls are open to explore. Make time, too, for the Red Mosque and the Church of the Holy Trinity, which has fabulous views down the valley.

Afternoon Push on for Përmet, 100 km (66 miles) to the southeast, where the Vjosa River weaves through town. There's opportunity to kayak or whitewater raft here, though for something a little more indulgent, take a soak at the nearby Bënjë thermal springs.

Evening Stop for the night in Gjirokastër *(p154)* and get to know this stunning mountain city by wandering some of its UNESCO-protected Ottoman-era streets. Visit the Cold War Tunnel before hunkering down in one of the city-centre restaurants serving hearty mountain dishes for dinner.

Day 3

Morning Before leaving town, be sure to visit Gjirokastër Castle *(p160)* at the top of the hill. Aside from its labyrinth of Byzantine chambers and dungeons, there are lovely views of a historic stone clock tower that rises up against the mountains of the Drino Valley.

Afternoon Continue on to the coast, making a pit stop at the remarkable Blue Eye *(p144)*. It's a 20-minute walk along forest paths to this natural attraction, with a handful of restaurants on the riverside available for a cold drink or a bite to eat. Then it's just over 35 km (22 miles) to the UNESCO-listed ruins at Butrint *(p116)*, where the remains of a Greek, Roman and later Ottoman settlement sit on an island in the middle of the Vivari Channel.

Evening End your journey through Albania's rich history at the nearby seaside town of Ksamil *(p118)* and raise a glass to the last few days at one of the beach bars down by the shore.

1 Rruga Kolë Idromeno in pretty central Shkodër.

2 Grunasi Waterfall, Theth National Park.

3 Church in Theth village.

4 Hiking from Theth to Valbonë.

5 DAYS
in the North

Day 1

Spend your first day in Albania's rugged northern climes soaking up the sights of Shkodër *(p88)*, the country's capital of culture. The city is focused around Shkodër Bazaar, with its tangle of well-preserved Ottoman-era streets. You can spend a pleasant morning browsing the independent shops on pedestrianized Rruga Kolë Idromeno, stopping for a strong Albanian coffee at one of its pavement cafés, and taking in the interesting exhibition at the Marubi National Museum of Photography. The afternoon can be dedicated to exploring Rozafa Castle *(p90)*, perched high above the city and dating back, in parts, to the 3rd century BCE. Alternatively, head to nearby Shkodër Lake *(p88)*, where you can while away the day at its sandy slip of beach and lakeside restaurant or on a flat, leisurely cycling trail.

Day 2

Make an early start for the 78-km (48-mile) journey northeast of Shkodër to the beautiful mountain village of Theth *(p92)*, which enjoys a tremendous setting deep in the Albanian Alps. Minibuses regularly make the run from Shkodër; the journey takes around three hours and covers some of the most stunning scenery in the country. On arrival, pick one of Theth's family-run restaurants for a lunch of traditional mountain cuisine – if you're lucky, you'll dine with views of the region's towering peaks. Spend the afternoon exploring the tiny village: look out for the 400-year-old *kulla* house – a type of tower house that was fortified to protect its original inhabitants from blood feuds – and a stone church sitting pretty against the wild landscape.

Day 3

Today is all about spending time in nature. Stretch your legs on one of the scenic marked hiking trails that lead off into the mountains of Theth National Park *(p92)* from Theth village. One of the most popular routes is the 24-km (15-mile) return hike along the Theth River to Blue Eye Kaprre, an irridescent blue pool fed by a small waterfall. There's an option to branch off the trail along the way to view the cascades at Grunasi Waterfall *(p95)*. Bring your active day to an end back in Theth with a hearty meal and a shot of home-distilled raki.

Day 4

You could take a taxi to the tiny, remote village of Valbonë *(p96)*, in the heart of breathtaking Valbonë National Park, but outdoor enthusiasts, especially, shouldn't miss the chance to tackle one of Albania's best day hikes. Starting in Theth, the waymarked route *(p92)* runs through the Valbonë Valley, past glacial lakes and rugged mountains, for 17 km (11 miles). The walk takes most of the day. On arrival in Valbonë, find a rustic guesthouse for a traditional meal and a well-deserved rest for the night.

Day 5

On your last day, hop on the morning bus service from Valbonë village to Fierze, where you can connect with the daily ferry across Komani Lake *(p98)*. An afternoon putter on its ethereally turquoise waters will take you below sheer cliffs and past an abundance of birdlife. The lake winds like a river to Komani village; stay the night or catch a minibus or transfer to Tirana.

7 DAYS

on the Riviera

Day 1

Spend a relaxing first day in Ksamil *(p118)*, hopping between the town's sheltered sandy bays. Two of the best are the ever popular Bora Bora Beach *(p118)* and Pema e Thatë, a quieter stretch 3.5 km (2 miles) outside of Ksamil.

Day 2

There's a change of pace as you leave the beach behind for the UNESCO-listed Butrint National Park *(p116)*. Spend the morning exploring the amphitheatre, temples and churches of this historic trade hub, a Greek city-state that was also ruled by Romans, Byzantines and Ottomans. Enjoy lunch at the nearby Mussel House *(p117)* before walking off these local delicacies at the famous Blue Eye *(p144)*, a mesmerizing deep spring in the Bistricë River, 37 km (23 miles) from Butrint, that shimmers unearthly shades of green and blue. From here, it's a short drive to the lively beach resort of Sarandë *(p120)*, in time for dinner on the waterfront as the sun sets over the Ionian Sea.

Day 3

Start the day with a coffee by Sarandë's marina, then drive (or take the bus) along the coast to Lukovë *(p143)*, a small town of orange-roofed buildings that appears to cling to the hillside. While away the day on a lounger on Lukovë Beach *(p143)* or hire a kayak to explore the sea caves in the area. Move on to Qeparo *(p142)*, where crumbling Upper Qeparo lies virtually abandoned on a hill; the castle here has some of the best sunset views on the Riviera. There are a handful of family-run guesthouses for an overnight stay in Lower Qeparo, down by the sea.

Day 4

From Qeparo, it's a short hop to Porto Palermo Castle *(p140)*, a dramatic fortress set on a peninsula, jutting into the Ionian Sea. Thick stone walls keep things cool and dark inside, creating an atmosphere befitting a former prison. Farther along the coast, Livadhi Beach *(p137)* gives off a completely different vibe, with flashy bars, restaurants and five-star hotels

1 Porto Palermo Castle.

2 Cycling through historic Vlöre Old Town.

3 The modern-looking Sfinksi promenade, Durrës.

4 Sunbathing on the beach at Ksamil.

5 Exploring the ruins at Butrint National Park.

lining its long stretch of pristine sand. Experience the Riviera's glitzy side during an afternoon here before moving on to Himarë *(p140)* for the night.

Day 5

Wander the streets of Himarë Old Town, crowned with the ruins of Himarë Castle, then make your way farther up the coast to Dhërmi *(p136)*, worth a stop for its far-reaching views over the hills towards the sea. Follow the road through Llogara National Park *(p132)*, stopping for lunch at Freskia *(p133)* to enjoy traditional Albanian mountain fare – lamb grilled on an open flame, say – amid pine trees. End the day in the coastal city of Vlorë *(p130)*, where there are plenty of options for a place to rest your head for the night.

Day 6

Turkish-style coffee and a flaky pastry is the perfect way to start the day on the Ottoman streets of Vlorë Old Town. Head from here to nearby Narta Lagoon, where the bucolic St Mary's Monastery *(p134)* sits on an island reached by a wooden walkway. It's then just another short journey, inland, to the sprawling ruins of Apollonia *(p134)*. Once a mighty city on a prehistoric trading route, Apollonia's rich history can be explored in the on-site archaeological museum. Push on for the buzzing port city of Durrës *(p126)*, farther north along the coast.

Day 7

Complete your trip along the Albanian Riviera by hitting the historic sights of Durrës. Its amphitheatre was once an entertainment venue for Romans, while the Archaeological Museum shows off Albania's vast and turbulent history, from the Illyrians to the communist era. Pop into Durrës' Venetian Tower, too, home to a state-of-the-art projection show that explains the history of the Venetian and Ottoman conquest of Durrës. End your final day by joining the local residents on a stroll along the Sfinksi promenade to watch the sun set over the Adriatic Sea.

Rushing Rivers

Over 150 rivers and streams course through Albania, and there might be just as many ways to enjoy them. Splash in the shallows of the Shalë River *(p102)* near Shkodër or go bird spotting in the Kunë-Vain-Tale Lagoon *(p103)* within the Drin river delta. Get up close to the mighty Vjosa *(p166)*, Europe's last wild river and Albania's newest national park, by kayaking down this stunning ancient waterway on a tour.

The winding Vjosa River, now a national park

ALBANIA FOR NATURAL WONDERS

The dramatic scenery of Albania is famous, and for good reason: trails through legendary mountains, thundering waterfalls and great lakes are all found here. There are few better places to enjoy the beauty and power of nature.

Spectacular Springs

Albania is famous for its topaz-coloured springs, called Syri i Kaltër or Blue Eyes. The most famous are the Blue Eyes near Sarandë *(p144)* and Theth *(p92)*; you'll need to trek through the Albanian Alps to reach the latter, but it's worth it for views of the pool and its waterfall.

→ The azure waters of Sarandë's Blue Eye, with its small waterfall

Lovely Lakes

Among Albania's hundreds of lakes, there are a few standouts. Take a boat tour across Lake Ohrid *(p180)*, a UNESCO World Heritage Site home to rare endemic species, or explore the past on Shkodër Lake *(p88)*, which has its own nature reserve where traditional fishing takes place.

→ The expansive Lake Ohrid, which straddles Albania and North Macedonia

Verdant Valleys

With so many mountains, stunning valleys abound in Albania. Hike through the Valbonë Valley *(p96)* and witness glacial streams become part of the mighty Valbonë River. Near Berat, the 26-km- (16-mile-) long Osumi River Canyon *(p172)* is one of the most famous valley regions here. Head out on a scenic hike through it or, to experience the canyon from the water, join a whitewater rafting tour.

← The impressive formations of the Osumi River Canyon

ECO-FRIENDLY TRAVEL TIPS

Keep to the path
Stay on designated hiking trails to protect delicate ecological environments.

Protect local species
Refrain from picking flowers or taking rocks and sand home.

Leave no trace
Avoid polluting the local environment by depositing your rubbish properly.

Respect the wildlife
Always observe any local wildlife you may encounter from a distance.

↑ Hiking route towards Grunasi Waterfall in Theth National Park

Mountain Escapes

Jagged peaks and unforgiving terrain lend the Albanian Alps their fearsome moniker: the Accursed Mountains *(p92)*. Now a national park, the mountains are a hub for mountaineering and fishing. For two-wheel exploration of the Albanian Alps, cycle along Albania's Trans Dinarica Cycle Route *(p182)*.

← Strolling down the palm-lined Sarandë Promenade

Seaside Walkways

Pedestrianized promenades and palm-lined boulevards are perfect for sunset strolls. Enjoy a drink by Sarandë Promenade *(p120)* or see the sunset from the cascading steps of the Sfinksi walkway *(p129)*.

ALBANIA FOR BEACHGOERS

The impressive blues of the Ionian and Adriatic seas meet white bays all along Albania's 470-km (290-mile) coastline. Between isolated coves and pristine stretches of sand, there's something for every beachgoer here.

Wonderfully Wild Beaches

While a lot of the Albanian coastline has been developed, it's still possible to find wild beaches, if you don't mind a hike or chartering a boat. The 20-minute hike to Gjipe Beach *(p142)* from the nearest car park is worthwhile: once you arrive at the beach, there are quiet, sandy shores to be enjoyed. The isolated bays of Krorëza and Kakoma, both north of Sarandë *(p120)*, are only accessible by boat, making these wonderfully tranquil.

↑ Pristine swathes of sand lining the shores of the wild Gjipe Beach

↑ Sunset beside one of the many seaside bars of the Albanian Riviera

Swish Beach Clubs and Bars

All along the coast, all-day beachside venues are de rigueur. For the best variety of venues, head to the beaches of the Albanian Riviera. Unwind by the water in Ksamil *(p118)*, where many bars offer sea-facing sun loungers and net beds that jut out over the water. Sarandë *(p120)* is home to beach clubs that pulse with music as the sun sets, while Livadhi Beach *(p137)* is where a glamorous crowd heads for cocktails and chilled beats.

INSIDER TIP
Shoulder Season

The height of the summer season sees the Albanian coast get incredibly busy. For a quieter escape, visit in spring or early autumn when it's easier to enjoy sun-drenched shores without the crowds.

Island Getaways

Head to the uninhabited islands of Albania for a fix of wild beaches, abundant birdlife and quiet woodland walks. Sazan Island, once a submarine base, is home to pristine beaches and the Karaburun-Sazan National Marine Park *(p130)*. The four islets of Ksamil *(p118)*, meanwhile, are home to undeveloped beaches, the smallest of which you can easily swim to from Ksamil.

→ One of the islets of Ksamil seen from above and *(inset)* a Great Egret

The huge façade of Tirana's National Historical Museum

ALBANIA FOR ARCHITECTURE

For a long time, Albanian architecture was defined by its occupiers, like the Venetians and Ottomans. Today, the historic sites they left behind can be seen among the concrete structures and glass towers of the last 150 years.

Towering Modernism

Since the 1990s, city skylines across Albania have changed rapidly. In Tirana, skyscrapers are hard to miss, like the 140-m- (460-ft-) high Downtown One *(Bulevardi Bajram Curri)*, with its distinctive, geometric façade. Another showstopper is the Arena Center Tower *(www.arenacenter.al)*. The red-and-black tower of this building is part of a larger complex, which is home to the city's main stadium.

The chequered façade of Tirana's looming Arena Center Tower

Socialist Realist Structures

As communism took hold in Albania, so too did the artistic style most associated with the ideology: socialist realism. Some common themes of this style include idealized figures and images of the proletariat, as seen in the looming mosaic decorating the entrance of Tirana's National Historical Museum *(p73)*. Socialist-era construction resulted in the old city of Kukës being flooded and turned into the Fierza Reservoir in 1976, making way for a new hydropower station. Today, you can stroll around modern Kukës *(p103)*, often referred to as New Kukës, which was built near the reservoir from concrete with numerous socialist realist touches, like the flag-bearing hero outside the Radio Kukesi site *(Rruga Gjalica 13)*.

← A socialist realist relief outside the headquarters of Radio Kukesi

TOP 3 BUILDINGS IN TIRANA

Arena Center Tower
Sheshi Italia 1
Tirana's Arena Center Tower is a hub of endless activity, home to a hotel, many restaurants and a music stadium.

Tirana Garden Building
Kavaja Street
With its grid-like frame, this industrial-style building stands out next to the historic sites of the city's main square.

Book Building
Rruga 28 Nëntori
Finished in 2024, the Book Building near Skanderbeg Square is in fact made up of three buildings. It's home to new shops, apartments and office spaces.

Did You Know?

Durrës' Venetian Tower was originally fortified with a number of cannons.

Venetian Legacies

The tiny Republic of Venice controlled a huge Adriatic empire, including parts of Albania. Hike around the pastoral ruins of Shkodër's Rozafa Castle *(p90)*, where the Venetians built a towering cathedral; it's now the Fatih Sultan Mehmet Mosque. In Durrës *(p126)*, see how the Venetians enlarged the original Byzantine castle walls in the port and take in the iconic Venetian Tower, which was used for maritime defence.

Walking past the grounds of the Venetian Rozafa Castle in Shkodër ↑

Impressive Street Art

Albania's lively street art scene owes much to former Tirana mayor and current Albanian prime minister Edi Rama. In the 2000s, Rama turned the post-communist capital into "a living museum", ordering entire tower blocks to be daubed with bright art. Today, see street art around areas like Pazari i Ri *(p74)*, where bookshelves, pop art portraits and animals adorn many buildings. Across Tirana *(p62)*, look out for works by the city's official street artist, Franko Dine; his pieces appear on many buildings across the city centre.

ALBANIA FOR ART AND CULTURE

Art and culture have thrived in Albania for thousands of years. Today, it's easy to find highlights from many important art periods, from Roman mosaics and medieval icons, to frescoed churches and modern street art.

↑ Big and bright iconostasis on display at the Ardenica Monastery

Medieval Art

When the Byzantine Empire was replaced by the Ottoman Empire, Albania was an artistic refuge for Orthodox artists. Key figures include Onufri and Kostandin Shpataraku, who painted ornate miniatures that can be seen in the 13th-century Ardenica Monastery *(Rrethi i Fierit)*. To see the works of the 17th-century painter David Selenica, there's no better stop than Korçë's National Museum of Medieval Art *(p170)*.

A towering work by one of Tirana's most famous street artists, Franko Dine

FRANKO DINE AND TIRANA'S STREET ART SCENE

Vlorë-native Franko Dine has played a big role in the transformation of Tirana's streets. His street art can be spotted in many places across the Albanian capital, covering walls with both playful and moving images. He became the first street artist to be officially hired by the city of Tirana to continue brightening its streets.

Modern Albanian Works

The 20th century saw a range of art styles flourish in Albania, from the realism of Kolë Idromeno to the socialist realism of Guri Madhi. See highlights of these periods in Tirana's soon-to-reopen National Gallery of Arts *(Blvd Dëshmorët e Kombit)*. Tirana's Skanderbeg sculpture *(p73)* is another key modern work, completed in 1968 by Odhise Paskali.

Motra Tone, a painting by the Albanian artist Kolë Idromeno

Ancient Mosaics

A common decorative feature in centuries past was the mosaic, and plenty remain to be seen today. Take in the 5-m- (16-ft-) wide *Beauty of Durrës* mosaic in the Durrës Archaeological Museum *(p127)*; the 4th-century BCE work features the head of a woman in the centre, with decorative elements around it. The 3rd-century CE Tirana Mosaic *(Rruga Sandër Prosi)* is the capital's oldest sight, which can be seen through the railings on a quiet Tirana street. Striking ancient mosaics decorate the interiors of the 6th-century Byzantine Church in Lin on Lake Ohrid *(p180)*.

An ancient mosaic decorating the floor of Lin's Byzantine Church

Polyphonic Vocals

One of Albania's oldest music traditions is iso-polyphony, a group chant that was first developed as a way for Illyrian shepherds to communicate while in the mountains. Get stuck into the history of this unique music style at Gjirokastër's café-museum Te Kubé *(Rruga Ismail Kadare)*, where recordings and displays shed light on the practice. Over at Vila Cofiel in Korçë *(Rruga Avni Rustemi)*, book a table to enjoy a live iso-polyphony performance over dinner.

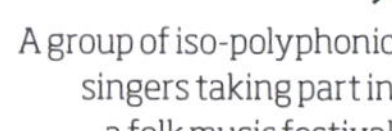

A group of iso-polyphonic singers taking part in a folk music festival

ALBANIA FOR MUSIC LOVERS

From centuries-old iso-polyphonic singing traditions to mood-lifting pop tunes, Albania has long been a hotbed of musical creativity. Discover some of the best of what it has to offer at informative cultural centres, lively music festivals and buzzing nightclubs.

Traditional Instruments

Traditional instruments are the backbone of Albania's folk music scene, and there are plenty on display at Gjirokastër's Ethnographic Museum *(p157)*. Look out for the *fyell brezi*, a double-ended flute, and the *çifteli*, a lute. To hear instruments like these in action, check for shows at the Tulla Culture Center *(www.tulla.tv)*.

Playing the *çifteli*, a traditional Albanian stringed instrument

MUST-HEAR ALBANIAN SONGS

Kenge Gjirokastrite
A timeless folk classic by Arian Shehu, the godfather of iso-polyphony.

Biçikleta (1971-2)
Françesk Radi's classic love song is a local favourite.

Mall (2018)
This love-at-first-sight ballad by Eugent Bushpepa serenaded Eurovision Song Contest viewers.

Local Musicians

In the 1970s, singer-songwriter Françesk Radi achieved legendary status with his own tunes and his modern takes on folk songs; today, you can see his memorial in the Grand Park of Tirana *(p79)*. The post-communist era saw a revival in traditional genres; listen to fresh takes on Albanian folk music by artists like Rosela Gjylbegu at festivals across the region.

← A statue of Albanian Françesk Radi, located in the Grand Park of Tirana

ALBANIA'S WORLD-FAMOUS POP ICONS

Some of the biggest pop stars that rock the world stage today – including Dua Lipa, Rita Ora and Bebe Rexha – have ties with Albania. Although many of these stars are based outside of Albania, they often perform at venues and festivals across the country. Dua Lipa ended her Future Nostalgia tour in Tirana on Albanian Independence Day in 2022, while Rita Ora performed a free show in Skanderbeg Square *(p72)* that same year.

↑ Festivalgoers enjoying a sunset party at the annual Unum Festival

Electronic Music Festivals

An epic roster of electronic music festivals rocks the Albanian coast in the summer months. In Dhërmi, the Ion Festival offers guided meditation and yoga as well as electronic DJ sets *(www.ionalbania.com)*. For buzzing house music, there's no better event than the Unum Festival, held each year near Shëngjin *(www.unumfestival.com)*.

Heart-Racing Hikes

Albania is the ideal place for a long-distance hike. Take on a section of the epic, long-distance Via Dinarica Trail, which passes through the Theth *(p92)* and Valbonë *(p96)* national parks in Northern Albania. The Mount Korab Trail is one of the highest routes, leading over to North Macedonia. Over in the south, the 74-km- (45-mile-) long Southern Coastal Trail leads walkers past verdant mountains and dramatic gorges of the Albanian Riviera.

→

Taking in the forest-filled mountain vistas of Valbonë National Park

ALBANIA FOR OUTDOOR ACTIVITIES

Dramatic and unspoiled, Albania's landscapes are made for adventure. The variety is endless: ski down alpine peaks, trek through valleys where glacial rivers flow clear or saddle up on an epic cycle route.

Scenic Rafting

Glacial rivers tumbling down from the Albanian Alps make for rocky rapids, ideal for whitewater rafting. Catch the best rapids in Përmët on the Vjosa River *(p166)*. Kayaking and rafting are the best ways to see Komani Lake *(p98)* and the Shala River *(p102)*, where sheer cliffs encase the impossibly blue water. In the Osumi River Canyon *(p172)*, a rafting adventure will take you past gushing riverside waterfalls.

Small rafts heading down one of Albania's aquamarine rivers

TOP 3 MOUNTAINS FOR CLIMBING

Dajti Mountain
Just outside Tirana, the Dajti summit is reached by taking a moderate 10-km (6-mile) hike.

Mount Tomorr
Found near Berat, this 2,400-m- (7,900-ft-) high summit is reached via a steep, rocky trail.

Mount Korab
Straddling the border between Albania and North Macedonia, Mount Korab is the highest peak in both countries.

Scenic Ski Slopes

Albanian ski slopes are enjoying a revival in popularity. Join locals and take to the ski lifts and scenic steep runs around Pukë *(p106)* and Korçe *(p170)*. Over in mountain villages like Shishtaveci and Voskopojë *(p178)*, enjoy a stellar terrain for some stunning cross-country skiing. At any of these destinations, expect a number of cosy, chalet-style guesthouses, where an après-ski raki almost always awaits.

← An off-piste skier enjoying some deep powder

Captivating Cycles

Dramatic switchbacks, epic climbs and panoramic views: Albania is a cyclist's dream. Once mainly made up of rugged roads braved only by seasoned cyclists, today the region has newer routes that range in difficulty and length. One of the most scenic is the Muzina Pass near Gjirokastër *(p154)*, which connects the Drino Valley with the laid-back beach towns of the Albanian Riviera.

→ Cycling through the green surrounds of a small village in the Albanian countryside

HIKING IN ALBANIA

From sections of long-distance hiking trails that cross multiple countries across the Balkans, to shorter day hikes through remote valleys, over mountains and around crystalline lakes, there are plenty of routes in Albania to keep keen walkers occupied. Whether you're hiking an overnighter or a challenging five-day trail, make sure you're properly equipped and have checked if the hiking route is best completed with a local guide.

Albania's most popular point-to-point hike, the 15-km (9-mile) **Valbonë to Theth** *trail leads through the valleys of the Albanian Alps between these two villages.*

The **Southern Coastal Trail** *is a long-distance hiking route through over 70 km (40 miles) of the Albanian Riviera. It runs from the pretty hillside village of Dhërmi to the inviting stretch of white beach at Lukovë.*

← Hikers enjoying a trail with mountain views in the Valbonë Valley

↑ Taking in the stunning vistas along the High Scardus Trail

The southeast of Albania is home to part of the multi-country ***High Scardus Trail*** *(p184). Follow the 17-km (10.5-mile) route from Stëblevë around the mountains of Shibenek-Jabllanicë National Park (p178).*

The Via Dinarica Trail is a multi-country route covering 1,200 km (750 miles) from Northern Albania through numerous Balkan countries. The main section that passes through Albania is the ***Via Dinarica White Trail****, which winds its way into Albania from the Montenegrin border.*

WAYMARKING ALONG ALBANIA'S HIKING TRAILS

Albania's designated walking routes tend to be waymarked with red and white paint, usually sprayed onto rocks or fence posts. Sometimes, small stone cairns mark the way along mountain paths. Many other hiking routes, often only known by local communities through word-of-mouth, are yet to be officially mapped, so it's a good idea to bring a GPS tracker when hiking through the region.

Marvellous Markets

Open-air markets sell fresh, local produce throughout Albania's towns and villages. Explore the streets of Tregu i Çamëve in Tirana, which are full of stalls piled high with seasonal produce like olives and figs. Walk along Rruga Jonianet in Sarandë *(p120)* on market days to see the street packed with produce, or explore the farmers' market of Shkodër *(p88)*, which has been in operation since the Middle Ages.

Choosing produce from a colourful selection at one of Tirana's markets

ALBANIA FOR FOODIES

Albanian cuisine is heavily influenced by the many historic empires that once occupied the region, and food traditions are well preserved. Its natural larder, too, is plentiful: from north to south, vegetable patches and fruit orchards abound and farm-to-table food spots are commonplace.

BLEDAR KOLA

Bledar Kola is one of Albania's best-known contemporary chefs. He has worked at sushi restaurants in London and the world-famous Noma restaurant in Copenhagen. After spending several years abroad, Kola returned to his homeland with a determination to put traditional Albanian cuisine on the world map. Today, he champions the natural produce of this Balkan region, showcasing the best local ingredients in his fine-dining menus at Mullixhiu in Tirana *(www.mullixhiu.al)*.

Local Seafood

Mullet, hake and bass fished in the nearby seas are served in towns along the Albanian Riviera daily, grilled fresh with just a squeeze of lemon. Try speciality mussels by the lagoon surrounding Butrint *(p116)*. Tuck into tasty carp at Shkodër Lake *(p88)* or Kunë-Vain-Tale Lagoon *(p103)*, or head to Lake Ohrid *(p180)* for its famous *koran* (Ohrid trout) dishes.

Wood-Fired Dishes

Some of the best of Albanian cuisine is still prepared in the traditional way: over a wood fire. Tuck into dishes like wild trout and clay-baked fish at the historic restaurant Tradita Geg & Tosk in Shkodër *(www.traditagt.com)*, served straight from the wood-fired oven. Over at Thethi Paradise Restaurant *(Rruga Gjecaj, Theth)*, enjoy tasty grilled meals alongside stunning mountain views. Here, classic dishes like delicious river fish, mountain lamb and lemon-infused chicken are all cooked over an open flame and served alfresco.

Meats being grilled over a burning wood fire

EAT

Mrizi i Zanave

This restaurant serves tasty dishes and drinks from its own winery.

C2 · Rruga Lezhë-Vau i Dejës, Fishtë · mrizizanave.al

Farma Sotira

With a farm on-site, Farma Sotira champions delicious slow food.

E6 · Rruga Nacionale Leskovik-Erseke, Leskovik · farmasotira.com

Serving a spread of Albanian cheese dishes and breads

Seafood specialities at a restaurant beside Lake Ohrid

Farm-to-Table Fare

Albania's farm-to-table restaurants and guesthouses embrace a food culture that has been in place for centuries, and there are plenty to choose from across the country. Enjoy fresh, local dishes at Uka Farm near Tirana *(www.ukafarm.com)*, where sustainable farming techniques are also taught. For slow meals in nature followed by horse riding, there's no better place than Agritourism Huqi *(www.agritourismhuqi.com)*.

Local Beers

In a country known for its historic winemaking, local beers still abound. Albania's first local beer brand, Birra Korça, dates back to 1928; try it at a lively bar like Duff Sports Bar *(Rruga Brigada e VIII, Tirana)*. At Taproom by Pan's Microbrewery *(Ish Uzina Dinamo e re)*, enjoy a pint from Tirana's first brewery to also serve its own beer.

←

Enjoying a pint at Taproom by Pan's Microbrewery in Tirana

ALBANIA

RAISE A GLASS

There's far more to Albanian drinks than meets the eye. Here, centuries-old drinking practices are carefully maintained. From a strong Turkish-style coffee to a delicious local wine, you'll be getting a taste of the country's long-standing traditions with every sip.

Historic Wines

Albania was made for winemaking: fertile soil, sun-drenched summers and cooling sea breezes result in delicious tipples. Head to Uka Farm, where ancient Cerujë grapes are fermented among others, for wine tastings *(www.ukafarm.com)*. Thirsty for more only-in-Albania experiences? Then stop by the Çobo Winery *(p174)* to indulge in bottles made from indigenous grape varieties, like Shesh i Zi red and Shesh i Bardhe white.

Did You Know?

Roman diarist Pliny the Younger described Albania's wines as "very sweet or luscious".

INSIDER TIP
Drinking Raki

Don't down a shot of raki - the clear spirit is meant to be sipped, often from tulip-shaped glasses. This allows the tongue to register its heat and fruity flavour.

↑ Raki being served in traditional tulip-shaped glasses, ideal for sipping

Balkan Spirit

Raki is a throat-tingling spirit brewed all over the Balkans from plums, figs and pears to a strength of at least 40 per cent ABV. Sample it at a specialist bar like Komiteti *(Rruga Papa Gjon Pali II, Tirana)*. To learn how it's made, book a tour at the Skrapar Distillery in Çorovodë *(www.kantinaepijeveskrapar.com)*. Here, raki is produced in the traditional way, using a historic copper still.

Mountain Tea

Mountain tea, or *çaj mali*, is a popular hot drink. Made from the *Sideritis raeseri* plant which grows in Albania's mountains, it's said to promote well-being. Hike through the Tomorr Mountain National Park *(p176)* to see it being sourced and dried in early summer, or buy a bunch of the herb at Pazar i Ri farmers' market *(p74)* to brew the sweet-tasting tea yourself.

← Brewing a fresh pot of Albanian mountain tea, or *çaj mali*

↑ A row of abundant grapevines on Uka Farm

Coffee Culture

A legacy of the Ottoman Empire, Turkish-style coffee is traditionally made by brewing grounds in a copper pot. Enjoy this strong concoction at a café like Ayla Bakllava & Kynefe *(Rruga Ibrahim Rugova, Tirana)*. To try a brew from a modern roastery, stop by Antigua *(Rruga Perlat Rexhepi 1001, Tirana)*.

→ A Turkish coffee being prepared in the traditional way, using a copper pot

Illyrian Roots

The group of tribes known as the Illyrians first appeared here around the 10th century BCE. At Byllis Archaeological Park near Hekal, see ruins left behind by the Bylliones tribe. Step back in time atop the Pogradec hilltop near Lake Ohrid and take in the Royal Tombs of Selca e Poshtme, where Illyrian kings were once laid to rest.

←

Ruins waiting to be explored at the Byllis Archaeological Park

ALBANIA FOR HISTORY BUFFS

Greek temples, Roman ruins, Byzantine frescoes and Ottoman mansions lie in wait throughout Albania, left behind by the many conquering empires that passed through it. With ancient mosques next to tea shops and Roman amphitheatres near beaches, there's no escaping the past here.

ISMAIL KADARE'S GJIROKASTËR HOME

Built in 1799, one of the best-preserved Ottoman-era homes in Gjirokastër is also the birthplace of Albanian writer Ismail Kadare *(p156)*. Preserved and open to visitors today, the old house sheds light on home life in Albania under the Ottomans. Visitors can see typical features of such historic houses, including bench-like sofas that line the grand salon and a fireplace that once warmed the house.

Ottoman Legacies

Nearly five centuries of Ottoman rule resulted in the spread of Turkish-influenced towns, bridges and cuisine all across Albania. The layout of Gjirokastër's houses *(p154)* offers great insight into Ottoman life. Elsewhere, architectural features like the curved Ottoman bridges dot the landscape; see a striking example in the historic town of Krujë *(p108)*.

→

Historic Ottoman-style houses lining the streets of Gjirokastër

Intricate patterns decorating the interior of Et'hem Bey Mosque

Changing Faiths

Faith has had a changing role in Albania - from the introduction of early Christianity under the Roman Empire to communist-era atheism of the 20th century - resulting in many religious sites in the region. See the Ottoman-era Et'hem Bey Mosque *(p72)*, with its ornate, nature-inspired frescoes rarely seen elsewhere. In Albania's traditionally Catholic north, the old Shkoder Cathedral *(Sheshi Gjon Pali II)* was built in the 19th century under Ottoman rule after intense local lobbying.

Did You Know?

King Zog I was the only Muslim king in modern Europe, sworn in on the Bible and the Qur'an.

Roman Ruins and Byzantine Relics

The Romans conquered then rebuilt Albania in their own image. New cities were built, while existing ones were added to in layers. Explore the Amphitheatre of Durrës *(p126)*, which once hosted 20,000-strong crowds until a Christian chapel was built on the same site. Butrint was first a Greek and then a Roman city, before becoming a Byzantine bishopric. See the Byzantine remains at Butrint National Park *(p116)*.

Butrint National Park and *(inset)* a mosaic in the park's baptistry

Folk Festivals

The unique traditions and identity of each town, village and county in Albania are celebrated in a series of folk festivals throughout the year. The biggest takes place in Gjirokastër Castle *(p160)* every five years, when locals in traditional dress dance to the music of instruments like the stringed *çifteli* and blow pipe. Other events include the Luleborë Song Festival in Shkodër *(p88)* and the Korçë Serenade in Korçë *(p170)*.

↑ Traditional folk dancing at an Albanian festival

ALBANIA FOR TRADITION

Albania has undergone many sweeping cultural changes over the centuries. In the face of numerous invasions and changing rulers, local traditions and folklore have managed to stand the test of time.

Religious Practices

Religion looms large in Albania. Visit sites such as Shkodër's Buşatlı Mehmet Pasha Mosque *(Rruga e Tabakëve 1)* and the Holy Trinity Church in Berat *(p162)* for a glimpse into the country's various faiths.

← The modern Ebu Bekër Mosque in Shkodër, completed in 1995

Myths and Legends

Albania is a land steeped in myth and legend. Mount Tomorr *(p176)* is personified in myth as an old man with a white beard; the top is said to be the home of the gods. Near Berat, the Osumi River Canyon *(p172)* is said to have been made by the tears of Osumi, a personified mountain.

→ A shrine topping the peak of myth-filled Mount Tomorr

Folkloric Dance and Music

Tradition is at the heart of folkloric dance and music across Albania, and many dances and melodies are linked to specific regions. These can be enjoyed at regional festivals, but another great way to experience them is at traditional restaurants. See the variety of local dance styles at popular venues like the Oda Garden *(p21)* in Tirana and Tradita Geg & Tosk in Shkodër *(www.traditagt.com)*.

← Musicians in national dress playing traditional folk instruments

ALBANIAN NATIONAL DRESS

Traditional dress can be found across much of the Balkan region. While it was once commonplace, today it's mainly worn for folk festivals and events. The dress varies widely between countries and regions: in Albania alone, there are said to be around 500 versions of traditional dress. Common elements of men's dress include the *qeleshe* hat and a *fustanella* skirt, and for women the *kapica* headdress. Another element worn by all is the *opinga*, distinctive leather shoes.

↑ Wearing traditional Albanian dress

Traditional Dress

Albanian regions each have a traditional national dress, complete with unique patterns and stylings. See displays of national dress at the ethnographic museums of Shkodër *(p88)* and Gjirokastër *(p157)* or at folk festivals throughout the year. Head to the Tradita Popullore folk dress workshop *(Casa Italia, Tirana)* to learn how these intricate garments are crafted and buy a unique piece as a souvenir from the on-site shop.

A YEAR IN ALBANIA

JANUARY

△ **New Year's Day** *(1 Jan)*. The first national holiday, following the ringing in of the New Year.

New Year's Holiday *(2 Jan)*. The second day of the year is also a public holiday, with the January festivities continuing across three days in total.

FEBRUARY

Annual Anniversary of Tirana *(11 Feb)*. A series of events and exhibitions across the city mark the anniversary of Tirana being declared the capital of Albania.

△ **Shkodër Carnival Festival** *(23–25 Feb)*. The streets of Shkodër fill with life and colour as locals don Venetian masks and attend cultural festivities.

MAY

Bylis-Fonia Festival *(mid-May)*. In the village of Bylis, this festival celebrates polyphonic singing.

△ **Tirana Street Food Festival** *(mid–late May)*. Tirana's Skanderbeg Square is filled with picnic tables and food trucks in this annual festival of street food from across the Balkans and beyond.

JUNE

△ **UNUM Festival** *(early Jun)*. A huge range of global acts take to the stage over six days for UNUM Festival, held in the village of Shëngjin.

Kala Music Festival *(early–mid-Jun)*. This popular music festival takes place each year in Dhërmi, with plenty of live performances, DJ sets and wellness experiences.

SEPTEMBER

ION Festival *(early Sep)*. Heavy beats fill the town of Dhërmi for this seven-day music festival.

△ **Tirana International Film Festival** *(mid–late Sep)*. New releases are screened across Tirana for this annual film festival.

Gjirokastër Folk Festival *(Sep)*. The biggest folk festival in Albania celebrates dance, music and art every five years; the next is scheduled for 2028.

OCTOBER

Elbasan Marathon *(early Oct)*. Runners choose between a marathon, half-marathon or 10-km (6-mile) race through the closed streets of Elbasan for this annual sports event.

△ **Tirana Marathon** *(late Oct)*. The streets of Tirana transform into a running track, welcoming competitors from across the world for the capital's annual marathon.

MARCH

△ National Festival of Urban Folk Songs *(early Mar).* Performers gather in Elbasan to showcase the folk music of their hometowns.

Dita e Verës *(14 Mar).* A national holiday with pagan roots, Dita e Veres is a celebration of the changing seasons.

Nevruz Day *(late Mar).* The spring equinox is a public holiday in Albania, celebrated primarily by people of the Bektaxhi religion.

APRIL

△ Vjosa n'Fest *(late Apr–early May).* This festival in Permët celebrates life by the mighty Vjosa River with shows, guided hikes and rafting experiences.

South Outdoor Festival *(late Apr–early May).* On the shores of Borsh Beach, this festival showcases the best adventure activities in Albania, from kayaking to mountain biking.

JULY

△ Berat City Festival *(mid-Jul).* This three-day event in Berat fills the city with live folk music performances, as well as stalls selling local beers and street food.

Turtle Fest *(late Jul).* Turtle Fest combines live music with nature conservation in Himarë.

AUGUST

△ Korçë Beer Festival *(mid-Aug).* Over five days, tens of thousands of people flock to the craft beer capital Korçë for this festival of beer.

Krujë Mountain Festival *(late Aug).* Crowds of believers and atheists alike make the pilgrimage to Krujë's Sari Salltik cave shrine every August.

NOVEMBER

Tirana Book Fair *(mid–late Nov).* This lively event celebrates the country's literary output, connecting publishers, authors and book enthusiasts.

△ Albanian Independence Day *(28 Nov).* Flags are draped from windows and huge parades take place across Albania for this yearly celebration.

DECEMBER

△ Christmas Market *(Dec–early Jan).* At the end of the year, Skanderbeg Square in Tirana is transformed into a lively hub. It's filled with buzzing market stalls, mulled wine spots and fun-fair rides.

Olive Festival Delvina *(20 Dec).* Originally a celebration of the town of Delvina's abundant olive oil production, the Olive Festival has expanded to showcase produce from the surrounding region.

A BRIEF HISTORY

Albania's story spans over 30,000 years, shaped by waves of invaders and occupiers, starting with the Illyrians. From Roman rule to the Third Reich, its history reflects a long struggle for liberty, with the nation now looking confidently to the future.

Prehistoric Albania

Archaeological finds, like those at the Kreçmoi Cave of Konispol, suggest that present-day Albania has been inhabited for at least 30,000 years. Remains also indicate that Neolithic farmers domesticated sheep and used flint tools in the region around 10,000 years ago. By the 10th century BCE, a group of tribes known as Illyrians populated the region's productive coastal plain; it's thought that modern Albanian heritage may trace back to these Illyrian roots. These groups include the Albanoi, who were mentioned again in 5th-century CE literature.

1 A map of Albania from the 16th century.

2 A battle between Romans and Illyrians.

3 The ruins of a baptistry in Butrint.

4 A Byzantine fresco in Lëkurësi Castle.

Timeline of events

30,000 BCE

Albania's earliest inhabitants occupy the area.

c 27,500 BCE

Remains of tools are left behind near Konispol.

3000 BCE

Indo-European populations begin to settle in the region.

7th century BCE

The ancient city of Apollonia is founded by Greek colonizers.

2

3

4

The Greeks and Romans

Despite the presence of the Illyrians, the first Greek colonies were established from around the 7th century BCE, laying the foundation for early settlement. However, the rise of Rome brought significant change. The Illyro-Roman Wars, fought during the 3rd to 2nd centuries BCE, ended with Albania's subjugation to Roman rule. Under the Romans, many cities played key roles: Butrint was used as a provisioning depot; Durrës acted as a staging post on a key trade route; and Apollonia was one of the first cities to embrace Christianity.

Between East and West

By the 4th century CE, the vast Roman Empire was split into two halves: the Western Roman Empire and Eastern Roman Empire, later known as the Byzantine Empire. Albania was tenuously ruled by the latter, but continued to take its religious lead from the Western Roman Empire. This divided rule continued until the 11th century CE, when Byzantine control weakened amid internal struggles, including the growing divide between Catholicism and Eastern Orthodoxy.

THE ILLYRIAN TRIBES UNITE

The 4th-century-BCE Illyrian King Bardylis ruled an empire which likely stretched between Lake Ohrid and Lake Prespa. Under his rule, Illyrian tribes united in a bid to fend off the growing threat of Philip II of Macedonia. Ultimately, it was Philip's son, Alexander the Great, who would gain control over the region under the Byzantine Empire.

335 BCE
Illyrian tribes are defeated by Alexander the Great at Pelium.

229 BCE
The Illyrian Queen Teuta initiates six decades of conflict against Rome.

167 BCE
The area occupied by modern Albania is conclusively conquered by the Roman Empire.

395 CE
Albania becomes part of the Byzantine branch of the Roman Empire.

1

2

Medieval Albania

By the 12th century, Byzantine authority in Albanian territories had crumbled. In its place, emerging powers in Sicily, Venice, Serbia and Bulgaria each threatened the region on all sides. From this chaos rose the Principality of Arbanon, a precursor to the modern Albanian state, in 1190. Its independence was fleeting, however, and from its ashes rose the Kingdom of Albania. This new kingdom was established not by locals, but by the Frankish King Charles of Anjou in 1271. During this time, Catholicism spread across Albania once again.

The Return of Byzantium

A resurgent Byzantine Empire sought to reclaim power over its territories, turning the Adriatic Sea into a warzone. This power tussle left the Kingdom of Albania unprepared to face the growing empires in the east, which began to look towards the country. By the mid-14th century, the Byzantine Empire lost its claim over Albania following a period of civil war. The Serbian Kingdom laid claim over the region soon after, before it was invaded by the Ottoman Empire at the end of the century.

MUHAMMAD ALI

Under Ottoman rule, ethnic Albanians filled the empire's military ranks. Muhammad Ali was one such military figure, who took control of Egypt on behalf of the Ottomans in 1805. As ruler here, he turned his back on the empire and sought to install his own dynasty instead. His descendants reigned from then on, until King Farouk was deposed in 1952.

Timeline of events

1190

The Principality of Arbanon is established in Albania.

1271

Durrës is occupied and the Kingdom of Albania is declared under King Charles of Anjou.

14th century

The Black Death kills 40 per cent of Europe's population, including many of Albania's Greek trading communities.

1335–1432

Four principalities are established across the Albanian region.

Ottoman Rule

Under the Albanian military commander Gjergj Kastrioti, known as Skanderbeg, Albania rebelled against Ottoman rule throughout the 15th century. Efforts were futile, however: after decades of resistance, Albania was conquered by the Ottoman Empire, which ruled the region via a network of pashas (officials). The Ottomans held onto power for over four centuries, up until 1912, shaping much of the country's culture and traditions.

An Independent Albania

In 1910, Albanian opposition groups challenged Ottoman rule through a series of uprisings. As the empire teetered, the nascent Albanian government fought off Serbs, Montenegrins and Greeks, who sought to claim the territory. In the aftermath of World War I, Albania's self-rule was secured in part thanks to the support of American president Woodrow Wilson at the Paris Peace Conference in 1919. From the late 1920s, King Zog I lent the country the stability it craved, but at the price of a dictatorship and later financial crisis.

1 The former military commander Skanderbeg. ↑

2 A battle scene in the Skanderbeg Museum.

3 A print of Ioannina.

4 Figures of the Ottoman Empire.

Did You Know?

Albanian leader Zog I was in fact never crowned; the title of "king" was self-proclaimed in 1928.

1385

Ottoman soldiers defeat Albanian militias at the Battle of Savra, with many local leaders becoming Ottoman vassals.

1444

Skanderbeg forms the League of Lezhë to unite the Albanian rebellion.

18th century

Many Albanians convert to Islam under the Ottomans.

1912

The statesman Ismail Qemali proclaims Albania's independence.

1928

Albania becomes a monarchy under Zog I.

1

World War II

The Kingdom of Albania swiftly fell in 1939, when the region was invaded by Italian forces. Italy's fascist leader Benito Mussolini hoped to carve out a modern Roman Empire in the 1930s and Albania, a former Roman province, became a prime target for invasion. When Italy began to fall to Allied forces from 1943 onwards, the Italian occupation of Albania ended and Nazi forces took its place. German occupation lasted until 1944, when Albanian partisans (who were mostly communists) successfully overthrew the Nazis and liberated Albania. Enver Hoxha, the Secretary General of the Albanian Communist Party, became national leader by default.

Did You Know?

Under communism, Albania became the first atheist state in the world in 1967.

Communist Leadership

Under Hoxha's leadership, the region became the People's Republic of Albania from 1946. At the beginning of communist rule, the government's socialist leaders sought to modernize the feudalist, war-weary country with rapid reform. From the 1950s, land and livestock agriculture was collectivized, other industries were nationalized and all opposition voices were

Timeline of events

1941

Enver Hohxa, a former grammar school teacher, becomes leader of the Albanian Communist Party.

1948

Albania cuts ties with communist Yugoslavia in favour of the Soviet Union.

1961

Albania builds a relationship with Chairman Mao's China.

1967

Religion is outlawed, and many religious sites are closed.

suppressed through persecution. One key policy was the outlawing of all religions, which was fully enforced by 1967. At the same time, Cold War tensions continued to mount, leading Albania to cut ties with other communist powers and build shelters in preparation for nuclear war; an estimated 175,000 bunkers were built during this time. As communism began to crumble across much of Eastern Europe, so too it fell in Albania; in 1992, over four decades of communist rule in the country came to an end when the first elections were held.

Albania Today

The 1990s were a time of significant upheaval, as Albania worked to transition into a modern democracy. Many Albanians emigrated from the country during this time – and continue to do so today. Albania has since strengthened its international ties, becoming a member of NATO in 2009 and pursuing membership of the European Union. A number of infrastructure projects are also underway to support a growing tourism industry, as reflected in the 10 million passengers who passed through Tirana Airport in 2024.

1 Benito Mussolini visiting Albania's front in 1941. ↑

2 General Enver Hoxha addressing a People's Congress in 1946.

3 The NATO Parliamentary Assembly's spring session held in Tirana in 2016.

4 Tourists enjoying one of Albania's seaside resorts.

1978

Albania cuts ties with communist China and becomes an isolationist state.

1992

Free elections end 47 years of communist rule in Albania.

2009

Albania becomes a full member of NATO.

2020

The European Union begins accession talks with Albania.

2025

Albania hosts the European Political Community summit.

FAITH IN ALBANIA

The presence of varied belief systems in Albania is in part thanks to its many historic rulers. Pagan customs have been maintained since the time of the ancient Illyrians, while Catholicism, Orthodox Christianity and Islam were all brought to the region by different conquerors. Eventually, with 20th-century communism came state-sanctioned atheism, which was overthrown in the 1990s along with the government. This long, multi-faith legacy means that, today, a whole host of religions are observed across Albania.

BYZANTINE PRESENCE

When the Christian faith began to split between Catholic and Orthodox factions from the 10th century CE, faith in the Albanian region was also divided. Areas in the north remained geographically and spiritually closer to Catholicism, while much of Albania's south observed the Orthodox faith. The southern city of Berat *(p162)* became a centre of Orthodox learning under the Byzantine Empire; as a result, many churches were decorated with the golden iconographic art of the Byzantine priest Onufri *(p163)*. Other cities, like Korçë *(p170)*, remain home to stunning Orthodox art and craftsmanship.

↑ A gold-painted icon in the Onufri Iconography Museum

TOP 3 RELIGIOUS BUILDINGS IN ALBANIA

Church of the Dormition of the Theotokos,
A striking Byzantine church in Labovë e Kryqit, this religious site dates back to the 6th century.

St Paul's Cathedral
Pope John Paul II laid the cornerstone of this modern cathedral in Tirana back in 1993 *(p76)*.

Bazaar Mosque
When religion was outlawed under communism in the 1960s, parts of Gjirokastër's Bazaar Mosque *(p154)* were used instead as a training hall for budding acrobats.

THE OTTOMANS BRING ISLAM

With the Ottoman conquest of Albania from the 14th century came Islam, the empire's dominant faith. Prominent Christian temples like St Stephen's Cathedral in Shkodër *(p88)* were turned into mosques, while hammams and religious schools were built in many cities and towns. Other key mosques were built during this time, including Tirana's Et'hem Bey Mosque *(p72)* and the Bazaar Mosque of Gjirokastër *(p154)*. The Ottoman Empire was multi-faith, and so there was some tolerance of other religions during this time.

COMMUNISM AND ITS AFTERMATH

Soon after the Ottoman Empire fell in Albania in the 20th century, it was succeeded by a communist government. In 1967, the Communist Party cracked down on faith and banned all religious activity; over 2,000 religious sites were desecrated or demolished. Worshippers continued to observe Islam and Christianity privately, taking care to avoid attracting attention. In 1991, the march of 10,000 people towards Tirana's Et'hem Bey Mosque *(p72)* precipitated the downfall of communism. Since then, religion has played a key role again and many religious sites – like Tirana's Namazgah Mosque, the largest of its kind in the Balkans – have been built.

THE BEKTASHI ORDER

Up to 10 per cent of Albanian Muslims today follow the legacy of Haji Bektash Veli, a 13th-century Islamic scholar. The Bektashi Order first became popular among the Ottoman Empire's elite Janissary corps, which was dominated by ethnic Albanians. As well as their five daily prayers, Bektashi Muslims pray at dawn and dusk and follow a *baba*, or a spiritual guide.

↑ Korçë's Resurrection of Christ Cathedral, home to stunning Byzantine art and woodwork

EXPERIENCE

Sunloungers along Dhërmi Beach

Tirana's Namazgah Mosque

TIRANA

Five centuries ago, Tirana was a mere village. By the 17th century, its Ottoman governor had added a hammam and mosque, but Tirana's promotion to town status came only at the start of the 19th century. It was then that the benefactor Molla Bey of Petrela funded the Et'hem Bey Mosque, which was named after his son and has been a key cultural landmark ever since. Molla Bey also later built the neighbouring Clock Tower, Tirana's tallest building for nearly two centuries.

Tirana still stayed small during this time; by 1900, its population hovered at around just 10,000 people. It was only in 1925, following mass migration caused by the Balkan Wars of 1912–13, that by-then fast-growing Tirana was proclaimed the newly independent country's permanent capital.

After first Italian then Nazi occupation during World War II, a communist government was established in 1946 under Enver Hoxha. The government oversaw the demolition of many of the city's historic buildings, and bazaars and churches were replaced with Soviet-style apartment blocks and factories. When the government was overthrown in 1991, Tirana became the epicentre of revolution; the first elections were held in 1992. As the political situation stabilized from 2000 onwards, the city experienced a boom in construction and tourism, which continues today.

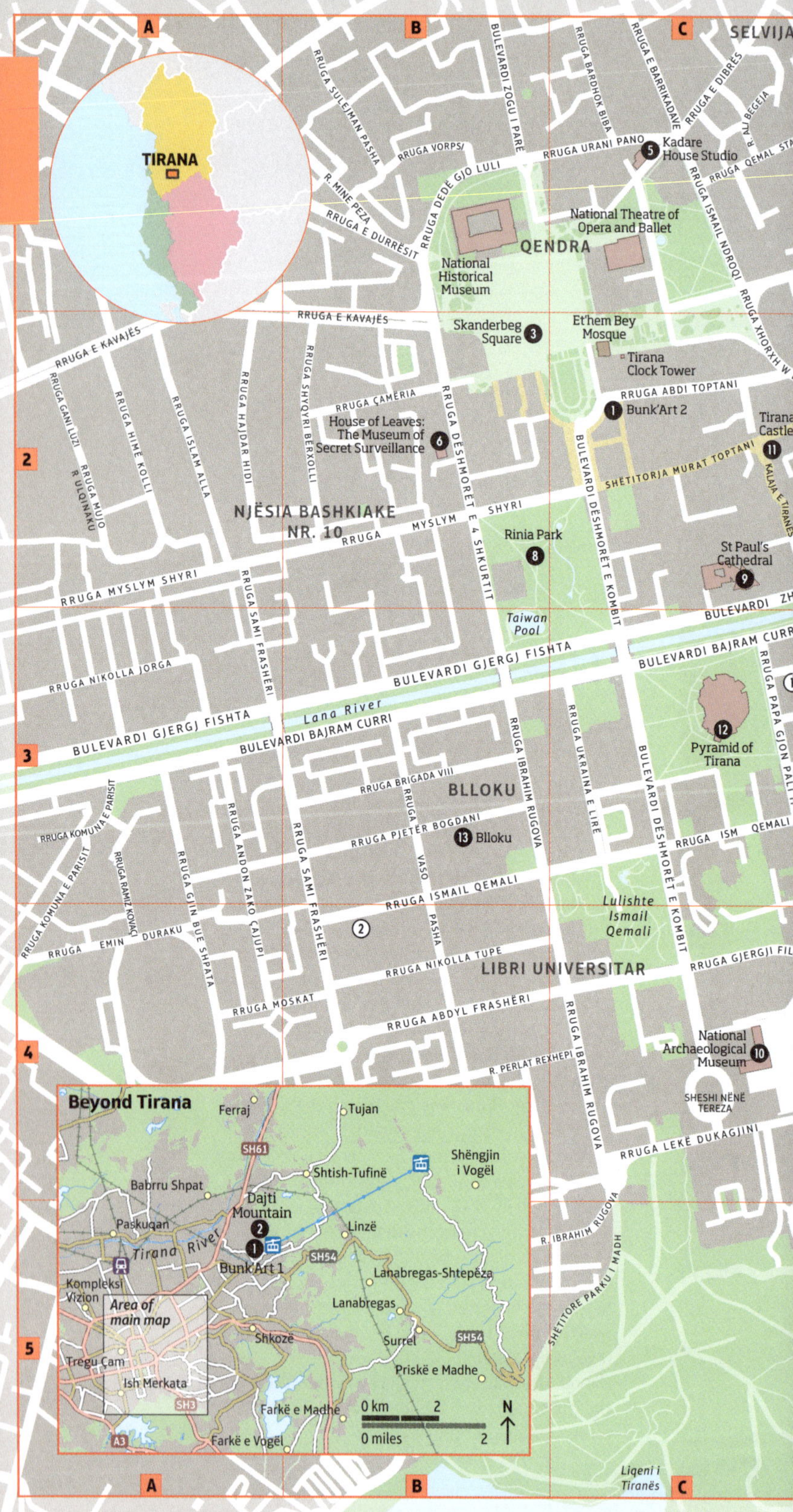

A
B
C
SELVIJA
TIRANA
Rruga Sulejman Pasha
Bulevardi Zogu I Parë
Rruga Bardhok Biba
Rruga e Barrikadave
Rruga e Dibrës
R. Ali Begeja
Rruga Vorps/
Rruga Urani Pano
Kadare House Studio
5
Rruga Qemal Sta
R. Mine Peza
Rruga e Durrësit
Rruga Dedë Gjo Luli
National Theatre of Opera and Ballet
QENDRA
National Historical Museum
Rruga Ismail Ndroqi
Rruga Xhorxh W
Rruga e Kavajës
Skanderbeg Square
3
Et'hem Bey Mosque
Tirana Clock Tower
Rruga Abdi Toptani
1
Bunk'Art 2
Tirana Castle
11
Rruga Çamëria
House of Leaves: The Museum of Secret Surveillance
6
Rruga Gani Luzi
R. Ulqinaku
Rruga Mujo
Rruga Himë Kolli
Rruga Islam Alla
Rruga Hajdar Hidi
Rruga Shyqyri Berxolli
Rruga Dëshmorët e 4 Shkurtit
Bulevardi Dëshmorët e Kombit
Shëtitorja Murat Toptani
Kalaja e Tiranës
2
NJËSIA BASHKIAKE NR. 10
Rruga Myslym Shyri
Rinia Park
8
St Paul's Cathedral
9
Rruga Sami Frashëri
Taiwan Pool
Bulevardi Zh
Bulevardi Bajram Curri
Rruga Nikolla Jorga
Bulevardi Gjergj Fishta
Lana River
Rruga Ukraina e Lirë
Rruga Papa Gjon Pali II
12
Pyramid of Tirana
3
Rruga Brigada VIII
BLLOKU
Rruga Ibrahim Rugova
Rruga Komuna e Parisit
Rruga Ramiz Kovaçi
Rruga Gjin Bue Shpata
Rruga Andon Zako Çajupi
Rruga Pjetër Bogdani
13
Blloku
Rruga Vaso Pasha
Rruga Ism Qemali
Rruga Ismail Qemali
2
Lulishte Ismail Qemali
Rruga Emin Duraku
Rruga Nikolla Tupe
LIBRI UNIVERSITAR
Rruga Gjergji Fil
Rruga Moskat
Rruga Abdyl Frashëri
4
R. Perlat Rexhepi
National Archaeological Museum
10
Sheshi Nënë Tereza
Rruga Lekë Dukagjini
R. Ibrahim Rugova
Shetitore Parku i Madh
5
Liqeni i Tiranës
Beyond Tirana
Ferraj
Tujan
SH61
Shtish-Tufinë
Shëngjin i Vogël
Babrru Shpat
Dajti Mountain
Paskuqan
Linzë
Tirana River
Bunk'Art 1
SH54
Lanabregas-Shtepëza
Kompleksi Vizion
Area of main map
Lanabregas
Shkozë
Surrel
Tregu Cam
Ish Merkata
Priskë e Madhe
SH3
Farkë e Madhe
0 km
2
0 miles
2
N
A3
Farkë e Vogël

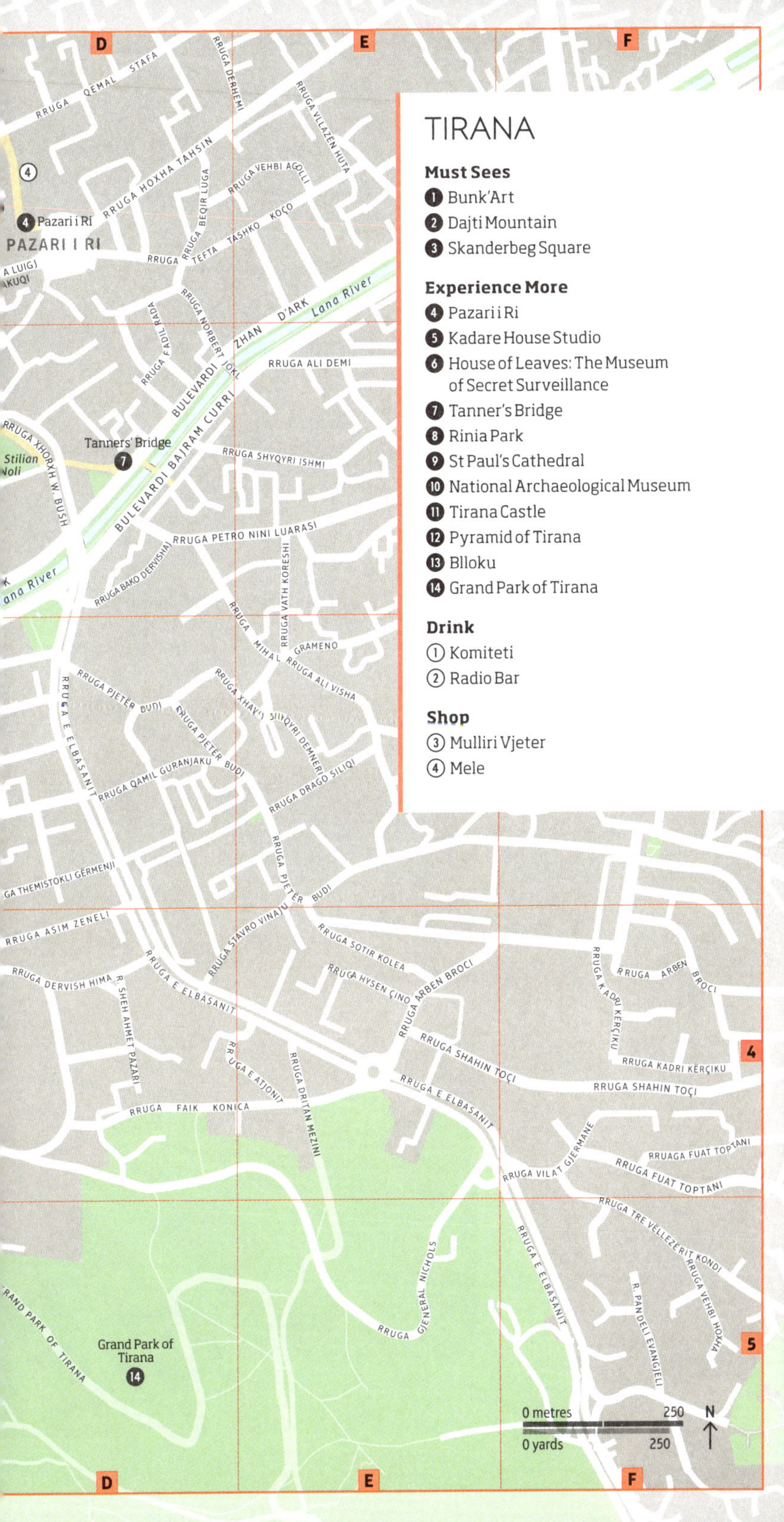
TIRANA
Must Sees
1 Bunk'Art
2 Dajti Mountain
3 Skanderbeg Square
Experience More
4 Pazari i Ri
5 Kadare House Studio
6 House of Leaves: The Museum of Secret Surveillance
7 Tanner's Bridge
8 Rinia Park
9 St Paul's Cathedral
10 National Archaeological Museum
11 Tirana Castle
12 Pyramid of Tirana
13 Blloku
14 Grand Park of Tirana
Drink
1 Komiteti
2 Radio Bar
Shop
3 Mulliri Vjeter
4 Mele
D
E
F
4
5
PAZARI I RI
Pazari i Ri
Tanners' Bridge
Grand Park of Tirana
Lana River
BULEVARDI ZHAN D'ARK
BULEVARDI BAJRAM CURRI
RRUGA QEMAL STAFA
RRUGA HOXHA TAHSIN
RRUGA DERHEMI
RRUGA VILLAZËN HUTA
RRUGA VEHBI AGOLLI
RRUGA BEQIR LUGA
RRUGA TEFTA TASHKO KOÇO
RRUGA NORBERT JOKL
RRUGA FADIL RADA
RRUGA ALI DEMI
RRUGA SHYQYRI ISHMI
RRUGA PETRO NINI LUARASI
RRUGA BAKO DERVISHAJ
RRUGA VATH KORESHI
RRUGA MIHAL GRAMENO
RRUGA ALI VISHA
RRUGA PJETËR BUDI
RRUGA XHAVIT SHQYRI DEMNERI
RRUGA E ELBASANIT
RRUGA QAMIL GURANJAKU
RRUGA DRAGO SILIQI
RRUGA THEMISTOKLI GËRMENJI
RRUGA ASIM ZENELI
RRUGA STAVRO VINAJU
RRUGA SOTIR KOLEA
RRUGA HYSEN ÇINO
RRUGA ARBEN BROCI
RRUGA DERVISH HIMA
R. SHEH AHMET PAZARI
RRUGA E ATJONIT
RRUGA DRITAN MEZINI
RRUGA SHAHIN TOÇI
RRUGA KADRI KËRÇIKU
RRUGA FAIK KONICA
RRUGA VILAT GJERMANE
RRUAGA FUAT TOPTANI
RRUGA FUAT TOPTANI
RRUGA TRE VELLEZËRIT KONDI
RRUGA VEHBI HOXHA
R. PANDELI EVANGJELI
RRUGA GJENERAL NICHOLS
GRAND PARK OF TIRANA
RRUGA XHORXH W. BUSH
0 metres 250
0 yards 250
N

1

BUNK'ART

Bunk'Art 1: A5 Rruga Fadil Deliu Bar Kafe Deliu 9:30am-4:30pm daily; Bunk'Art 2: C2 Rruga Abdi Toptani Parku Rinia 9:30am-8pm daily bunkart.al

In the face of rising Cold War tensions in the late 20th century, Albanian leader Enver Hoxha oversaw the building of cavernous underground bunkers across the country. Now disused, many have been repurposed; today, two of Tirana's larger complexes are now the Bunk'Art museums, where displays shed light on this communist past.

Opened in 2014 and 2016, Tirana's Bunk'Art museums are found inside two of the city's former military bunkers. Defence structures like these were continually built across Albania from the 1960s for decades until the decline of the communist regime in the 1980s. The Bunk'Art sites represent just a small portion of these: there are thought to be over 175,000 disused bunkers across the country. Today, the Bunk'Art spaces have been repurposed to house interactive exhibition spaces.

Bunk'Art 1

Away from Tirana's centre, under the shadow of Dajti Mountain *(p70)*, lies the first of the city's two Bunk'Art sites. Unlike smaller ones across Tirana, this bunker was intended as a huge, subterranean settlement for senior officials in the event of all-out nuclear war.

Inside, the past is brought to life through interactive displays on communism in Albania from the 1930s. Visitors can also see Enver Hoxha's preserved personal quarters here.

THE SIGURIMI: ALBANIA'S FORMER SECRET POLICE

The Directorate of State Security (Drejtoria e Sigurimit të Shtetit) was a ruthlessly effective secret police force that operated during the entire communist period, from 1945 until 1991. Known as the Sigurimi for short, the organization oversaw prison camps, press censorship and, above all, state-sanctioned espionage. Albanian agents were originally taught by Soviet instructors. The Sigurimi used these surveillance skills in all kinds of public spaces, from cultural venues like cinemas to public transport. The force did its best to quell uprisings in 1990 and 1991, before being disbanded.

Did You Know?

Bunker builders were moved from project to project once a month to ensure absolute confidentiality.

Inside the main domed space of the underground Bunk'Art site ↑

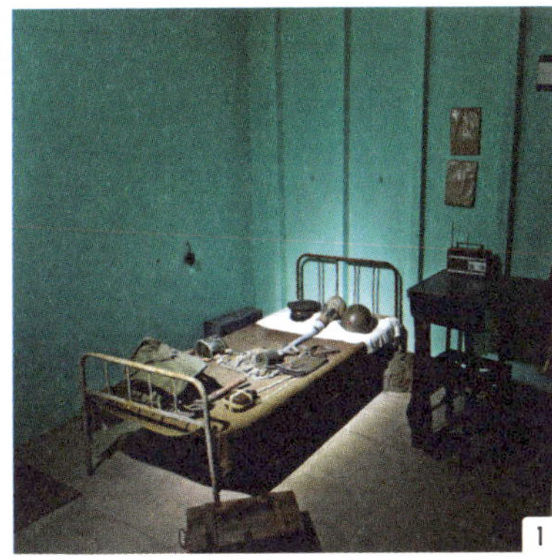

1 One of the re-created living quarters inside Bunk'Art 1.

2 The tunnel entrance to Bunk'Art 1, leading through to the exhibition inside.

3 Visitors engaging with the displays in Bunk'Art 1, which explores Albania's communist history.

Bunk'Art 2

The second site of the Bunk'Art project, Bunk'Art 2 is a massive, 24-room nuclear bunker located right below the centre of Tirana. One of the last mega-structures planned by Enver Hoxha, it was off-limits to the public from when the communist government fell in the 1990s until 2016, when the museum was opened. Beneath its domed entrance, burrowed several storeys below the building of the former Ministry of Internal Affairs, lies an exhibition space dedicated to the history of the ministry and the work of the secret police force known as the Sigurimi *(p66)*.

Visitors to Bunk'Art 2 can follow an underground route through the museum's many rooms, which chronicle the claustrophobic monitoring that took place across late 20th-century Albania. Displays explore different aspects of Sigurimi surveillance. One room shows how foreign capital was used to source 4-cm- (1.5-inch-) long eavesdropping bugs produced in East Germany; these were hidden in everyday objects, like ashtrays or bicycle pumps, to allow covert monitoring to take place.

Aside from monitoring the Albanian population during this period, another one of the ministry's principal aims was to prevent people from leaving the country; more displays throughout the museum space shed light on some of the tactics that were used to track down people attempting to flee.

The second site of the Bunk'Art project, Bunk'Art 2 is a massive, 24-room nuclear bunker located right below the centre of Tirana.

Historic monitoring devices on display inside the rooms of Bunk'Art 2

↑ One of the preserved rooms in the underground Bunk'Art museums

TOP 3 BUNKER EXPERIENCES

Keq Marku Tattoo
Km 3 Koplik, near Shkodër
06 7556 3852
This tattoo parlour operates out of a small, concrete bunker.

Gjirokastër's Cold War Tunnel
Sheshi Çerçiz Topulli, Gjirokastër
Now a museum *(p155)*, locals only knew about this 800-m- (2,600-ft-) long bunker in the 1990s.

Beach Bunkers of Lake Ohrid
Pogradec
Around Lake Ohrid, disused bunkers have been repurposed and made into beach bars.

The distinctive domed entrance to Bunk'Art 2 in the centre of Tirana

DAJTI MOUNTAIN

A5 Teleferik Cable car: 9am-7pm Wed-Mon (until 7:30pm Sat & Sun)
dajtiekspres.com

Looming 1,600 m (5,200 ft) over Albania's capital city, Dajti is both a mountain peak and a national park with a thick forest of oak, beech and juniper trees. Its cable car is the easiest and most popular way to take in the peak's beautiful views.

Dajti Mountain National Park (Parku Kombëtar Mali i Dajtit) is the green oasis near Tirana, covering nearly 300 sq km (115 sq miles). It's a popular getaway from the city centre, in part thanks to the thrilling cable-car journey up to its peak. It whisks passengers from a Tirana suburb to the top in just 15 minutes, gliding high above lakes, vineyards, orchards and the first green shoots of Tirana's rural outskirts.

At the summit, an array of activities await near the cable-car terminus. Visitors can enjoy a rose garden, children's park and mini golf, as well as cafés and breathtaking views of Tirana. There is also a tree-top Adventure Park, with zip lines and rope bridges for all ages.

Hikers, meanwhile, can explore the forests with a pre-arranged mountain guide; care should be taken along the way, as wild boars, wildcats and brown bears all roam here. Serious trekkers can also follow a red-and-white marked trail to the park's breathtaking Col of Qershia viewpoint, two hours away.

Dajti Mountain is a popular getaway from Tirana's city centre, in part thanks to the thrilling cable-car journey up to its peak.

Did You Know?

The yellow house near Dajti's cable-car terminus once belonged to a scouts-style youth camp.

EAT

Ballkoni Dajtit

For a delicious lunch with an epic view, make your way to this restaurant near Dajti Mountain's cable-car terminus. The restaurant serves home-style Albanian classics, including chicken and walnut risotto, stuffed pickles and crispy spinach *byrek*.

Mali i Dajtit 11am-6:30pm Wed-Mon
67 401 1021

↑ A cable car pulling in to the stop at the top of Dajti Mountain

↑ Abandoned bunkers located among Dajti Mountain's green forests

3

SKANDERBEG SQUARE

B2 Biblioteka

Tirana's main plaza, Skanderbeg Square (Sheshi Skënderbej) is named after the Albanian national hero. The huge square is a bustling pedestrian hub, ringed by restaurants and the capital's star attractions.

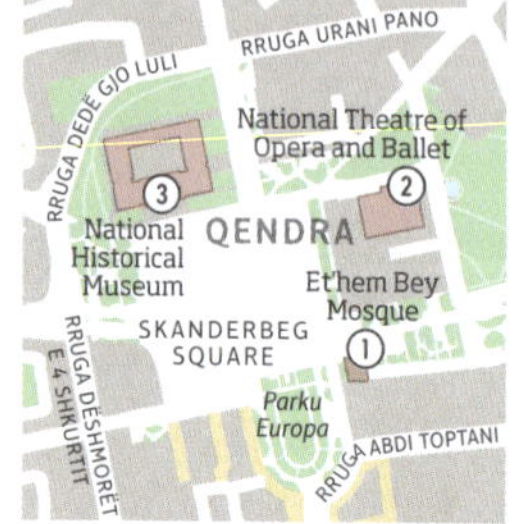

①

Et'hem Bey Mosque

Sheshi Skënderbej 1
9am-noon & 2-4pm Sat-Thu, 2:30-4pm Fri

One of Tirana's few remaining historic sights, the small but beautiful Et'hem Bey Mosque (Xhamia e Haxhi Et'hem Beut) was completed around 1821. It was spared during the communist absolutism of the 1960s – when many churches, monasteries and religious buildings were torn down or repurposed – although its doors remained closed to the public during this time. As the dictatorship teetered, the mosque's closure was tested, and in January 1991, some 10,000 worshippers flooded into the mosque in an act of defiance.

Today, visitors can step inside the cool interior, which reveals a lesson in Islamic art. Its main prayer hall is the most ornate room, decorated with intricate frescoes seldom seen in mosques. Trees, flowers, waterfalls and bridges spiral up many of the interior walls. The mosque welcomes sightseers until sunset, in happy disregard to the official opening hours.

Also part of the Et'hem Bey Mosque structure is the **Clock Tower** (Kulla e Sahatit). The 35-m- (115-ft-) tall tower was built in 1822 by Haxhi Et'hem Bey Mollaj, the poet and power behind the Et'hem Bey Mosque next door; it remained the tallest building in the city until the 1970s.

The 90 claustrophobic steps up the landmark lead

STAY

Choose Balkans Apartments
This travel agency has trendy apartments near Skanderbeg Square.
Bulevardi Dëshmorët e Kombit
chooseballkans.com

Destil B&B
This guesthouse offers four boutique, en-suite rooms, with a small shared kitchen.
Rruga Ismail Qemali 8
69 756 5237

to one of Tirana's most scenic viewpoints. If you ascend the stairs on the hour, hearing the clock tower's loud ring up close is unavoidable.

Clock Tower
9am-6pm Mon-Fri, 9am-2pm Sat

National Theatre of Opera and Ballet

Muzeu Kombëtar
Performance times vary, check website for details
tkob.gov.al

The capital's National Theatre of Opera and Ballet (Teatri i Operas dhe Baletit) is one of the cultural hearts of Tirana. Albania's largest performing arts centre, it opened in 1966 at a time when the city was almost completely devoid of such venues. Today, operas, ballets and musicals are performed year-round, ranging from a Puccini season and Baroque recitals to concerts featuring music by the British rock band Queen.

The opera house occupies the northern half of the Palace of Culture (Pallati i Kulturës), built in 1963. Beneath its grand façade are popular restaurants and shops. To the rear of the palace is the **National Library of Albania** (Biblioteka Kombëtare e Shqipërisë), another important cultural institution in the capital still used by students today.

National Library of Albania
9:30am-7:30pm daily

SKANDERBEG

Albania's national hero, the military figure Skanderbeg (1405-68) challenged, and frequently defeated, the Ottoman Empire at its zenith. Born Gjergj Kastrioti, he was known as İskender bey (Lord Alexander), perhaps a nod to his military skills which channelled Alexander the Great. Skanderbeg's victories are said to have delayed further Ottoman expansion into Europe by decades.

Dusk descending over Tirana's pedestrianized Skanderbeg Square

National Historical Museum

Muzeu Kombëtar
Temporarily for refurbishment until 2028 **mhk.gov.al**

Opened in 1981, the National Historical Museum (Muzeu Historik Kombëtar) is one of the country's most important museums of Albanian artifacts. Currently undergoing a renovation, it will showcase a visual timeline of Albanian culture, starting in ancient Illyria, when it reopens in 2028.

The museum collection holds many objects from key periods in Albanian history: ornate silver coins and vibrant mosaics of Illyrian kings, Greek pottery, Roman statues and medieval artworks. One of the museum's most colourful collections includes artworks painted by Onufri *(p163)*, a 16th-century priest born in Albania who carried on the Byzantine tradition of icon painting into the Renaissance period.

The recent past is covered here, too, with displays on Albanian-born Mother Teresa *(p77)* and the 20th-century communist regime. Visitors can also gaze up at the socialist realist mosaic, *The Albanians*, which dominates the museum's façade. This looming, colourful work depicts statesman Ismail Qemali and Ottoman resistance fighters, among others.

EXPERIENCE MORE

Pazari i Ri

D1 Pazari i Ri
8am-9pm daily
pazariiri.com

Pazari i Ri (New Market) is a busy market neighbourhood alive with hawkers' cries and fragrant foodie aromas. Street stalls supplying downtown Tirana have existed here for centuries, alongside a surrounding cluster of cafés, bars and restaurants. Today, the bazaar's main function remains the same: selling delicious Berat olives, Adriatic octopus, mountain butter, homemade raki and other culinary delights.

The district's market area has a glass roof, beneath which cooking presentations are hosted, food kiosks serve tasty street food and market stalls sell produce. Shoppers can sample fresh fruit and vegetables like apricots or walnuts before purchasing, depending on what's in season. Souvenirs are also sold here, such as olivewood breadboards and traditional woollen slippers, as well as smaller items like fridge magnets and hats emblazoned with the Albanian eagle. The market supplies most establishments in the area, making Pazari i Ri a great place to stop for refreshments between sights.

Today, the bazaar's main function remains the same: selling delicious Berat olives, Adriatic octopus, mountain butter, homemade raki and other culinary delights.

SHOP

Mulliri Vjeter

You can smell this coffee roaster before you see it. There are grinds for sale suited to a range of coffee makers, from traditional Turkish pots to Nespresso machines. There's also a great café on site.

D1 Pazari i Ri
mullirivjeter.al

Mele

This superb shop has a great selection of traditional Albanian cheeses. It's possible to try before buying, with available varieties including *djath i bardhë* village feta and a cheddar-style cheese from Gjirokastër.

D1 Pazari i Ri

5 Kadare House Studio

C1 Rruga e Dibrës 25
Muzeu Kombëtar
10am-5pm Tue-Fri, 10am-3pm Sat Mon & Sun
shtepiakadare.tirana.al

The Kadare House Studio (Muzeu Kadare), located in the former Tirana home of prolific 20th-century Albanian author Ismail Kadare *(p159)*, serves as a museum dedicated to his life and work. Kadare, who died in July 2024, is renowned for his novels warning of the dangers of totalitarianism. Through the use of legend, metaphor and double meanings, he skilfully

navigated Albania's strict censorship at the time. The highlight of the museum is Kadare's personal library, which contains around 1,000 books, unpublished manuscripts and poems translated into English.

The building itself, one side of which is brightly painted, is easy to find; the museum's opening hours, however, can be erratic.

House of Leaves: The Museum of Secret Surveillance

B2 Rruga Dëshmorët e 4 Shkurtit Parku Rinian 9am-7pm daily muzeugjethi.gov.al

A basement entrance to one of the exhibition spaces at Tirana's House of Leaves museum

The House of Leaves (Shtëpia me Gjethe: Muzeu i Përgjimeve të Sigurimit të Shtetit) is located in a townhouse obscured by trees, the inspiration behind its name. In the 20th century, it was the little-known headquarters of Albania's secret police, known as the Sigurimi *(p66)*. It has since been made into one of Tirana's most interesting museums, where visitors can learn more about the surveillance that took place in communist Albania. Displays showcase historic monitoring devices that were used, such as microphones, mini-cameras and wire-tapping kits. They also highlight ways in which these methods were ineffective; in 1970s Tirana, only around 1,500 households out of 175,000 had phones that could be tapped in the first place.

Tanner's Bridge

D2 Parlamenti

The pretty Tanner's Bridge (Ura e Tabakëve) may be small, but it holds a significant place in Tirana's history. In the 18th century, the footbridge was part of the main road into Tirana. It spanned a river and its main traffic was livestock, with cows and sheep herded across on their way to the butchers' and leather-makers' quarters a few blocks north, near Pazari i Ri; today, it no longer crosses any waterways. As one of the few surviving older structures in Tirana, the bridge stands as a reminder of the city's past, much of which was lost during five centuries of Ottoman rule.

Pazari i Ri's glass-roofed market and *(inset)* a stall selling olivewood goods

↑ An artificial lake with plenty of greenery in Tirana's Rinia Park

Rinia Park

B2 Parku Rinia

Rinia Park (Parku Rinia) was built in the 1950s, creating a family-friendly green square in the city. Since then, the square has been reimagined and upgraded into a modern outdoor space.

Today, it's filled with fountains, walkways, climbing frames and a photo-ready sign spelling out the city's name. There are also plenty of casual food venues in and around the square, serving light refreshments. The square makes for an ideal stop-off point while sightseeing in Tirana, connecting the centrally located Skanderbeg Square *(p72)* to some of the popular sights near the Pyramid of Tirana *(p78)* and National Archaeological Museum.

PICTURE PERFECT
Tirana Cloud

Known as *The Cloud,* this art installation by Sou Fujimoto near Rinia Park is made up of thin rods which create a cloud-like form. It makes for stunning photos, both within and outside the structure.

St Paul's Cathedral

C2 Bulevardi Zhan d'Ark Piramida 7am-7pm daily

Near the banks of the Lana River stands the striking Modernist-style St Paul's Cathedral (Katedralja Katolike Shën Pali). The cornerstone of this Catholic cathedral was laid by Pope John Paul II in 1993 and it was eventually consecrated in 2002. Since then, the site has become a place of pilgrimage, where visiting Catholics can also take mass in English.

The cathedral departs from tradition in its layout by using symbolic triangular and circular shapes in its floor plan instead of the more common cruciform shape. This adds to the contemporary feel of the building.

The inside space is austere, devoid of the usual detailed decorations associated with this type of religious building. Stained-glass windows, some of which depict popes Francis and John Paul II, bathe the interior in colour. Outside the cathedral stands a well-visited

→ A statue of the sainted Mother Teresa, located outside St Paul's Cathedral

MOTHER TERESA

Mother Teresa (1910-97) is one of the most famous Albanians in history. The sainted nun was born Anjezë Gonxhe Bojaxhiu in 1910 in Skopje (North Macedonia) to a Kosovar-Albanian family. She moved to Ireland to join the Sisters of Loreto in 1928. After the rise of communism in Albania in 1944, she wasn't able to return to the region for a long period due to the government's stance on religion. Later, as a Catholic missionary, she was sent to Kolkata, India. Mother Teresa eventually returned to Albania in 1991 to open a charity and take up citizenship. She died in 1997.

statue of Mother Teresa, or Nënë Tereza, the world-famous missionary nun.

National Archaeological Museum

C4 Sheshi Nënë Tereza 3 Rektorati 9am-2pm daily asa.edu.al

The artifact-rich National Archaeological Museum (Muzeu Arkeologjik Kombëtar) opened in 1948. Its extensive collection is displayed over five capacious halls, beginning with objects from the Bronze Age, when the ancient Illyrians moved into the Albanian region. There are plenty of items from the Roman era here, too: as the region sat on the Via Egnatia (the historic highway between Constantinople and Rome), daggers, urns, Roman-era jewellery and the like have been unearthed at over 100 sites of archaeological significance. Many of the artifacts on display were discovered by European excavators, until international collaboration ceased in the 1950s. The museum's display of Roman busts includes a depiction of Emperor Hadrian, who founded the town of Hadrianopolis in the present-day Albania.

11   

Tirana Castle

C2 Shëtitorja Murat Toptani Parlamenti 7am-2am daily kalajaetiranes.al

The towering 6-m- (20-ft-) high walls in the city centre may not look like a typical fortress, but they are all that remains of Tirana Castle (Kalanë e Tiranës). The original fortifications were built by Ottoman occupiers on top of 14th-century Byzantine remnants and were known as the Fortress of Justinian.

In the 21st century, restaurants and ice-cream shops have opened inside, as well as a popular bazaar where traditional textiles and olivewood carvings are sold. The bustling atmosphere carries through to the rest of the street, with its many outdoor restaurants and cafés.

→ Enjoying the many cafés and shops in the grounds of Tirana Castle

DRINK

Komiteti
Decked out in nostalgic décor, this atmospheric spot is known for its great raki selection.
C3 Rruga Papa Gjon Pali II
69 445 2772

Radio Bar
This gem of a bar serves tasty cocktails amid a collection of antique TVs and typewriters.
B3 Rruga Ismail Qemali 29 radiobar.al

Pyramid of Tirana

C3 Bulevardi Dëshmorët e Kombit 5 Piramida piramida.edu.al

Built in 1988, the Pyramid of Tirana was constructed as a museum dedicated to the life of dictator Enver Hoxha following his death in 1985. Within a few years, it was used for much more, becoming a conference centre and even a filming location for a horror movie.

In 2023, the Pyramid underwent its latest and most ground-breaking reinvention, when it was transformed into an architectural symbol of a modern Albania. New exhibition spaces, cafés and viewing platforms have been added to the structure, all of which can be accessed via a series of white metal staircases. There are a variety of venues to enjoy on-site, while concrete slides allow visitors to whizz back down to ground level. At the day's end, it's possible to enjoy fabulous views over the Tirana skyline from here. Down below, regular outdoor performances take place in the Pyramid's leafy grounds.

Blloku

B3

Just a 10-minute stroll from Tirana's city centre lies the elegant Blloku neighbourhood, a storied district buzzing with modern energy. Once the exclusive domain of Albania's political elite during the communist period of the 20th century, Blloku's pretty, tree-lined streets were mainly reserved for high-ranking officials, including then-leader Enver Hoxha. His former residence, a three-storey villa, still stands on Rruga Ismail Qemali, although today it's closed to the public.

Venues inside the Pyramid of Tirana and *(inset)* the structure's conical exterior

↑ Strolling along a leafy path within the Grand Park of Tirana

Today, Blloku attracts a vibrant crowd, drawn to its swanky hotels, bustling bakeries and independent boutiques. The popular neighbourhood is especially known for its thriving food and drink scene, offering everything from seafood spots where you can pick your own fish to hipster coffeehouses. It's also a hub for Tirana nightlife, and home to several lively LGBTQ+ bars.

The district is perfect for leisurely city walks and people-watching, with locals gathering at swish pavement cafés throughout its streets. Blloku's trendy vibes have also spread to nearby roads, bringing a fresh wave of fashionable venues and well-heeled visitors to the area.

HISTORY OF COFFEE CULTURE IN ALBANIA

Coffee culture has thrived in Albania for centuries. Traditional coffee-making goes back to the time of the Ottoman Empire, when coffee was made in the Turkish manner: finely ground coffee beans would be cooked in small copper pots, producing a strong brew. Today, the ritual of sharing *kahve* (coffee) remains ingrained in Albanian culture, and traditional coffee is easy to find in most cafés.

14  

Grand Park of Tirana

D5 Rruga Herman Gmeiner Rektorati aprtirana.al

South of trendy Blloku is Tirana's green lung, the Grand Park of Tirana (Parku i Madh). This large, leafy outdoors space was first laid out in 1956 in what was then the city limits. Its impressive 289 hectares (714 acres) – about the size of 500 football pitches – of green space are home to approximately 120 plant and animal species, including turtles, lizards and snakes. At the heart of the park is its massive artificial lake, complete with a functioning dam, which was completed in the 1950s.

The Grand Park of Tirana, a large, leafy outdoors space, was first laid out in 1956 in what was then the city limits.

Among all the greenery and nature, there are a number of notable structures. The 1970s amphitheatre hosts regular events, while children's playgrounds, sports grounds and designated cycle paths offer recreational activities for all ages. There is also a church and a zoo.

Look out, too, for the many monuments here, including a Holocaust memorial located near the park's main entrance. Unveiled in 2020, it was produced by Holocaust survivor Stephen Jacobs to commemorate the efforts of Albanians who aided their Jewish neighbours during the time of Nazi occupation in Albania.

Bordering the park grounds is the Palace of Brigades (Pallati i Brigadave), which was originally built in the 20th century for the former ruler King Zog I.

A SHORT WALK DOWNTOWN TIRANA

Distance 2 km (1.3 miles) **Walking time** Approx 30 minutes

Locator Map
TIRANA
Downtown Tirana

See p64

Downtown Tirana is centred around Skanderbeg Square *(p72)*, where some of the capital's most popular sights can be found. Stroll around the square and onto its connecting boulevards and pedestrian streets to take in the architectural highlights and cultural offerings of the area. There is a huge variety of buildings to be enjoyed here, from historic mosques to towering modern skyscrapers.

RRUGA ISMAIL NDROQI

Start at Tirana's centre, **Skanderbeg Square** *(p72), which hosts a range of events throughout the year.*

START

RRUGA ABDI TOPTANI

Spot the minaret of the historic **Et'hem Bey Mosque** *(p72) before making your way to the south of the square.*

0 metre 200
0 yards 200
N

Pass by the museum and art space **Bunk'Art 2** *(p66), home to exhibits on Albania's communist past.*

Strolling through Skanderbeg Square, with its mix of architectural styles

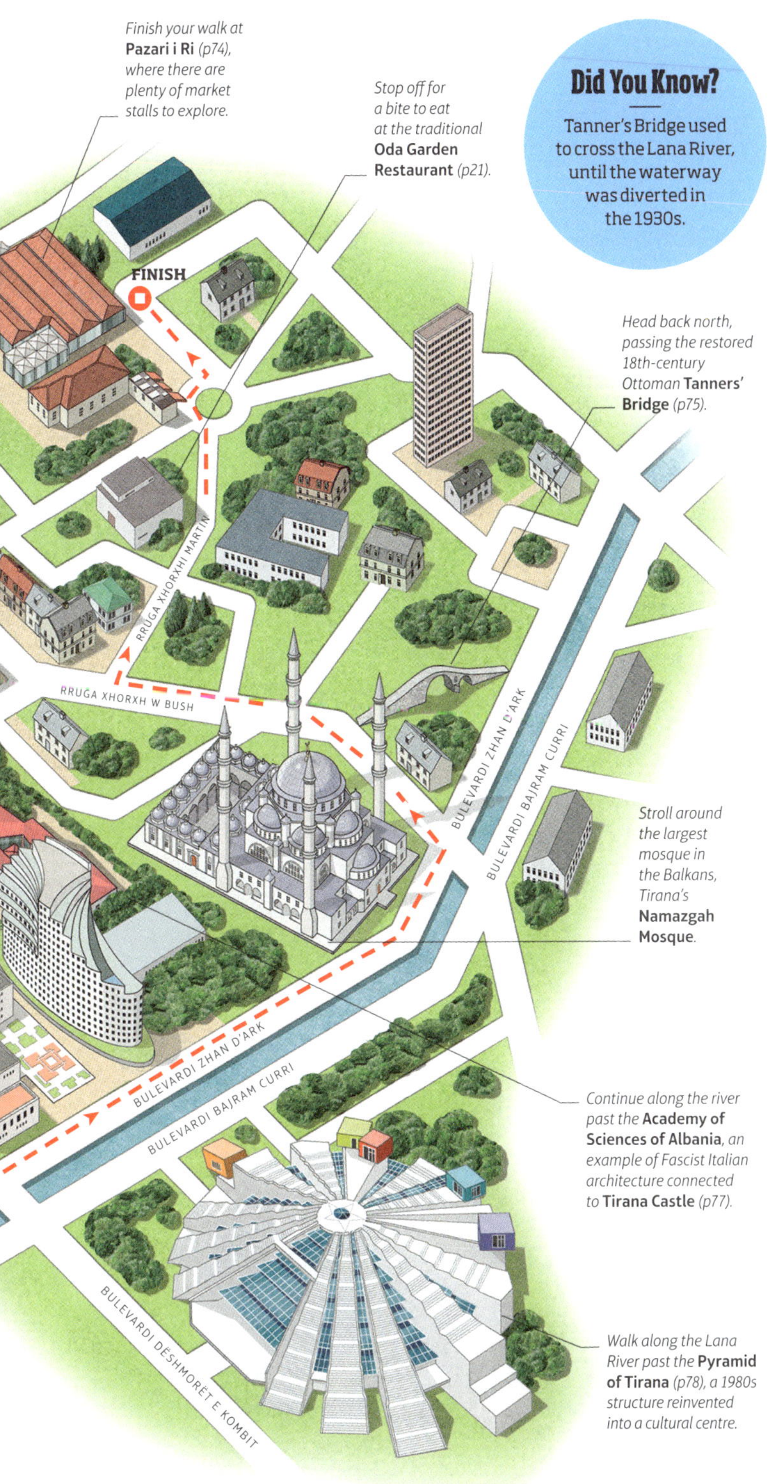

Finish your walk at **Pazari i Ri** *(p74), where there are plenty of market stalls to explore.*

Stop off for a bite to eat at the traditional **Oda Garden Restaurant** *(p21).*

Did You Know?

Tanner's Bridge used to cross the Lana River, until the waterway was diverted in the 1930s.

Head back north, passing the restored 18th-century Ottoman **Tanners' Bridge** *(p75).*

Stroll around the largest mosque in the Balkans, Tirana's **Namazgah Mosque**.

Continue along the river past the **Academy of Sciences of Albania**, *an example of Fascist Italian architecture connected to* **Tirana Castle** *(p77).*

Walk along the Lana River past the **Pyramid of Tirana** *(p78), a 1980s structure reinvented into a cultural centre.*

A SHORT WALK

GRAND PARK OF TIRANA

Distance 1.5 km (1 mile) **Walking time** Approx 20 minutes

With nearly 300 hectares (over 700 acres) of open space, shaded by lofty oaks, cedars and cypress trees, the Grand Park of Tirana *(p79)* is the capital's green lungs. With plenty of quiet spots to be enjoyed as well as popular venues and sights, this verdant area offer locals and visitors a moment of respite from the busy city. Take a short stroll past morning joggers or afternoon walkers near the park's large artificial lake and take in some of the key sights found here, from moving memorials to useful recreation centres.

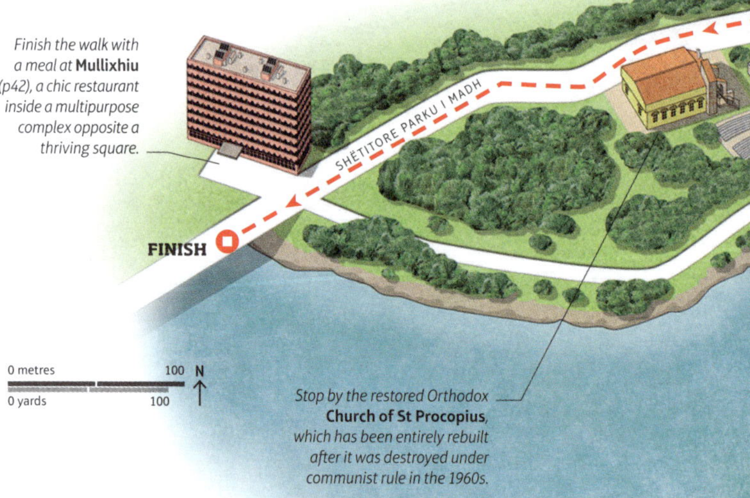

Walk past the memorial to musician **Françesk Radi** *(p37), who was popular in the 1970s and remains a key cultural figure.*

Finish the walk with a meal at **Mullixhiu** *(p42), a chic restaurant inside a multipurpose complex opposite a thriving square.*

Stop by the restored Orthodox **Church of St Procopius**, *which has been entirely rebuilt after it was destroyed under communist rule in the 1960s.*

← Enjoying the green paths in the Grand Park of Tirana

Did You Know?

The Grand Park of Tirana's lake is a great place to spot birds like grebes, kingfishers and moorhens.

TIRANA
Grand Park of Tirana

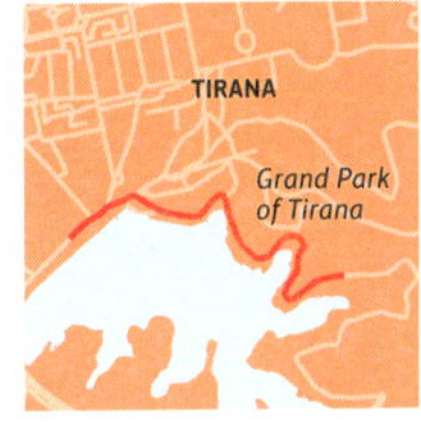

Locator Map
See p64

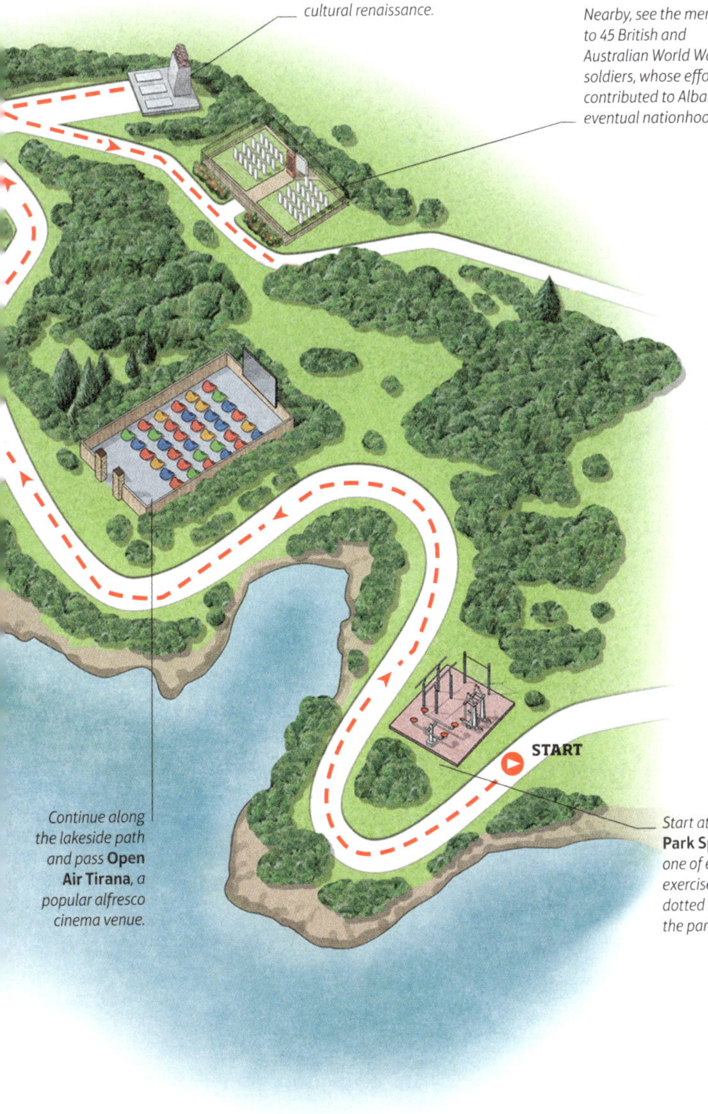

Stop by the **Naim Frashëri cenotaph**, *dedicated to the writer (p158) who led Albania's 19th-century cultural renaissance.*
Nearby, see the memorial to 45 British and Australian World War II soldiers, whose efforts contributed to Albania's eventual nationhood.
START
Start at the **Park Sportiv**, *one of eight exercise points dotted through the park.*
Continue along the lakeside path and pass **Open Air Tirana**, *a popular alfresco cinema venue.*

Traditional farmhouses near Theth Village

NORTHERN ALBANIA

A natural barrier on the border with Montenegro and Kosovo, Albania's Accursed Mountains kept much of Northern Albania isolated from its neighbours, although parts of the region bear the same hallmarks of occupation as the rest of the country. The Illyrians had populated as far south as Burrel, just 62 km (39 miles) northeast of Tirana, by the 10th century BCE, making Shkodër their capital under King Gentius in the 3rd century BCE. Remnants of their reign survive in Rozafa Castle, on Shkodër's southern fringes, which was rebuilt in the 14th century by the Venetians and houses an old Ottoman mosque. The region also played an important part in the Albanian hero Skanderbeg's fight for independence in the 15th century, with skirmishes against the Ottoman Empire taking place in the town of Krujë, 40 km (25 miles) north of Tirana, and around Preza.

Away from the cities, life has barely changed in centuries, although with Northern Albania's mountains attracting more and more adventurous travellers, the villages are not as isolated as they once were. In places like Theth, Valbonë and Dragobi, traditional *kulla* towers, used for sanctuary in times of blood feuds, have been renovated into cosy B&Bs and guesthouses. There are a few established hiking trails here, but many routes remain word-of-mouth, passed down by generations of shepherds and goat herders. The result is a wilderness that feels almost untouched – and is always beautiful.

NORTHERN ALBANIA

Must Sees

1. Shkodër
2. Theth National Park
3. Valbonë National Park
4. Komani Lake
5. Bovilla Lake

Experience More

6. Preza Castle
7. Shala River
8. Lurë-Dejë Mountain National Park
9. Kukës
10. Kunë-Vain-Tale Lagoon
11. Burrel
12. Pukë
13. Lezhë
14. Mesi Bridge
15. Krujë

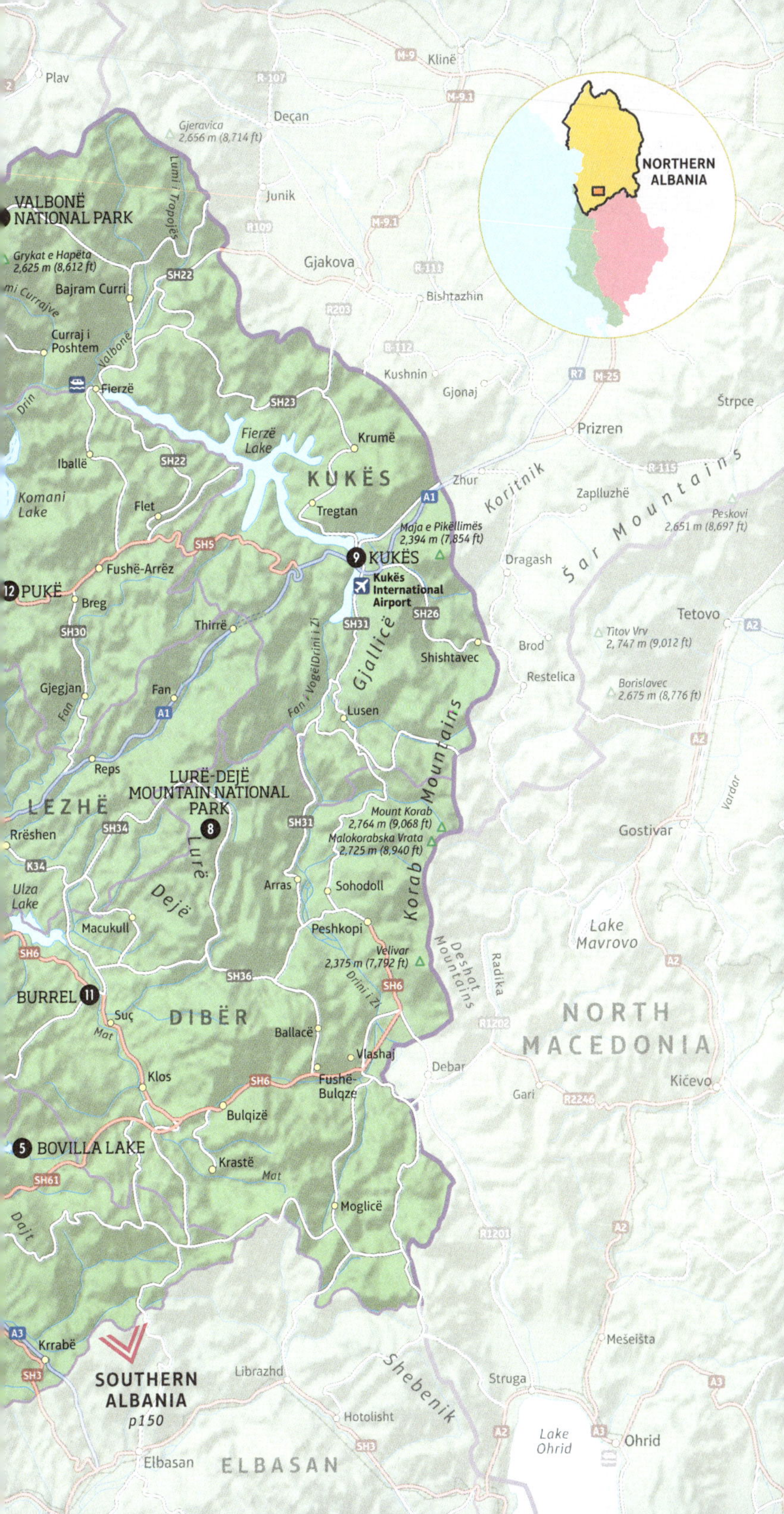

NORTHERN ALBANIA
VALBONË NATIONAL PARK
KUKËS
9 KUKËS
Kukës International Airport
12 PUKË
LURË-DEJË MOUNTAIN NATIONAL PARK
8
LEZHË
DIBËR
BURREL 11
5 BOVILLA LAKE
SOUTHERN ALBANIA p150
NORTH MACEDONIA
ELBASAN
Plav
Klinë
Deçan
Gjeravica 2,656 m (8,714 ft)
Junik
Gjakova
Bishtazhin
Kushnin
Gjonaj
Prizren
Štrpce
Zhur
Koritnik
Zaplluzhë
Šar Mountains
Peskovi 2,651 m (8,697 ft)
Dragash
Tetovo
Titov Vrv 2,747 m (9,012 ft)
Borislavec 2,675 m (8,776 ft)
Brod
Restelica
Gostivar
Vardar
Lake Mavrovo
Radika
Debar
Gari
Kičevo
Mešeišta
Struga
Lake Ohrid
Ohrid
Librazhd
Hotolisht
Shebenik
Elbasan
Grykat e Hapëta 2,625 m (8,612 ft)
Lumi i Tropojës
Bajram Curri
Lumi Currajve
Curraj i Poshtem
Valbonë
Fierzë
Drin
Fierzë Lake
Krumë
Iballë
Komani Lake
Flet
Tregtan
Maja e Pikëllimës 2,394 m (7,854 ft)
Fushë-Arrëz
Breg
Thirrë
Shishtavec
Gjallicë
Fan i Vogël/Drini i Zi
Gjegjan
Fan
Lusen
Reps
Korab Mountains
Mount Korab 2,764 m (9,068 ft)
Malokorabska Vrata 2,725 m (8,940 ft)
Rrëshen
Lurë
Dejë
Arras
Sohodoll
Ulza Lake
Macukull
Peshkopi
Velivar 2,375 m (7,792 ft)
Deshat Mountains
Drini i Zi
Suç
Mat
Ballacë
Vlashaj
Klos
Fushë-Bulqzë
Bulqizë
Krastë
Moglicë
Dajt
Krrabë
M-9
R-107
M-9.1
R109
R-111
R203
R-112
R7
M-25
R-115
A1
SH22
SH23
SH5
SH31
SH26
SH30
SH34
K34
SH6
SH36
SH61
A3
SH3
A2
R1202
R2246
R1201

1

SHKODËR

C2 100 km (62 miles) N of Tirana Shkodër Bus Station, Rruga Teuta Shkodër Train Station, Rruga Revolucioni Antikomunist Hungarez Rruga Teuta; www.visitshkoder.org

Close to the border with Montenegro, Shkodër is a city steeped in history. Parts of Rozafa Castle date back to the 3rd century BCE, while Roman documents cite Shkodër as the capital of the Illyrian king Gentius until it was taken by the Roman Empire in 168 BCE. Since then, it has been held by the Byzantines, Bulgars, Serbs and Turks, and was sold to Venice in 1396. The resulting mishmash of historic architectural styles is on display in the city's charming centre.

①

Shkodër Lake

From Rruga Teuta

Shkodër is dominated to its west by the lake of the same name, which spans the border between Albania and Montenegro. Formed by the collapse of a series of caves due to the movement of tectonic plates millions of years ago, Shkodër Lake is the largest lake in all of Southern Europe. It now lies within protected parkland on both sides of the border: a nature reserve in Albania and a national park in Montenegro.

Shkodër Lake is something of an ornithologist's paradise. Its open waters, reedy banks and surrounding verdant marshland provide refuge for over 240 species of birds, including the endangered Dalmatian pelican – the lake is home to one of the few nesting sites in the world.

In summer, the sandy and pebbly lakeshore acts as an alternative beach destination to the coast, from where sunbathers and swimmers can enjoy

Did You Know?

On the Albanian side, the lake is known as Shkodër Lake; in Montenegro, it's called Skadar Lake.

The Buna River, emptying into Shkodër Lake west of the city

views of the lake framed by distant jagged mountains.

A quiet road runs along the lake from the city of Shkodër to the charming lakeside town of Shiroka. It's a popular route to cycle. Plenty of restaurants line this stretch of lakefront, their chefs making the most of the diversity of flora and fauna that live in the clear waters – eel, carp, bass, and an edible lotus plant that flowers in the summer rain.

Zdrale Market

Rruga Evlija Celebiu
6am-3pm daily

Lying on an ancient trade route between the Aegean Sea and the Danube River, Shkodër has always had a busy bazaar, and even after the city expanded beyond its central marketplace, it remained an area where mountain farmers and craftspeople from Northern Albania gathered to sell their wares. Stalls and hole-in-the-wall shops selling mountain produce such as cheese, walnuts and honey prevail to this day, many of them clustered together in the bazaar-like Zdrale Market. The market at the centre of an atmospheric tangle of preserved Ottoman streets, where coffee shops and bars spill out onto the pavement.

INSIDER TIP
To Montenegro

Buses run several times a day from Shkodër to the Montenegrin capital of Podgorica, 60 km (37 miles) away, or you can cross the border through the foothills of the Albanian Alps by car.

EAT

Arti'Zanave

Delicious traditional Albanian fare, with a focus on locally sourced produce and - a rarity in Albania - plenty of vegetarian options. Proceeds from craft sales help victims of domestic abuse.

Rruga Berdicej
9am-11pm daily
67 376 6211

Agroturizëm Faqedol

This farm-to-table restaurant benefits from a big outdoor terrace overlooking Rozafa Castle. Slow-food dishes embrace North Albanian cooking.

Rruga Shpija e Gjyshit
7am-11pm daily
69 602 5777

3 

Rruga Kolë Idromeno

Running right through the heart of central Shkodër, pedestrianized Rruga Kolë Idromeno presents a picture-perfect scene and is a popular meeting point for locals, who gather to chat, sip coffees and watch the world go by at the plentiful cafés and restaurants here. It's a great place to take in the history of the city, with a rainbow of renovated Ottoman-style buildings fringing both sides of the street. Kolë Idromeno is also home to some of the city's best eating, drinking and shopping options and is a popular spot throughout the day. The street is bookended by the Ebu Bekër Mosque, which looks like a modern version of Istanbul's Hagia Sophia in miniature, and a statue of Mother Teresa.

4 

Rozafa Castle

Rruga Rozafa **Rruga Teuta** **9am-8:30pm daily**

Cresting a hilltop enclosed by the Drin and Buna rivers, just outside the southern fringes of the city, Rozafa Castle (Kalaja e Rozafës) was built in the 3rd century BCE, when the area was an Illyrian capital. The oldest fortified walls of the castle date back to this time, although the majority of what remains today was constructed by the Venetians in the 14th century. The castle spans a series of courtyards and vast, well-preserved ruins, including a Venetian Catholic church turned Ottoman mosque. There are also incredible views down over the stunning Lake Shkodër.

The castle has a chequered history and is steeped in folklore – it's believed that its walls provided sanctuary for people hiding from blood feuds, and rumours that human sacrifices were made here still swirl around the ruins. According to the most famous legend, the three brothers who built Rozafa Castle were cursed. The story goes that the brothers spent every day constructing their

Rozafa Castle, perching on a hill south of Shkodër

A display at the Marubi National Museum of Photography

castle, only for the walls to fall down each night. A wise old local man told the brothers that a human sacrifice was required to lift the curse, so they buried one of their wives, Rozafa, within the walls of the castle – but with one breast exposed so she could continue to feed her infant son.

It is 3.5 km (just over 2 miles) from Shkodër to Rozafa Castle. Buses stop at the turning to the castle, or it's a pleasant cycle from the city centre.

Marubi National Museum of Photography

Rruga Kole Idromeno
9am-7pm daily
marubi.gov.al

True to its roots as a centre of culture in Albania, Shkodër boasts an excellent selection of local museums, and the Marubi National Museum of Photography (Muzeu Kombëtar i Fotografisë Marubi) is one of the city's best. It features the photographic works of the Marubi family – Albania's answer to the Gettys – alongside changing exhibitions from local photographers

The collection includes Albania's first photograph, a portrait of an Ottoman soldier taken by Pjetër Marubi in 1858, as well as street scenes from a bygone time and portraits and photojournalism covering the rise and fall of communism across the country.

Venice Art Mask Factory

Rruga Inxh. Gjovalin Gjadri **8am-5pm daily**
68 406 7481

A nod to the Venetian history of Shkodër, the Venice Art Mask Factory showcases the craftsmanship of Edmond Angoni, a local who emigrated to Italy in the 1990s to learn the art of mask making. Gilded, intricate and designed by the most skilful of hands, each mask is a work of art. Angoni's masks are renowned worldwide and were worn by Tom Cruise and other actors in the Stanley Kubrick film *Eyes Wide Shut*. Some of the 2,500 or so masks on display include the Harlequin mask, inspired by a character from the Commedia dell'arte, the "Bauta" mask made famous by Casanova, and the beaked "Plague Doctor" mask, which was worn by doctors during the Black Plague.

The factory is a mix of artist's studio and souvenir shop. You can peruse the beautiful masks to buy or spend time watching a master craftsman at work.

A skilfully crafted mask from the Venice Art Mask Factory

2

THETH NATIONAL PARK

D1 76 km (47 miles) NE of Shkodër From Shkodër to Jezerca Market

At just over 25 sq km (10 sq miles), Theth is one of Albania's smallest national parks, but it is also one of its most beautiful, taking in a dramatic section of the rugged Accursed Mountains.

The main base for exploring Theth National Park is the charming village of Theth, with its picture-perfect church surrounded by sky-scraping mountains. Family-run guesthouses, in the style of ski chalets, offer accommodation, and most have restaurants serving home-cooked Albanian mountain fare. The park itself encompasses jagged mountains and the verdant Shala Valley, where the turquoise Shala River cuts through the landscape in dramatic fashion.

Outdoor Adventure

Theth is a playground for outdoor enthusiasts, with hiking trails (marked by red and white paint) leading from the village up to waterfalls, craggy mountain summits and otherworldly blue pools. The air is fresh and energizing, making the lung-busting ascents up the mountain trails feel truly exhilarating.

HIKES IN THETH

Valbonë Valley Trail
The most popular hike in national-park land, this 17-km (11-mile) trail *(p110)* connects Theth with Valbonë, leading through wildflower meadows and a cliff-lined valley.

Theth Waterfall Trail
This trail starts in Theth and runs for 6.5 km (4 miles), past mountain peaks and farms, ending with a view of the 30-m- (98-ft-) high Grunasi Waterfall *(p95)*.

Theth Blue Eye
Theth's Blue Eye Kaprre is just as mesmerizing as its famous southern counterpart *(p144)*. From Theth village, it's a 12-km (7.5-mile) hike to the ethereally blue pool.

Theth is a playground for outdoor enthusiasts, with hiking trails leading from the village up to waterfalls, craggy mountain summits and otherworldly blue pools.

←

Theth National Park and *(inset)* hiking the Valbonë Valley Trail

↑ Cooling off at Blue Eye Kaprre, better known as Theth Blue Eye

EXPLORING THETH NATIONAL PARK

An asphalt road connects Theth with Shkodër, and minibuses regularly ply the route between the two settlements. For a long time, the only way to reach Theth was by gravel and dirt roads, and this idyllic mountain village was completely cut off from the rest of Albania in winter; Theth's restaurants and hotels still shut up shop between November and February. Boat trips run along the Shala River, and there are opportunities to kayak or try whitewater rafting.

MONTENEGRO
Theth National Park
Area of main map
ALBANIA

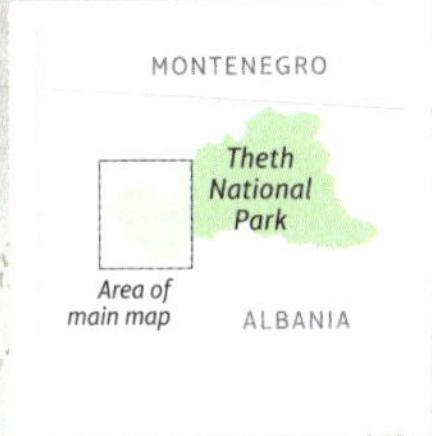

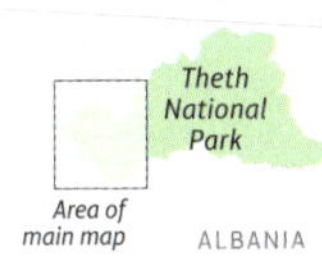

Locator Map
For more detail see p90

0 km 1
0 miles 1
N
Maja e Harapit 2,218 m (7,277 ft)
Maja e Kokërhanes 2,495 m (8,186 ft)
Maja e Jezercës 2,694 m (8,839 ft)
Maja e Radohimës 2,568 m (8,425 ft)
Maja Popluqes 2,569 m (8,428. ft)
Maja Alijes 2,471 m (8,107 ft)
Okol
Nikgjonaj
Lumi i Thethi
Lumi i Thethit
Maja Valbonës 1,965 m (6,447 ft)
Gjeçaj
Hardedaj
Theth
Nënreth
Lock-in Tower
Maja Rukës 1,620 m (5,315 ft)
Grunasi
Grunasi Waterfall
Maja Kij Zhariellave 1,713 m (5,620 ft)
Maja e Zorzit 1,663 m (5,456 ft)
Theth Blue Eye
Stone Groves of Nderlysaj
Nderlysaj

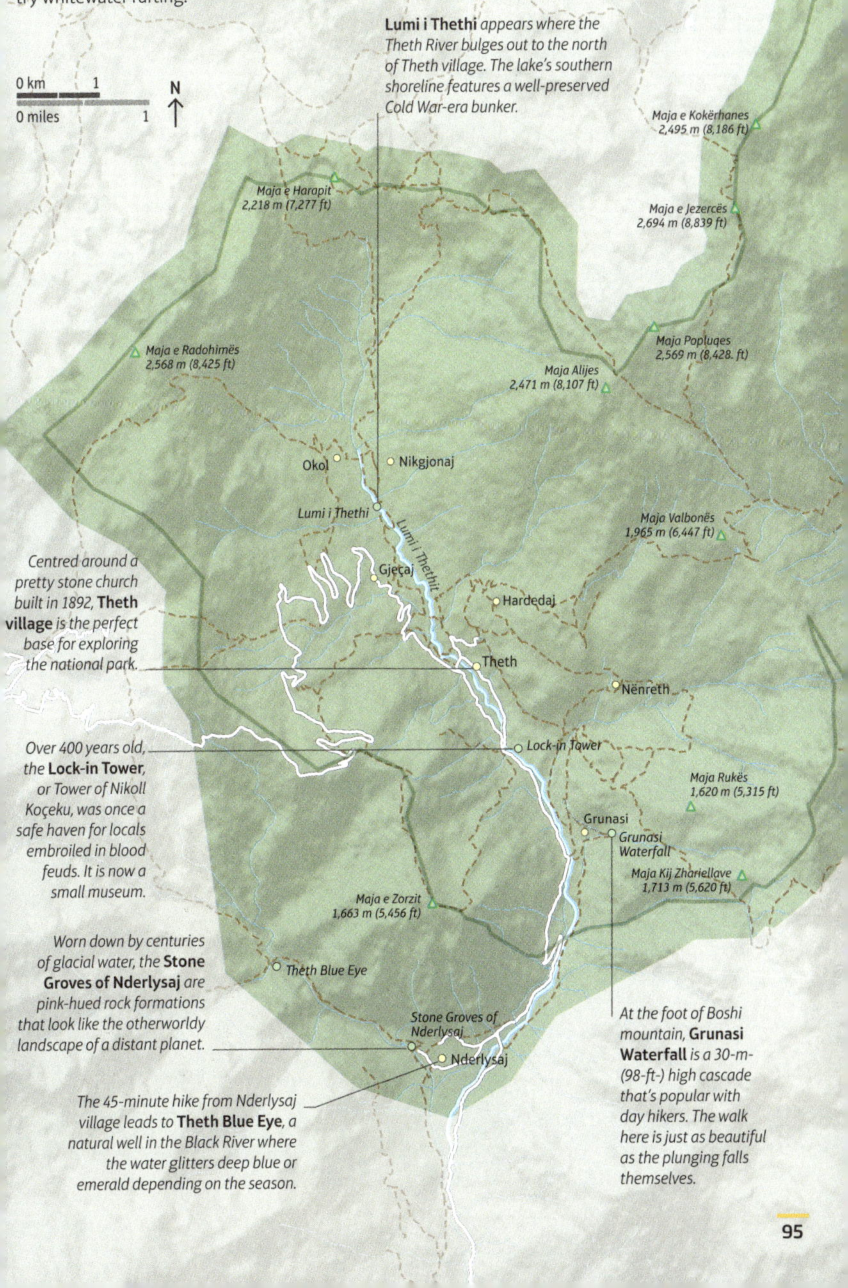

Lumi i Thethi *appears where the Theth River bulges out to the north of Theth village. The lake's southern shoreline features a well-preserved Cold War-era bunker.*

Centred around a pretty stone church built in 1892, **Theth village** *is the perfect base for exploring the national park.*

Over 400 years old, the **Lock-in Tower**, *or Tower of Nikoll Koçeku, was once a safe haven for locals embroiled in blood feuds. It is now a small museum.*

Worn down by centuries of glacial water, the **Stone Groves of Nderlysaj** *are pink-hued rock formations that look like the otherworldly landscape of a distant planet.*

The 45-minute hike from Nderlysaj village leads to **Theth Blue Eye**, *a natural well in the Black River where the water glitters deep blue or emerald depending on the season.*

At the foot of Boshi mountain, **Grunasi Waterfall** *is a 30-m- (98-ft-) high cascade that's popular with day hikers. The walk here is just as beautiful as the plunging falls themselves.*

3

VALBONË NATIONAL PARK

D1 Valbonë, 17 km (10.5 miles) NE of Theth Albania Bus runs a daily bus to Fierzë to meet the Komani Lake ferry

Set within the stunning Accursed Mountains (or Albanian Alps), Valbonë National Park is centred around the Valbonë Valley, where a glacial river has scored its way through the mountains over millennia.

The Valbonë National Park is home to some of the most impressive nature of the Albanian Alps. Within its 80 sq km (30 sq miles), there are clear springs, tumbling waterfalls and forests to be explored, with quiet hiking trails winding through them. These trails follow old mule tracks through the park's protected landscape, where it's rare to see anyone else – apart from the occasional shepherd moving herds of sheep and goats between crumbling stone outhouses.

Wildlife thrives within the abundant and varied landscapes of the park. Golden eagles – the emblem of Albania – make their home here; sightings of these birds are, however, growing rarer. Other local species include brown bears, lynxes and wild goats, which roam throughout the park. With just a few nearby villages – like Çerem and Dragobi – offering traditional accommodation options, like historic *kulla* houses, this national park is an ideal place to truly escape into nature.

BEARS IN ALBANIA

Between 180 and 200 brown bears make their home in Albania's mountainous north. Brown bears are protected in Albania, but illegal poaching is unfortunately still practised, and the species is consequently under threat. Bears stick to the more remote regions of Northern Albania and are unused to humans, so sightings are rare – but not impossible.

PICTURE PERFECT

Kulla Houses

These tower houses were mostly built using stone from nearby river beds and were fortified to protect inhabitants from blood feuds. They cast a striking silhouette, isolated against the rugged mountain backdrop.

1 The Valbonë River, threading through the Valbonë Valley.

2 A tall, stone *kulla* house nestled into the Valbonë Valley.

3 Crossing a wooden bridge near the village of Dragobi, Valbonë National Park.

↑ Dramatic mountain scenery in Valbonë National Park

4 

KOMANI LAKE

D2 58 km (36 miles) E of Shkodër From Shkodër to Komani Bus Stop on the SH25

Mountains plummet to a shimmering green expanse of water, still as glass, at Komani Lake. The idyllic scene is no accident: the lake was created by the communist regime between 1979 and 1988 to power a hydroelectric dam on the Drin River.

Komani Lake weaves like a wide river between the sheer verdant cliffs of the Drin River Valley. Most people visit to take a boat trip: car ferries, passenger boats and day cruises putter across the lake's calm surface, mostly traversing the picturesque stretch of water between the hydroelectric power station in Komani and the small town of Fierzë.

Apart from a few villages and farmsteads on the lakefront, and a couple of restaurants by the terminal near the power station, the area feels untouched by humanity. The mountains surrounding the lake are home to a number of mammals, including badgers, polecats and golden jackals – although the latter are extremely rare – while the lake itself is a rich hunting ground for bird-spotters, with a variety of species found here.

INSIDER TIP

Getting Here

Komani Lake Ferry *(komanilakeferry.com)* runs minibuses from Shkodër and Tirana that connect with its ferry departure from Komani. It also runs a shuttle between Fierzë and Valbonë village *(p96)*.

←

The emerald waters of Komani Lake, hemmed in by verdant cliffs

→

An iridescent-blue common kingfisher

Hydroelectric power station at Komani ↓

TOP 4 BIRDS TO SPOT

Common Kingfisher
A glimpse of shimmering teal marks the presence of this beautiful bird.

Grey Heron
With long legs and a streamlined beak, grey herons hunt small fish in the lake's shallows.

Great Spotted Woodpecker
Woodpeckers can be heard drilling into the trees fringing the lake.

Alpine Swift
These agile birds, which spend almost all of their life in the air, soar high above the lakeshore.

BOVILLA LAKE

D3 19 km (36 miles) NE of Tirana

An hour's drive from Tirana, Bovilla Lake is a teal-hued reservoir that cuts an impressive picture at the foot of Gamti Mountain. It's an easy day trip from the capital to this popular beauty spot.

The product of a dam in the Tërkuzë River, Bovilla Lake was formed in the 1990s. It is located within Dajti National Park, and was protected in order to preserve the flora and fauna that thrives around its shores. The lake's waters may look invitingly blue but swimming is not permitted – though it's true many people ignore this in summer. Rock climbing is a popular activity in the area and experienced climbers can often be spotted scaling routes up the sheer cliffs that surround the lake. A more sedate way to experience the Dajti Mountains is to follow the short (signed) hiking trail that leads up from the lake's western shoreline to a lookout point on Gamti Mountain. The route features metal stairs built into the mountainside and ends at a rocky outcrop, where a hole in the rocks makes a natural picture frame for capturing the glorious lake and mountain views.

↑ One of several caves that pockmark the cliffs around the lake

← Admiring the view from the cliffs that surround Bovilla Lake

↑ Yellow mountain plants flowering on the slopes above the lake

EXPERIENCE MORE

Preza Castle's striking 19th-century clock tower

Preza Castle

C3 Off Rruga Preze Palaq, Preza

The ancient stronghold of Preza Castle (Kalaja e Prezës) looks out over the idyllic village of Preza, a 40-minute drive northwest of Tirana. The castle was built by the Byzantine emperor Justinian I around 550 CE and was expanded in the 14th century by the Topias, the local feudal family. It was an important strategic point for the Albanian hero Skanderbeg during the 15th-century resistance against the Ottoman Empire. The mighty fortification is reminiscent of a child's drawing of a castle, with thick, crenulated walls bookended by a tower at each corner. The striking clock tower was added in the 19th century. You can walk the walls and grassy courtyards and peer through arrowslits that perfectly frame the Dajti Mountains and the sprawling shape of Tirana in the distance. A restaurant within the walls serves simple meals and drinks.

Shala River

D1-2 Rruga e Molles, Pepsumaj Shala River Boat Tours

An offshoot of the Drin River where it runs into Komani Lake *(p98)*, the tranquil Shala River meanders through a dramatic canyon where sheer rocks rise from the banks like karst pinnacles. The only way to reach this beautiful stretch of bright blue water is by boat from Komani Lake, with Shala River Boat Tours *(shalarivertrip.com)* or from Fierzë. You can stay overnight on the riverfront in one of a cluster of small, chalet-style guesthouses, where there is also the chance to zip-line over the river and embark on hiking trails into the mountains.

Lurë-Dejë Mountain National Park

D3 66 km (41 miles) NE of Burrel

Spread over 200 sq km (77 sq miles) of protected land, Lurë-Dejë Mountain National Park includes the seven lakes of Lurë and the impressive peak of Dejë Mountain. Hills and mountains thick with pine and fir forests shelter an abundance of birdlife and endemic mammals including the European brown bear, Eurasian lynx and grey wolf.

A forest-fringed lake in Lurë-Dejë Mountain National Park

DAY TRIPS TO KOSOVO

Kukës is less than 20 km (15.5 miles) from the border with Kosovo. Day trips to the beautiful Kosovan city of Prizren, just 19 km (15 miles) farther on, are popular, offering visitors the chance to explore the charming old town, with its fine mosque and stone bridge. Direct buses run from Kukës to Prizren several times a day, clearing the border at Morine-Vermice in just 15 minutes or so.

Following the fall of communism in the 1990s, logging decimated the area's biodiversity, and it is estimated that around 50 per cent of what is now national-park land was destroyed. Efforts have been made to reforest Lurë-Dejë, but it is non-government organizations made up of passionate locals that are currently tending to the ecological needs of the forest, valleys and rivers that make up this lovely national park.

Kukës

E2 150 km (93 miles) E of Shkodër

You won't find preserved Ottoman streets or Byzantine churches in Kukës. Under the regime of Enver Hoxha, the old town of Kukës was completely engulfed by the waters of Lake Fierzë to create a reservoir. A new town was built on its banks, and today the streets of this newer Kukës serve as a time capsule of 1970s Soviet-style architecture.

During the Kosovan War, Kukës gained fame as the first city nominated for a Nobel Peace Prize, for its welcoming of Kosovan refugees. This event is marked by the imposing **Kulla Monument**, which has a photographic exhibition and ethnographic museum inside.

Tourism is only just starting to take hold in Kukës and is focused around hiking trips to the Sharr Mountains that rise up around the city, but there are also plans to open Kukës' network of underground Cold War tunnels to the public in the future.

Kulla Monument
Rruga Eksod 99
8am-5pm Mon-Sat

10  

Kunë-Vain-Tale Lagoon

C3 48.5 km (30 miles) N of Tirana To Talë, then 25-minute walk

This protected area of marshes sits at the delta of the Drin River on the Adriatic Sea. Free from human interference, the lagoon attracts migratory birds such as yellow ospreys, common kingfishers, pygmy cormorants and even a colony of greater flamingos. A trail loops around the lagoon, and there's an information hut at the park's entrance that provides guidance for spotting birds – the best place is the lookout tower. The area is also a foodies' paradise. Its rich, well-nourished soil makes it ideal for agriculture, and there are also a number of farm-to-table restaurants serving delicious local dishes scattered among the marshland and forest around the lagoon.

EAT

Trëndafili Mistik
Dishes cooked simply on a wood-fired grill, with daily-changing fresh-fish options. Views over the Kunë-Vain-Tale Lagoon are a bonus.

C3 Rruga Vaini, Laguna e Vainit Noon-8pm daily 68 226 7107

ⓁⓁⓁ

Restorant Peshkatari
Spot flamingos and kingfishers while enjoying fresh lake fish at wooden tables set along the shore.

D3 Rruga Dede Shabani, Lezhë 10am-10pm daily 69 392 5744

ⓁⓁⓁ

Rana Shëngjin
Fine dining and craft cocktails, in a warehouse-sized interior or on the beach out front.

C3 Rruga Shëngjin-Kunë 7am-11:30pm daily 69 978 2310

ⓁⓁⓁ

The Shala River, flowing between cliffs near Komani Lake

11

Burrel

D3 99 km (62 miles) SE of Skodër

Around the 10th century BCE, the area surrounding Burrel was an Illyrian enclave, and the wild countryside of what today makes up Mat County still hides evidence of this ancient civilization. Following hiking trails that are often used by local walkers, you might stumble across an ancient Illyrian burial site or an Iron Age fort, although note that these sights have not yet been fully excavated or curated for the public.

You'll have greater success finding out more about the area's past in Burrel itself, where the interesting **Mat Historical Museum** (Muzeu Historik Mat) charts the region's history through displays of local Illyrian artifacts. Burrel is centred around a charming main square with a number of outdoor cafés. A statue of Skanderberg *(p73)* stands in the centre, making this small town feel a little like Tirana in miniature.

Mat Historical Museum
Rruga Qamil Xhika
10am-2pm & 5-7pm daily

12

Pukë

D2 60 km (37 miles) E of Shkodër Stacioni Autobuzave Pukë

Perched in the northern mountains at 838 m (2,783 ft) above sea level, the town of Pukë boasts one of the highest elevations in Albania. It is steeped in tradition and still lives by an old set of Albanian laws known as the Kanuni i Pukë (Canon of Pukë). Pukë is home to a handful of restaurants and coffee shops, a peaceful lake ideal for strolling, and a hotel with its own microbrewery where Puka Beer is made.

The town's claim to fame is its winter sports scene. Surrounded by Alpine forests and towering massifs, this is Albania's main ski destination. In summer, though, it's all about the hiking. Around 12 km (4.5 miles) from the town centre, a moderate-to-challenging trail leads to the summit of Murga Peak, affording beautiful views over nearby Komani Lake *(p98)*. Alternatively, make the more leisurely hike to Kryeziu Waterfall, which tumbles into a crystal-clear plunge pool – a popular wild swimming spot.

SKIING IN ALBANIA

During the communist era, skiing was a popular pastime in Albania, but since then, many of the pistes have been reclaimed by nature. Today, the mountains around Pukë are the best place to ski in the country, with Marenglen Laci featuring a 600-m (1,968-ft) piste, which cuts through forest, as well as ski hire. There are also a few ski villages around Korçë *(p70)* where skiing is possible: Dardha, Shishtaveci and Voskopojë.

13

Lezhë

D3 38 km (24 miles) S of Shkodër Stacioni i Furgonave, Lezhë

Located on Albania's north coast, the historic town of Lezhë enjoys a stretch of beach beside the Adriatic and in close proximity to the verdant Kunë-Vain-Tale Lagoon *(p103)*. It is home to one of Albania's few functioning train stations, connecting it by old, slow trains to Shkodër.

Lezhë secured its place in history during the Ottoman era, when the 1444 League of Lezhë united Albania's princes under the banner of resistance leader Skanderbeg

The Albanian flag inside the Skanderbeg Memorial in Lezhë

(p73) who battled to overcome Ottoman rule. A memorial to the man himself stands pride of place in the centre of town.

The **Lezhë Ethnographic Museum** (Muzeu Etnografik Lezhë) showcases the great ethnographic and archaeological heritage of Lezhë and its surroundings.

Presiding over it all from a hill above town, **Lezhë Castle** dates back to the Byzantine period. Its crumbling walls afford fine views: a sprawling landscape of fields and farmhouses juxtaposed with the built-up Communist-era centre of Lezhë itself.

In the fertile landscape around town, you'll find some of Northern Albania's best wineries. The area has a rich terroir, producing grapes like the ancient Kallmet for deliciously dry reds. Try them, along with distilled raki, on a tour of a family-run vineyard.

Lezhë Ethnographic Museum
Pallati i Kulturës, Sheshi Gjergj Kastrioti 8am-6pm daily 356 0006

Lezhë Castle
Rruga Verosh

14

Mesi Bridge

C2 Rruga Mesit Postribe, Mes

Just 8.5 km (5 miles) northeast of Shkodër, the village of Mes is a pleasant place to stop and admire Albania's past, preserved perfectly in stone. Dating back to around 1770, Mesi Bridge was built by the local Ottoman pasha, Kara Mahmud, a member of the Albanian Ottoman Bushati family, as part of the trade road leading to Pristina in modern-day Kosovo. Crossing the Kir River, the bridge features 13 stone arches and makes for a pretty picture as the milky-blue river rushes beneath its historic stonework. However, it is currently at risk after floods caused cracks in the arches on its right-hand side.

DRINK

Kallmeti Kantina
This family-run winery near Lezhë is known for its dry red made from 100 per cent Kallmet, an ancient Albanian variety.

C3 Rruga Lezhë-Vau i Dejës, Kallmet i Madh 8am-4pm Mon-Sat kantinakallmeti.com

Kantina Arberi
Almost all of the wines at this vineyard near Lezhë are made from Albanian grapes. There are stone cellars, and a state-of-the-art tasting room.

D3 Rruga Rreshen-Kurbnesh, Rreshen-Mirdite 8am-4pm Mon-Fri 69 443 3773

Mesi Bridge, crossing the Kir River near the village of Mes

Krujë Castle, overlooking the charming Ottoman town of Krujë

15

Krujë

D3 40 km (25 miles) N of Tirana From Tirana & Tirana Airport

Around an hour's drive from Tirana, the picturesque town of Krujë makes a popular day-trip destination from the capital – for Albanians and tourists alike. Its cobblestoned streets are lined with restored Ottoman-era shopfronts, creating a buzzing bazaar of souvenir shops, craft stalls and open-fronted premises that sell all manner of intricately made items from across Northern Albania. If you want to stay overnight, Krujë's Hotel Panorama *(hotelpanoramakruje.com)* makes a fine option; one of the first luxury lodgings in Albania, it is notable for its curvy architecture and far-reaching views of the surrounding mountains.

Krujë has deep ties with Skanderbeg *(p73)*, Albania's national hero. It was here that he fought for his country's independence against the Ottoman Turks in the 15th century. A statue of him, erected in 1959, stands in the town's centre, while a museum dedicated to his life sits within the walls of **Krujë Castle** (Kalaja e Krujës) perched at the top of the winding streets that crawl up the hillside from the town centre. Part museum and part memorial, it's an architectural marvel, rising up from the castle ruins in like a historic fortification itself. A carving of Skanderbeg and his army greets visitors at the entrance; inside is a collection of Ottoman weaponry, armour, traditional clothing and ceramics, alongside colourful frescoes depicting Skanderbeg's life. The castle, once a fortified bastion that held off countless Ottoman sieges, is also home to the **Ethnographic Museum of Krujë** (Muzeum Etnografik i Krujës), housed in a building dating to 1764 and one of the most intriguing museums of its kind in Albania. Admiring the view from up here, it's easy to see why its original owner, Ismail Pashë Toptani, chose this location for his family home. Life in 18th-century Albania is re-created within this Ottoman-style villa, with the social history of Krujë told across its 15 rooms, including a stable and workshop on the ground floor and grand family rooms upstairs.

Several hiking trails wind into the mountains from Krujë, including a popular pilgrimage route to the shrine of Sari Salltik, a 13th century Sufi saint. The walk takes around an hour and ends in a visit to his cave shrine at the bottom of some stone steps.

Krujë Castle
Rruga Kala
Open 24 hours

Ethnographic Museum of Krujë
Rruga Kala
9am-6pm daily
muzeumet-kruje.com

SHOP

Silver Shop Berhami

Aida Berhami's original shop - there's a second branch in Tirana - specializes in coffee pots and jewellery.

D3 Rruga Albanopolis, Krujë
9am-8pm daily
69 214 0902

Qeleshe Punes Hyseni

This shop has seen seven generations of the same family weave wool slippers.

D3 Rruga Albanopolis, Krujë
8am-9pm daily
69 674 0473

NORTHERN ALBANIAN CUISINE

The remoteness of Albania's mountainous north has kept cooking methods even more traditional here than elsewhere in the country. Hearty dishes are the order of the day, usually based around grilled lamb or goat, salty cheeses and fish (hake and sea bass on the coast, carp from Shkodër Lake). Here are three stand-outs.

JANI ME FASULE

A staple of northern Albanian cuisine, this hearty bean soup has few ingredients - white beans and fresh vegetables in a rich stock flavoured with wild mountain herbs - but is ideal fuel for a hike.

PESHK NË ZGARË

Meaning "fish on the grill", this dish is ubiquitous in the seafood restaurants of the Northern Albanian coast and around Lake Shkodër. Fresh fish such as carp, bass and mullet are grilled whole in olive oil and parsley and served with a squeeze of lemon.

FËRGESË

This dish has been gracing the tables of Albania for centuries. An oven-baked medley of peppers, tomatoes, onions and cheese (usually feta but also sometimes ricotta), it's a culinary ode to Northern Albania's agricultural history.

↑ A bowl of hearty *jani me fasule* (white-bean soup)

↑ *Fërgesë*, a simple but satisfying dish with peppers and tomatoes

Grilled fish, a staple of seafood restaurants all along the coast ↑

A LONG WALK
VALBONË VALLEY TRAIL

Length 17 km (11 miles) **Stopping-off points** There are cafés at Rragami Waterfall and Fushë e Gjeshë **Terrain** Moderate to challenging - steep ascents and rocky trails

This popular hike through the spectacular Valbonë Valley, linking the villages of Theth and Valbonë, is the most famous single-day trail in Albania. Depending on weather conditions and fitness levels, it can take anywhere between 5 and 10 hours. It reaches its peak, in more ways than one, at the Valbonë Pass, the highest point on the trail, which tops out at 1,756 m (5,760 ft).

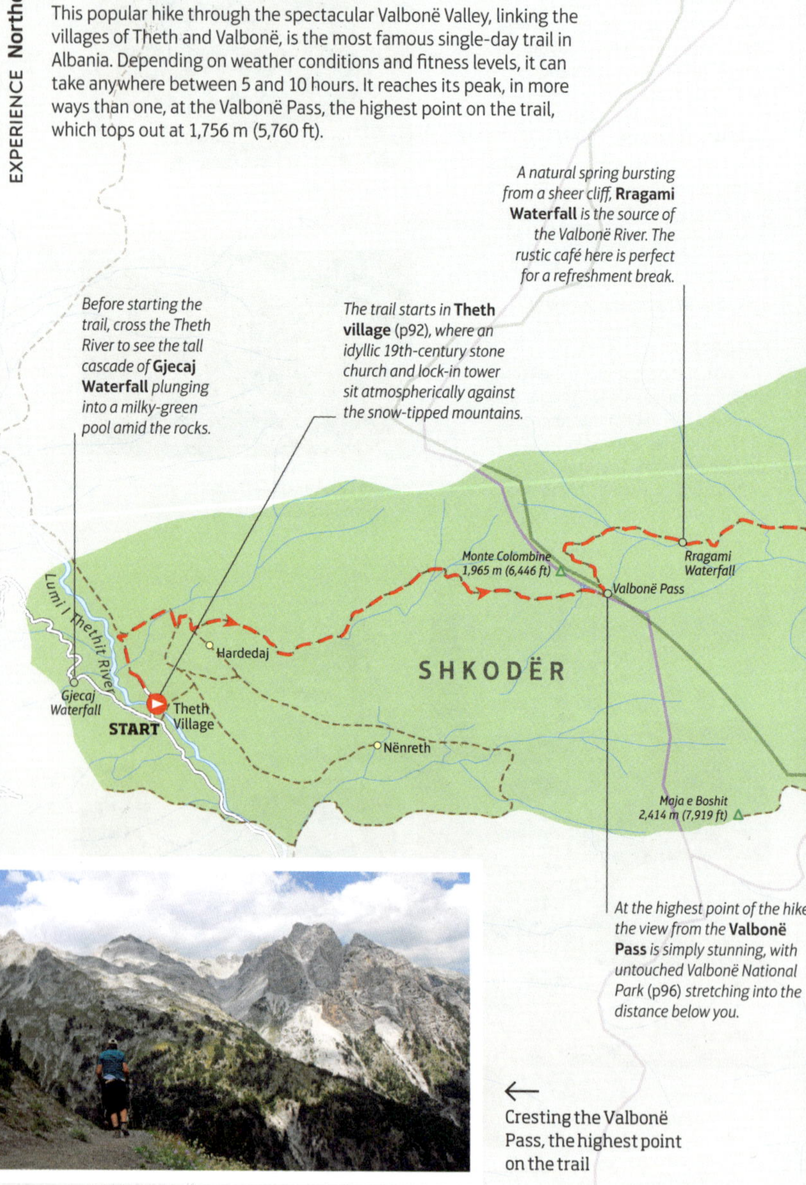

← Cresting the Valbonë Pass, the highest point on the trail

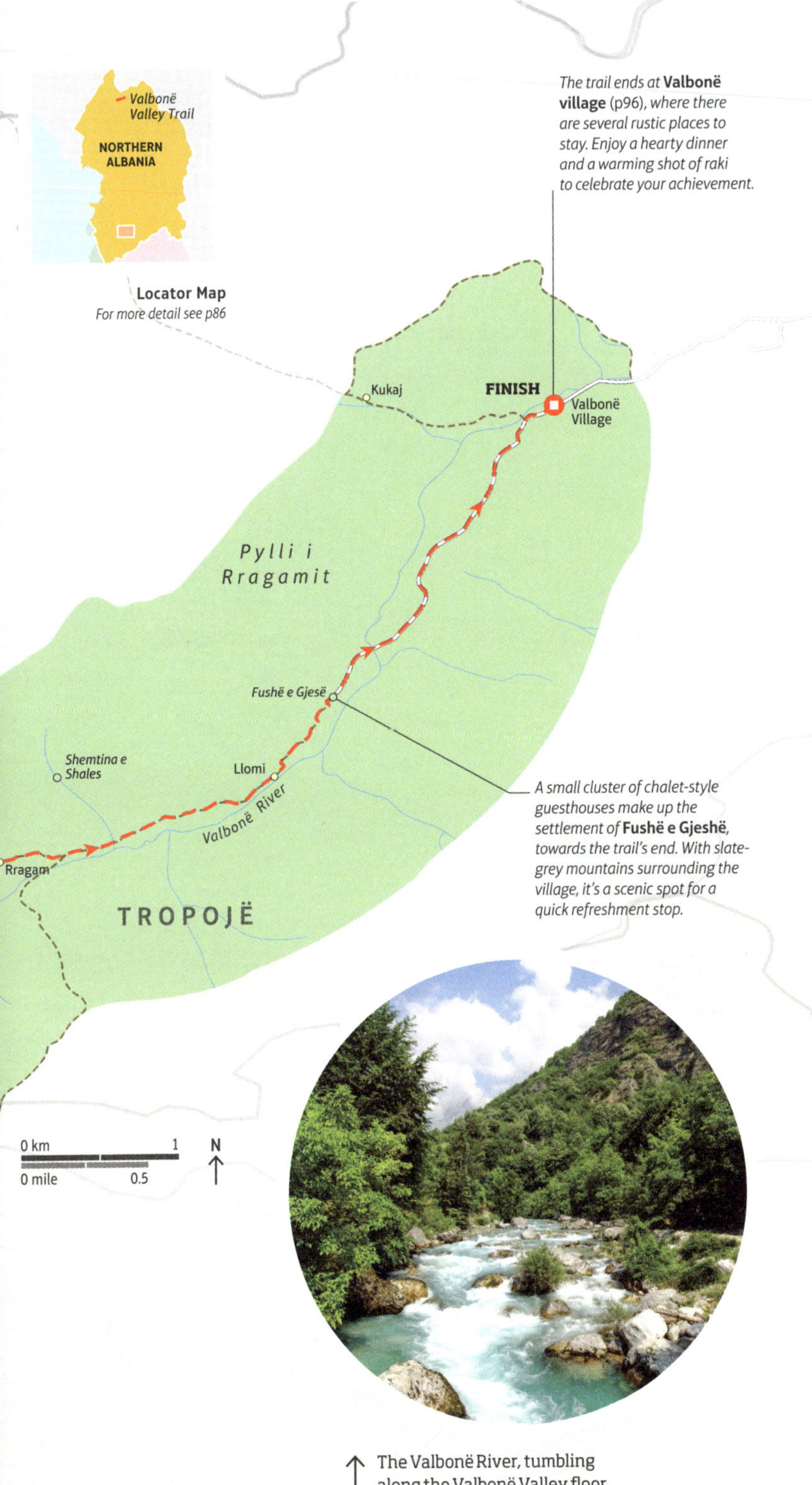

The trail ends at ***Valbonë village*** *(p96), where there are several rustic places to stay. Enjoy a hearty dinner and a warming shot of raki to celebrate your achievement.*

A small cluster of chalet-style guesthouses make up the settlement of ***Fushë e Gjeshë****, towards the trail's end. With slate-grey mountains surrounding the village, it's a scenic spot for a quick refreshment stop.*

↑ The Valbonë River, tumbling along the Valbonë Valley floor

Azure waters off Ksamil Beach

THE ALBANIAN RIVIERA

The Albanian Riviera is fast gaining recognition for its picturesque beaches, buzzing seaside towns and mountains that plunge from sky to sea, but people have been drawn to this region for thousands of years. The Illyrians settled the coast in the 10th century BCE, followed by Greeks from Corinth, Corfu and Chaonia, who colonized pockets of land between 800 BCE and 44 BCE. As a result, the remains of Greek amphitheatres and columned buildings dot the landscape. Romans invaded the area around 50 BCE – their influence can still be seen in the UNESCO-listed ruins at Butrint National Park and historical sites of Durrës – and by the Middle Ages, the Byzantines had constructed religious buildings on hilltops and in secluded bays. The Venetians arrived in the 15th century but were usurped by the Ottomans, who ruled the region through pashas (feudal lords) until the early 20th century. Albania declared independence in the coastal city of Vlorë in 1912, but decades of war and an isolated dictatorship under Enver Hoxha kept this coastline completely cut off from the rest of Europe until the 1990s.

Today, the number of visitors is rapidly growing, drawn by easy-going beach bars and a range of luxury hotels, but plenty of bays remain undeveloped, reachable only on foot or by boat.

NORTHERN ALBANIA p84
TIRANA p62
DURRËS 4
Durrës Bay
Kamez
Tirana
TIRANA
Krrabë
Kavaja
Cape Lagji
Rrogozhinë
Peqin
Shkumb
0 kilometres 20
0 miles 20
N
Divjakë
Karavasta Bay
Karavasta Lagoon
Lushnja
Belsh
Rezervuar i Murizit
Myzeqe
Seman
Kuçovë
Dimal
FIER
Roskovec
APOLLONIA 7
Fier
Patos
Vjosa
Novosele
Ballsh
Selenicë
Adriatic Sea
Narta Lagoon
8 ST MARY'S MONASTERY
Poçem
Vlorë Bay
5 VLORË
Gribe Mountain
Cape Gjuhëza
Kotë
Shushica
Dukat Bay
Karaburun Peninsula
9 ORIKUM
VLORË
Dukat
Brataj
LLOGARA NATIONAL PARK 6
Çikë
10 DHËRMI
DHËRMI BEACH 11
LIVADHI BEACH
GJIPE BEACH 18
12
13 HIMARË
PORTO PALERMO CASTLE 14
15
UPPER QEPARO AND LOWER QEPARO 17
16
Piqeras
BORSCH BEACH
LUKOVË 19
20
LUKOVË BEACH
Ereikoussa
Othonoi
Diakopo
Sidari
Kassiopi
Mathraki
Agios Stefanos Avliotes
Corfu
Ionian Sea
Palaiokastritsa
Gouvia

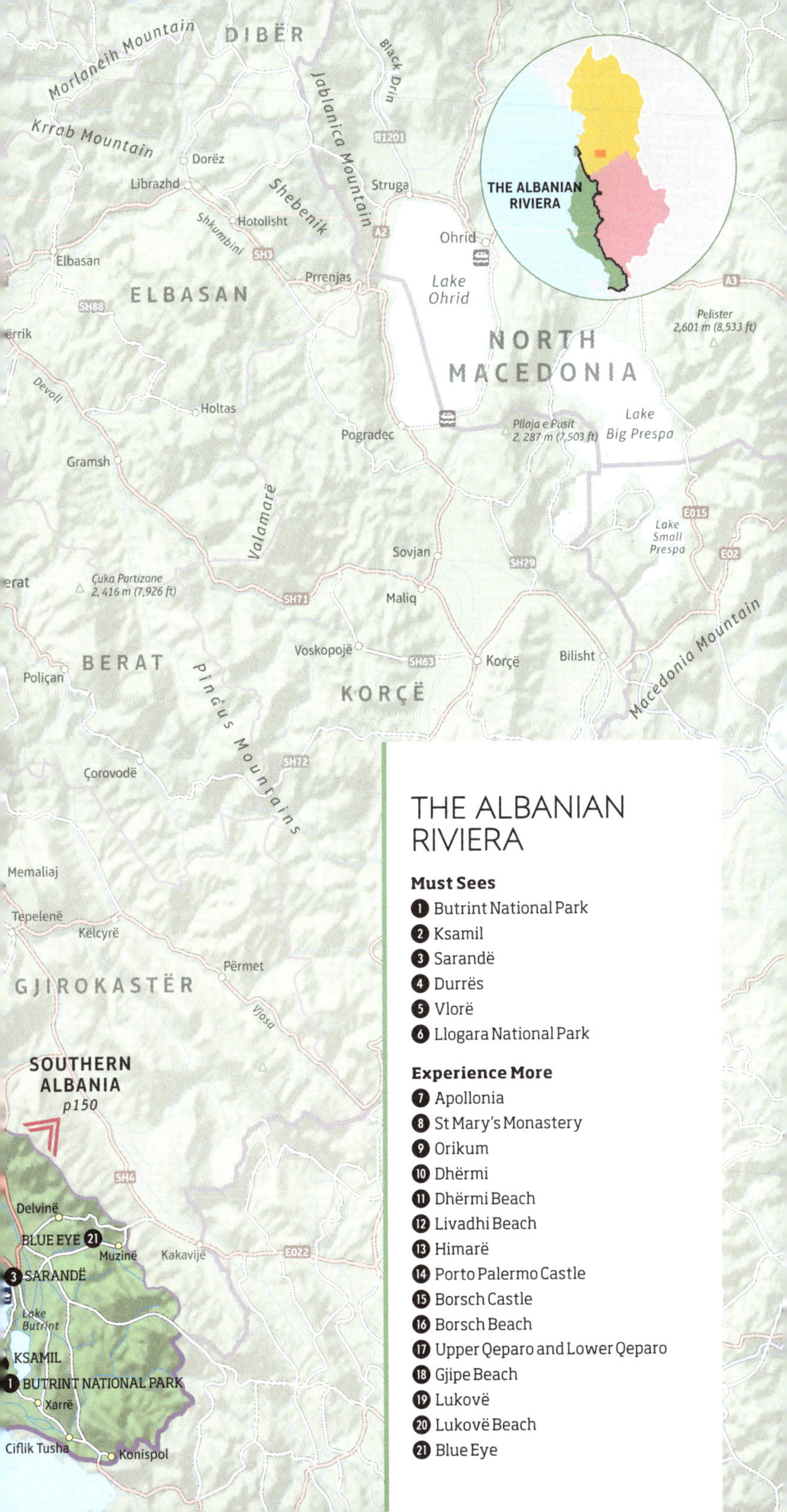
THE ALBANIAN RIVIERA
Must Sees
1 Butrint National Park
2 Ksamil
3 Sarandë
4 Durrës
5 Vlorë
6 Llogara National Park
Experience More
7 Apollonia
8 St Mary's Monastery
9 Orikum
10 Dhërmi
11 Dhërmi Beach
12 Livadhi Beach
13 Himarë
14 Porto Palermo Castle
15 Borsch Castle
16 Borsch Beach
17 Upper Qeparo and Lower Qeparo
18 Gjipe Beach
19 Lukovë
20 Lukovë Beach
21 Blue Eye
THE ALBANIAN RIVIERA
SOUTHERN ALBANIA
p150
DIBËR
ELBASAN
NORTH MACEDONIA
BERAT
KORÇË
GJIROKASTËR
Morlaneih Mountain
Krrab Mountain
Jablanica Mountain
Shebenik
Pindus Mountains
Macedonia Mountain
Valamarë
Black Drin
Shkumbini
Devoll
Vjosa
Lake Ohrid
Lake Big Prespa
Lake Small Prespa
Lake Butrint
Pelister
2,601 m (8,533 ft)
Pllaja e Pusit
2, 287 m (7,503 ft)
Çuka Partizane
2, 416 m (7,926 ft)
Dorëz
Librazhd
Hotolisht
Struga
Ohrid
Elbasan
Prrenjas
Holtas
Pogradec
Gramsh
Sovjan
Maliq
Voskopojë
Korçë
Bilisht
Poliçan
Çorovodë
Memaliaj
Tepelenë
Këlcyrë
Përmet
Delvinë
BLUE EYE 21
Muzinë
Kakavijë
3 SARANDË
KSAMIL
1 BUTRINT NATIONAL PARK
Xarrë
Ciflik Tusha
Konispol
R1201
A2
SH3
SH88
A3
E015
E02
SH79
SH71
SH63
SH72
SH4
E022

BUTRINT NATIONAL PARK

D7 4 km (2.5 miles) SE of Ksamil From Sarandë and Ksamil
9am-7pm daily butrint.al

A site of great historical significance, Butrint is also a biodiversity hot spot. Its forests, wetlands and lagoons are rich in birdlife, while mammals found here include the Mediterranean monk seal.

Butrint National Park's biggest draw is the sprawling ruins of the fortified city of Butrint itself, a UNESCO World Heritage Site since 1992. First occupied in 50,000 BCE, the site spans the Greeks, Romans, Byzantines, Venetians and Ottomans. Wandering the ruins, you can see the marks these myriad rulers left on Butrint over the centuries. A well-preserved Greek amphitheatre stands alongside Roman bathhouses, Byzantine churches and Venetian towers; look out, too, for the Lion Gate, one of six entrances within the city's Hellenistic walls. One highlight is the Roman Theatre of Asclepius, a sanctuary to which people would make pilgrimages and pay tribute to the god of Healing.

A well-preserved Greek amphitheatre stands alongside Roman bathhouses, cross-shaped Byzantine churches and Venetian towers.

← The ruins at Butrint, including a preserved Greek amphitheatre

EAT

The Mussel House
This is the spot to try lagoon-fresh mussels from Lake Butrint, steamed or grilled, on an alfresco deck jutting out over the water.

Ruga Sarandë-Butrint, Qafa e Hartes
noon-10pm daily
69 232 9231

ⓁⓁⓁ

Restaurant Kalivoi
Seafood fresh from the lagoon is served at this place on the shores of Lake Butrint. Expect flaky fish, eel and plates of grilled mussels.

Shëndëlli
8am-10pm daily
69 872 9066

ⓁⓁⓁ

A BRIEF HISTORY

Butrint was occupied as far back as 50,000 BCE, but what can be seen today dates to when the ancient Greek Chaonians settled here around 800 BCE. The Romans arrived in 44 BCE, expanding the site and building an aqueduct across the Vivari Channel. It was abandoned in the Middle Ages but reconstructed under the Byzantines in 800 CE. Butrint came under Venetian control in the 14th century. The last addition to the site was when the Ottoman ruler Ali Pasha added a fortress at the mouth of the Vivari Channel in the early 19th century.

2

KSAMIL

D7 Ksamil Bus Station ksamil.al

Almost at the border with Greece, the coastal town of Ksamil sets the scene for a laid-back and slow-paced beach trip. The town has several stretches of sand along the crystal-clear shallows of the Ionian Sea; just beyond the uninhabited islets that float off Ksamil lies the hazy blue silhouette of the Greek island of Corfu.

Marking the southern tip of the Albanian Riviera, Ksamil may have the feel of an old, traditional fishing village about it, but it was in fact built under the communist regime in the 1960s. Once isolated and undiscovered, Ksamil has seen a huge rise in visitor numbers in the early 21st century, during which time it has transformed into a destination beach town. Today, scores of holidaymakers stretch out on loungers or over-water beds, sipping cocktails from the myriad beach bars and taking day trips to the uninhabited islands just offshore or to the UNESCO-listed ruins at nearby Butrint National Park *(p116)*.

The town gets very busy in summer, when its nightlife scene bursts into life with live sets from international DJs, fairground attractions and club nights.

Ksamil's Beaches

Several sweeps of snow-white pebble and coarse-sand beaches grace the town, including the central section known, rather imaginatively, as Bora Bora Beach, after the island paradise in French Polynesia. As well as the beaches here, one of Ksamil's quiet, forested islands can be reached by swimming from the calm shallows of Bora Bora Beach.

DRINK

The Black Pearl Beach Club

This beach club enjoys an enviable position on Bora Bora Beach, with fishing-net beds poking out over the sea. Fresh seafood accompanies a slew of cocktails.

Rruga Vaçe Zela
May-Oct: 8am-11:30pm daily
69 966 9750

Ohana Beach Bar

Ohana's luxury loungers dominate a slice of Last Bay. Craft cocktails can be enjoyed with some of the best seafood in Ksamil.

Rruga Riviera Zela
May-Oct: 7:30am-11:30pm daily
69 707 0757

KSAMIL'S ISLETS

If all the islets of Ksamil were merged together, they would only cover around 99,000 sq m (1 million sq ft). All four sit within the confines of Butrint National Park *(p116)*, and thus remain blissfully undeveloped. In summer, locals set up pop-up bars on the islands' otherwise deserted beaches, providing refreshments for those making the journey over here by boat, paddleboard, jet-ski or pedalo from Ksamil. Boatmen in town offer day trips (no need to book); or it's a short, easy swim to the closest island from Bora Bora Beach in Ksamil.

↑ Sunloungers on a pontoon jutting into the turquoise waters at Bora Bora Beach

↑ Sunset turning the sky pink above the beach in central Ksamil town

← Ksamil town, and two of its four islets, just offshore

3

SARANDË

D7 Sarandë Bus Station Port of Sarandë
7 Rruga Skënderbeu; www.saranda.al

With a buzzing centre packed full of cafés, cocktail bars and DJ-hosting nightclubs, Sarandë is the unofficial capital of the Albanian Riviera – during summer, sunseekers flock to its all-day beach clubs, and the town's handful of sand-and-pebble strips are filled with sunloungers. Sarandë has changed hands many times over the centuries, from the Greeks to the Romans around the 1st century CE, and then to the Ottomans in the 15th century, when it was used as a commercial harbour. The town's population has doubled since the 1990s, and it continues to swell in peak season, when ferries from Greece bring in bargain-hunting partygoers.

Sarandë Promenade

Shëtitorja Naim Frashëri
Rruga Onhezmi Bus Stop

Sarandë's attractive promenade, also known as the Sarandë Embankment, runs along the waterfront in the centre of town, stretching east for 1 km (0.5 miles) from the ferry terminal in the Port of Sarandë, at the head of the bay. Dotted with palm trees, this traffic-free route is perfect for a stroll, passing along the way sandy beaches, and tiny marinas where boats bob about in the clear blue waters. Shops full of beach-holiday necessities and general souvenirs line the boulevard for most of its length, and there are plenty of seafood restaurants, waterfront bars and stylish coffee shops in which to relax over a meal or a drink and watch the world go by. Evening is the most popular time to visit the promenade, when locals partake in the *xhiro* – an evening walk that is the Albanian version of the Spanish *paseo* and the Italian *passeggiata* – along the seafront as the sun sets.

INSIDER TIP
Fly to Greece

The closest airport to Sarandë is actually Corfu Airport, in Greece. From the ferry terminal in Corfu Town, you can catch the 35-minute hydrofoil that runs several times a day to the Port of Sarandë, at the western end of Sarandë Promenade.

 Cafés lining a boat-filled marina on Sarandë Promenade

DRINK

Mango Club

White-curtained cabana beds, with chilled-out beats by day and DJ sets at night.

Rruga Turizmi Kanali i 'Çukës
7am-midnight daily
discomango.com

Jericho Cocktail Bar

First-class mixologists, and a rooftop on the waterfront offering superb sunset views.

Shëtitorja Naim Frashëri
8am-2am daily
jerichorooms.com

②

Sarandë Synagogue Complex

7 Rruga Skënderbeu
Sarandë Bus Station
visitsaranda.net/see/synagogue-complex

Located right in the centre of Sarandë, these ruins are all that remains of what was once the largest synagogue in the Balkans. The small excavated site is free to enter, although there is scant signage, leaving visitors to interpret the ruins for themselves. The main part of the complex is the ancient synagogue itself, which dates to the 5th or 6th century CE. Two long mosaic pavements are a highlight, although you can also make out the walls of what were once dwellings and shops, whose history has been traced back to the Roman era, around 1 BCE.

↑ Umbrellas lining the sands at Mango Beach

Mango Beach

Rruga Turizmi Kanali i'Çukës **SH81 Bus Stop**

This amenity-packed beach at the southern end of Sarandë is named after the trendy private beach club *(p121)* that occupies the majority of the shoreline here, as is commonly the case along the sandy sections of the southern Albanian coast. It's an undeniably beautiful stretch of beach, where a warm, clear sea laps at a white shore, but there's very little room to put a towel down, as most of the sand is taken up by loungers from the various beach clubs that have cropped up here over the years. To secure your spot, you'll need to pay the daily lounger fee.

Monastery of 40 Saints

Rruga 40 Shenjtoret
Sarandë-Ksamil-Butrint Bus (Rruga Butrinti Stop)
9am-6pm daily

Once an important Byzantine pilgrimage site, this isolated

↓ Ruins of the Monastery of 40 Saints and *(inset)* the remains of an arch

Did You Know?

Sarandë owes its name to the 40 Martyrs of Sebaste - Saranda is Greek for "forty".

hilltop monastery has since slowly disintegrated into the atmospheric ruins that can be seen here today. It was originally constructed in the 6th century and named after the 40 Martyrs of Sebaste. In 320 CE, these Christian Roman soldiers, refusing to give up their faith, were condemned to freeze to death, naked. In honour of its namesakes, the monastery consisted of 40 small underground chapels, each one dedicated to a different martyr. The building remained relatively intact until Allied forces bombed it during World War II, after which it was used as a military base during the communist regime. Visitors today are free to wander through the stone ruins and take in the fine views down over Sarandë and the Ionian Sea. An information panel at the entrance shows what the monastery would have looked like before it fell into disrepair. It is still of religious significance, and followers of the Greek Orthodox faith continue to leave flowers here. The site is 3 km (2 miles) east of Sarandë, around a 45-minute to an hour-long walk from the waterfront.

Gjiri i Midhjeve

Rruga Mbreteresha Teute Sarandë-Ksamil-Butrint Bus (SH81 Bus Stop)

Gjiri i Midhjeve, which translates to "Mussel Beach", is found just south of Sarandë. Protected by a horseshoe-shaped bay, the water here is constantly calm and so clear that the seafloor is often visible – perfect for swimming. Stone steps lead down from the car park to the pebble and rough-sand shore, where most of the space is taken up by paid-for loungers. Although it can get busy in summer, this is still among the more peaceful beaches along the Albanian Riviera.

STAY

Demi Hotel

The VIP suite has a hot tub on the terrace, but even the most basic rooms come with a sea view at Demi Hotel. The highlight is the hotel's sun terrace, jutting out over the Ionian Sea.

2 Rruga Butrinti
demi.al

Hotel Brilant

Plush rooms with sea-view balconies belie the mid-range price of this central hotel. Breakfast is served on the top floor, where the maritime panorama lets you know that the seafront is no more than a few footsteps away.

4 Rruga Bilal Golemi
brilanthotel.al

ⓁⓁⓁ

6

LËKURËSI CASTLE

Lëkurësi Hill **Feniq Bus Stop** **visitsaranda.net/see/lekursi-castle**

When Lëkurësi Castle was built in 1537, Suleyman the Magnificent was no doubt thinking about strategic vantage points rather than sunsets over the sea, but this is now a super spot to watch the sun go down.

Lëkurësi Castle's fortified walls with round watchtowers used to encase old Lëkurës village, but a series of raids and neglect over the centuries have left little of the original structure aside from its external walls. However, some faded Byzantine frescoes remain, and a restaurant has been sympathetically constructed in the same grey-hued stone as the castle. You'll also find the mushroom-like concrete remains of Cold War bunkers, now home to stray cats and the occasional passing tortoise.

EAT

Restaurant Kalaja e Lëkurësit

Within the thick walls of the castle, this restaurant has seating scattered across the terrace with a glorious view at sunset. The menu is a mix of Italian pasta dishes, Greek salads and seafood.

Lëkurësi Hill, Sarandë
9am-10pm Mon-Fri, 11am-11pm Sat & Sun
lekursi-castle.al

ⓁⓁⓁ

GREAT VIEW
Terrace Sunsets

On a clear evening, the terrace at Lëkurësi Castle is one of the best places in Sarandë to watch the sunset.

The walls of Lëkurësi Castle, now home to a restaurant with a view

Detail from a Byzantine fresco on the walls of Lëkurësi Castle

A concrete Cold War bunker near the castle on Lëkurësi Hill

The terraced seating of curving Durrës Amphitheatre

4

DURRËS

C4 Durrës Bus Terminal, Rruga Hafiz Podgorica
Durrës Port, Rruga Pavaresia durres.gov.al

The northern gateway to the Albanian Riviera, Durrës was founded in 627 BCE, when the Illyrian territory of Taulantians was colonized by Corinthians from what is now Corfu. More recently, it was the summer home of King Zog, whose once-lavish villa still presides over the city.

Durrës Amphitheatre

Rruga Kalase Durrës Bus Terminal Apr-Sep: 9am-6pm daily; Oct-Mar: 9am-4:30pm daily

Durrës' remarkable Roman amphitheatre is the city's most significant sight. Construction began under Emperor Trajan and was finished in the 2nd century BCE. Originally used for gladiatorial contests, the amphitheatre was damaged by two earthquakes, the second one burying it underground in the 10th century; it was only found again in 1966. You can still make out the terraced seating, which once held up to 20,000 people, and venture into the tunnels where the gladiators would have awaited their fate all those centuries ago.

When the amphitheatre was abandoned, a small Christian chapel was built inside the complex; it features several well-preserved mosaics.

Royal Villa of Durrës

Rruga Kont Urani Durrës Beach Bus Stop, Rruga Taulantia To the public

The summer residence of the infamous King Zog and his family until the abolition of the monarchy in 1945, the Royal Villa of Durrës is worth a stop

KING ZOG

"King Zog" was born Ahmed Muhtar Zogolli in 1895. Elected as Albania's first president in 1925, he was effectively a dictator, and in 1928 he declared himself to be Zog I, King of the Albanians. In April 1939, Mussolini's Italy (with whom Zog had allied himself) invaded Albania and the royal family fled to Greece, taking a considerable amount of gold with them. Zog died in exile in France in 1961.

Did You Know?

King Zog also took the name Skanderbeg III to highlight his family ties to Albania's national hero.

to admire its kitsch pink-and-white façade. During communism, the villa was used to accommodate diplomats and world leaders like Nikita Khrushchev and Jimmy Carter.

Archaeological Museum

Rruga Taulantia 32 Durrës Centre Bus Stop, Rruga Pavarësi May-Oct: 9am-7pm daily; Nov-Apr: 9am-4pm Tue-Sun

This is the largest archaeological museum in Albania, with collections that span a multitude of eras and empires, from the Hellenistic periods to the Roman conquest of the region and beyond. It was built in the 1950s and has been undergoing major reconstruction and renovation for most of the 2020s. Slowly, a sleek, modern space with impeccably curated artifacts from the ancient sites of Dürres and its surrounding region is emerging. Some parts of the museum may be periodically closed to the public as renovation work continues, but you'll always find pockets of interest and intrigue amid the Roman funeral stones and sarcophagi. The museum's highlight is the *Beauty of Durrës*, a colourful, elliptical mosaic spanning 9 sq m (97 sq ft), some 5.1m (17 ft) at its widest, and depicting a woman's head on a floral background. Discovered in 1916, it was created in the second half of the 4th century BCE to decorate the courtyard of one of Durrës' many fine villas of the time.

EAT

Mema House

The menu of fresh seafood and grilled meats celebrates local produce, while the interior has hints of old Albania while staying stylish.

Rruga Taulantia 33
10am-11pm daily
69 754 1068

LLL

Kodra e Kuajve

Just outside the city but worth the journey, this upmarket restaurant enjoys fine views over Durrës. Local delicacies are served with finesse.

Off SH4, Golem
8am-9pm daily
kodrakuajve.com

LLL

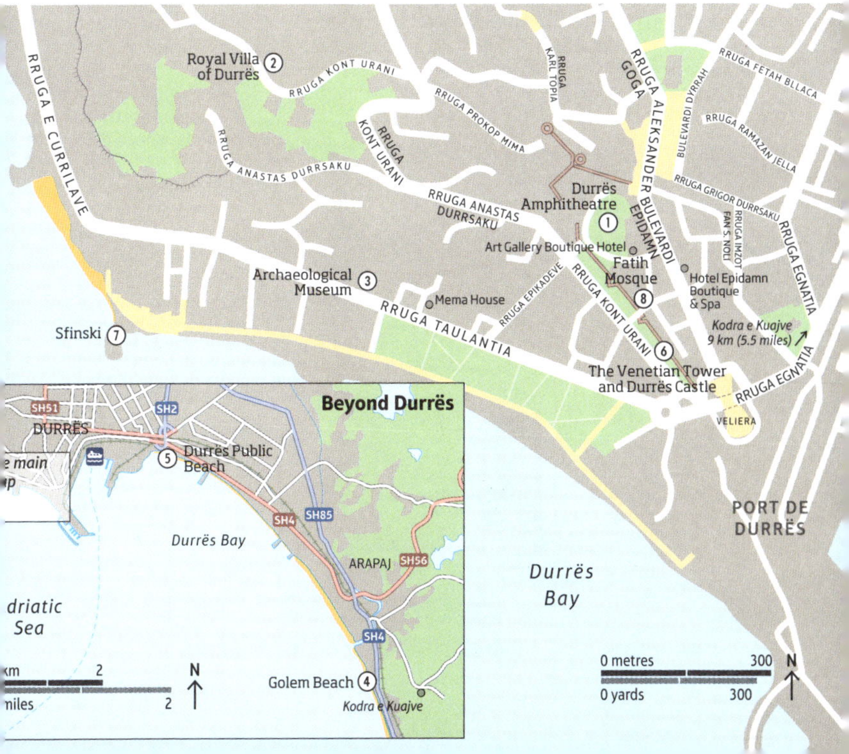

④

Golem Beach

Bulevardi i Pishave
Hotel Fari, Rruga Qemal Stafa Kompleksi Fari

Its proximity to Durrës makes Golem Beach one of the most popular on the Albanian Riviera. Its sunloungers fill up quickly in summer, and the clear, warm sea is a hive of activity, from jet-skiing to inflatable obstacle courses.

⑤

Durrës Public Beach

Rruga Porta e Detit
Durrës Beach Bus Stop, Rruga Taulantia

Parts of Durrës' central beach are open to the public, a rarity on the built-up sections of Albania's coast. While there are a still a lot of private areas, marked by sunloungers belonging to local restaurants and bars, you can still find a patch of lounger-less sand at several points along the shore. The sand is a shade of fawn brown and the sea is clear and calm and an array of vendors provide all manner of water-sports equipment, from inflatables to paddleboards to jet skis. Some parts of the beach have yet to be developed for tourism; locals make the most of the crumbling concrete rubble jutting out like a pier here, dangling fishing rods in the shallows. There is an actual pier, too, a stark Modernist construction, but it is closed to the public.

INSIDER TIP
Flight-free

The easiest way to get to Albania from the UK without flying is to go by rail to Bari in Italy, from where daily ferries head across the Adriatic to Durrës, taking eight hours or so.

⑥ 

The Venetian Tower and Durrës Castle

Rruga Kont Urani
Durrës Bus Terminal
9am-7pm daily

The Venetian Tower sits within the historical complex known as Durrës Castle (Kalaja e Durrësit), a Byzantine fortress whose 6-m- (15-ft-) high walls were constructed in the late 5th century. They were reconstructed in the 15th century, when the tower was added by the Venetians to serve as a lookout point and weapons store. For years, the Venetian Tower stood as an interesting but undeveloped monument in the centre of Durrës, but thanks to an injection of funding from the European Union, it now offers a virtual-reality tour, where the history of Dürres and its castle is projected onto the walls of the Venetian Tower's main hall in a state-of-the-art display. Up on the rooftop, there are great views out to sea and information on the area's history is provided at each lookout point – guard posts when Durrës was under Venetian rule.

The long stretch of Durrës' central public beach

The Venetian Tower, now home to a virtual-reality tour

Sfinksi

Rruga Taulantia
Durrës Beach Bus Stop, Rruga Taulantia

At the end of Durrës' seaside promenade, the Sfinksi was created as a social space and is dotted with street art. Concrete steps, shaped like a pyramid, lead to the water, where people gather to talk or fish. It's vaguely Brutalist in style, making it feel like a public work of art. There are several sculptures here, including a socialist realist soldier that commemorates the struggle against Italian fascism in 1939.

Fatih Mosque

Rruga Xhamia **Durrës Centre Bus Stop, Rruga Pavarësi** **6-9:45am daily**

Dating back to the 16th century, when Ottoman Turks controlled Durrës, Fatih Mosque is one of the few religious buildings that survived the switch to an atheist state during Albania's communist era. The imposing façade with its spiky minaret is a beautiful addition to the central Durrës skyline. Inside, it's a haven of quiet reverie, with peaceful gardens and a pretty fountain for ablutions.

↑ Fatih Mosque, with its slender minaret and ablutions fountain

STAY

Art Gallery Boutique

A sweeping external staircase sets a tone of grandeur that continues in the art-filled corridors inside. Boudoir-style rooms overlook Durrës Amphitheatre.

Rruga Kalase
artgalleryboutiquehotel.com

ⓁⓁⓁ

Hotel Epidamn Boutique & Spa

Right next door to Durrës Amphitheatre, this boutique hotel embraces Ottoman-esque splendour.

Boulevardi Epidamn
epidamn.al

ⓁⓁⓁ

5

VLORË

C6 Intracity Bus Station, Rruga Enver Jaho Vlorë Port, Rruga Hektor Shyti vlora.gov.al

Vlorë was founded around the 10th century BCE by Illyrians, drawn to its protected position, nestled as it is in a bay. The allure is still the calm sea, but for swimming rather than maritime endeavours.

HIDDEN GEM

Karaburun-Sazan National Marine Park

Formerly used as a German submarine base, this biodiverse park of deserted beaches can be reached by boat on day trips from Vlorë marina.

Vlorë Old Town

Rruga Justin Godar, Vlorë Bus Station Cole, Rruga Demokracia

For a city dating back to the Illyrian era, Vlorë's Old Town is comparatively new. A rainbow of Venetian-style buildings with wooden shutters line the mostly pedestrianized streets, with stringed lights illuminating the narrow walkways in the evening; the whole area is a hub of pavement cafés and bars serving alfresco Turkish coffee and raki. The Old Town is centred around the main Independence Square, which is dominated by a Neo-classical clocktower. Here, towering monuments created by sculpters Muntaz Dhrami and Kristaq Rama in 1972 pay homage to Albania's independence from the Ottoman Empire in 1912.

Museum of Independence

Bulevardi Vlorë -Skelë Bus Station Tulla - Uji i Ftohtë, Rruga Çamëria Apr-Sep: 9am-5pm daily; Oct-Mar: 9am-5pm Tue-Sat, 10am-2pm Sun

This unassuming yellow building in the heart of Vlorë played a huge role in the history of Albania. It was here, in 1912, that Ismail Qemari (1844–1919) raised the distinctive black-and-red flag of an independent Albania for the first time. For the following six months, this house was the base of operations for the first Albanian government. Today, it's an intriguing museum with exhibitions dedicated to the country's fight for independence across two

→ Bronze bust of Mehmet Pashe Derralla, Museum of Independence

↑ Plazhi i Vjeter, Vlorë's long stretch of town beach

floors of collections. Bronze busts of the ministers who formed Albania's first government line the museum's front garden.

Muradie Mosque

🏠 Rruga Justin Godar
🚌 Bus Station South, Rruga Liria

One of Albania's oldest mosques, Muradie was built in 1537, during the reign of Suleyman the Magnificent, and is said to have been designed by leading Ottoman mosque builder Mimar Sinan. Although dwarfed by modern buildings, it is a striking construction, with two-toned stonework of white and rose stripes and floral carvings inspired by Byzantine designs.

Plazhi i Vjeter

🏠 Rruga Rebi Alikaj
🚌 Plazhi i Vjeter Bus Stop, Rruga Sazan

Stretching around 800 m (2,625 ft) along the coast of Vlorë, Plazhi i Vjeter beach features soft sand, warm waters and a view of the hills that cocoon the city. A few high-rise hotels have cropped up over the years, and the shore is lined with sunloungers, but the large amount of space here means it doesn't feel as built up as you might expect from a city beach.

Plazhi i Ri

🏠 Rruga Aleksandër Moisiu
🚌 Stacioni i Autobusit Akademia e Marines

A series of boardwalks and promenades makes palm-tree-lined Plazhi i Ri beach an ideal spot for an evening stroll, especially as the sun sets over the Adriatic Sea. Spend the day dipping in and out of the pleasingly blue water – if you don't mind paying for a lounger spot – finished off with a cocktail at a bar on the sand.

EAT

Pizeri Amantia
Feast on Italian-style dishes, plus seafood from the Adriatic.

🏠 Boulevard Ismail Qemali 🕒 10am-1:30am daily 📞 69 216 9507

Novus Traditional Food Restaurant
This buffet-style diner serves traditional Albanian dishes.

🏠 Rruga Çamëria 🕒 noon-11pm daily (from 9am Sun) 📞 69 996 9111

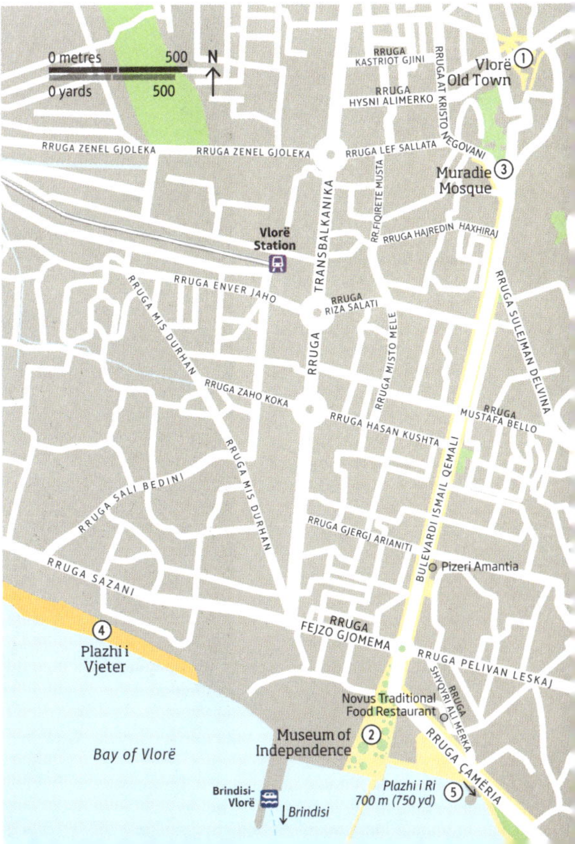

LLOGARA NATIONAL PARK

C6 40 km (25 miles) S of Vlorë Vlorë-Himarë (request stop)

Thanks to its position on the Albanian Riviera, Llogara is one of the most visited national parks in the country. It's also one of Albania's smallest protected areas at just over 10 sq km (4 sq miles). Despite its diminutive size, the landscape is varied, encompassing alpine meadows, sheer cliffs, towering mountains and dense forests.

Located in the Ceraunian Mountains, Llogara National Park makes a pleasant change from the baking coast, and even in the height of summer the air here is chilled and refreshing. It's a popular place to stop off on the drive along the coast between Vlorë and Himarë, with several country-style restaurants serving farm-to-table fare amid the peace of the pine trees. If you want to stay longer to hit some of the hiking trails, there are a few small hotels and campsites within the national park, most of them enjoying beautiful mountain and sea views. You might spot deer, wild boar and – if you're really lucky – an elusive Eurasian wolf up on the thick forested peaks, while the evergreen trees rustle with birdlife.

TOP 3 HIKES IN LLOGARA

Mount Çikë Trail
This challenging 13.2-km (8.2-mile) circular trail summits Mount Çikë, 2,045 m (6,709 ft) above sea level. The trail is marked, but it's advisable to take a GPS map with you.

Maja Thanasit Trail
This out-and-back trail has beautiful views of the sea from high up in the mountains and is a good option for seeing alpine wildflowers. It's 7.4 km (4.6 miles) each way; turn back at the old radio tower.

Pass of Caesar (Qafa e Qesarit)
This route passes through thick forest and takes in the site where Julius Caesar is alleged to have set up camp during the Battle of Pharsalus in 43 BCE.

Did You Know?

Llogara is famous for its honey. Local beekeepers sell their wares from stalls by the roadside.

EAT

Freskia

The place to try mountain lamb, slowly roasted on a spit over hot coals. Outdoor dining here comes with a backdrop of birdsong, and the tables are dotted between towering pine trees.

Off SH8, Llogara National Park Orikum Bus Stop Noon-9pm daily 69 650 4892

ⓁⓁⓁ

↑ The park's visitor centre, where you can pick up information on hiking trails

← Wild mountain goat, climbing a tree within the park

← Hikers taking a breather on one of Llogara National Park's many scenic trails

EXPERIENCE MORE

Apollonia

C5 Pojan Pojan Bus Stop May-Sep: 8am-8pm daily; Oct-Apr: 9am-4pm Tue-Sun apollonia archaeologicalpark.al

The ancient port city of Apollonia once sat at the crossroads of a prehistoric trading route and was used as an Illyrian trading post before Corinthians colonized it around 600 BCE. It became a centre for culture under the Roman Empire, with a school of philosophy and rhetoric – Augustus, the first Roman Emperor, studied here in his youth. The city's significance declined after an earthquake in 234 CE silted up the harbour and turned the River Vjosa into a malaria-infested bog, and Apollonia was abandoned by the 4th century CE.

Parts of the site were destroyed during World War II, and in the 1960s the construction of some 400 military bunkers in the area irrevocably damaged the ruins. Since the turn of the millennia, however, steps have been made to preserve the site, and in April 2003 Apollonia was designated an archaeological park. While most of the remains still lie buried underground, the columned façade of the administrative building has been renovated and it's a pleasant stroll among what has been unearthed, following the pathway between old olive trees and crumbling walls. Housed in the 13th-century Byzantine church and St Mary's monastery, the Archaeological Museum of Apollonia details the site's history up to the Roman era. Displays include restored porticoes, a Roman mosaic and a collection of ceramics decorated with mythological Hellenic images.

PROTECTING APOLLONIA

After being left to ruin for centuries, Apollonia drew archaeological interest in the early 20th century, when classicists from the Austrian Empire began investigating the site. Many relics were protected in the on-site Archaeological Museum of Apollonia and in the National Historical Museum in Tirana *(p73)*, but after the collapse of the Hoxha dictatorship in the 1990s, the treasure was raided and much of it sold off to collectors in other countries. In 2011, Apollonia's museum reopened, dedicated to protecting the site's artifacts, and French-Albanian archaeological teams continue to excavate the ruins.

St Mary's Monastery

C5 Zvërnec Island, Vlorë Plazhi i Vjeter Bus Stop, then 4-km (2.5-mile) walk

Dating back to the 13th century, the Byzantine Manastiri i Shën Mërisë (monastery of St Mary) sits alone on the larger of the two Zvërnec islands, in the middle of the Narta Lagoon. The red-roofed stone building can easily be made out from the mainland, poking above the island's verdant green forest – ask the caretaker to open the locked metal gate for a walk in the woods. The monastery features a typical cross-shaped floor plan and houses an icon of St Mary by the famous 18th-century Albanian artist Tërpo Zografi. Its cluster of stone buildings is an ode to the ascetic way of life: dormitories, a workshop, a stable, a warehouse, a small football pitch and a tiny graveyard are the only signs of life here. The entire island measures a mere 400 m (1,400 ft) by 300 m (1,000 ft), and apart from the clearing

St Mary's, which houses Apollonia's museum, and *(inset)* its exterior

that was made for the complex, it is completely covered in fragrant pine trees. You can access the monastery along a wooden walkway, which stretches over the lagoon and out to the island, starting at a car park 11 km (7 miles) northwest of the centre of Vlorë.

9

Orikum

C6 Orikum Bus Station

Just under 24 km (15 miles) south along the bay from Vlorë lies the fast-developing beach town of Orikum. There's a Miami Beach vibe to its palm-fringed beachfront, where some of the Albanian Riviera's best seafood restaurants open out to a flat strip of sand and the milky blue water is calm enough to swim in. It's worth venturing 5 km (3 miles) west of town to the ruins of **Ancient Orikum**, the original settlement after which the new town is named. Julius Caesar set up camp here with his vast army during the Roman Civil War in 48 BCE. You can see the remains of bathhouses, dwellings and shops, and cows and sheep grazing between the ruins.

Ancient Orikum

Orikum Archaeological Park

EAT

Oriku Restorant

"Fresh" is the watchword at Oriku, whether that's salads packed with local vegetables or seafood caught from the Ionian Sea every morning. Dine inside or take a seat in the garden area out front.

C6 Rruga Pashaliman, Orikum
8am-10pm daily
oriku.al

LLL

Fish House

Less is more at this no-fuss restaurant on Orikum's seafront. Catch of the day, from fat prawns to lightly fried whole fish, is simply seasoned with salt and a squeeze of lemon.

C6 Rruga Pashaliman, Orikum
8am-11pm daily
69 321 1355

LLL

The beach at Orikum, backed by palm trees and overlooking the Bay of Vlorë

Dhërmi

C6 50 km (31 miles) SE of Vlorë Dhermi Bus Stop, SH8

Wonderfully picturesque Dhërmi village looks like it's about to tumble from the mountainside. Red-roofed villas and houses cling to the rocks, staggering up the slopes away from the main coastal road. Dhërmi's most eye-catching building is the **Church of St Spyridon**, with its white façade and blue-domed clocktower rising against the mountains.

GREAT VIEW

Dhërmi Skyline

For a stunning view of Dhërmi's blue-domed church and its jumble of houses ranged against the rugged mountains, head up the winding road from the village to the Monastery of St Mary, perched higher up the mountainside.

There's a slew of family-run guesthouses and traditional grill restaurants serving mountain-style fare, most of which have terraces that enjoy fabulous views out to the sea from their mountainside vantage points. From the village, it's a ten-minute walk down to Dhërmi Beach, or you can venture a little farther on to reach Drymades Beach, which remains largely undeveloped. Alternatively, the scenic Mills Hiking Trail offers another way to reach the sea from the village, via a series of rugged paths and metal walkways. The short trail passes several waterfalls and, of course, old mills, which are slowly being reclaimed by nature. Just outside Dhërmi, the **Monastery of St Mary** sits on a hilltop above the village and is worth a visit for the colourful 18th-century frescoes of saints that adorn its walls.

Church of St Spyridon

Kisha e Shën Spiridhonit

Monastery of St Mary

Rruga Vlladas

Dhërmi Beach

C6 Rruga Jaliskari, Dhërmi Dhermi Bus Stop, SH8

Dhërmi Beach looks postcard-perfect, with its glass-clear turquoise water slipping into a deeper azure behind a sweep of ivory-white pebbles. A crop of sun loungers provide (paid) spots to while away the day; in the peak of summer, you'll need to get here early to find public space to lay down your towel. Several boutique hotels and restaurants are dotted between Dhërmi village and Dhërmi Beach, between the olive groves and pine trees.

Did You Know?

Petro Marko, one of the founders of modern Albanian prose, was born in Dhërmi in 1913.

Dhërmi village, with its blue-domed Church of St Spyridon

Livadhi Beach

D6 Himarë-Livadhi Road, Himarë

Just north of Himarë, Livadhi is the region's premier luxury beach destination. While this long stretch of coast could hardly be described as undiscovered – five-star hotels and luxury boutique accommodation have sprouted up all along the seafront – staying here means days spent padding from pool to beach lounger, swimming in the gorgeous sea and taking advantage of the many watersports on offer. Day-trippers can pay for a lounger and while away the day sipping cocktails with enviable views of pure turquoise shallows. The farthest end of Livadhi Beach has been taken over by private hotels and beach bars, and you'll be hard-pressed to find a spot of free-to-access sands unless you visit in the shoulder or low season. From Livadhi Beach, however, you can hike the coastal path to Aquarium Beach in less than half an hour. Blissfully undeveloped and often deserted, this is one of the few remaining wild beaches in Albania.

ALBANIA'S BEACHES

Albania's beaches have received a lot of attention on social media for their soft white sands, although most are coarse sand or pebble. Influencers are also careful to crop out the high-rise hotels and private beach bars that now claim large parts of the coast. However, there are still some wild beaches accessible only by boat or on foot, and if you visit outside the peak season, you'll find that many pop-up bars have closed and their paid-for sunloungers are stacked up until next summer.

STAY

La Brisa Boutique

Five-star hotel right on Dhërmi Beach, with an infinity pool that catches the sunset.

C6 Rruga Jaliskarii, Dhërmi labrisa.al

ⓁⓁⓁ

Gogo's Boutique Hotel

Close to Drymades Beach, this rather lavish boutique hotel also has stylish apartments.

C6 Rruga Perivolo, Dhërmi gogoshotel dhermi.com

ⓁⓁⓁ

Roots Dhërmi

Self-catering in a stone house in old Dhërmi village, a 15-minute walk from the beach.

C6 Rruga Allonja, Dhërmi rootsdhermi.com

ⓁⓁⓁ

Sunloungers line the sand at Livadhi Beach, where the water is a striking shade of blue

Soaking up the views from the hillside village of old Dhërmi

↑ Wandering the pretty cobblestoned alleyways of Himarë's Old Town

STAY

Geo & Art Boutique Hotel
Just across the road from the beach in central Himarë, this family-run hotel offers boutique bedrooms with sea views.

Ⓐ D6 Ⓐ Sfageio Beach, SH8 Ⓦ geoarthotel.com

Amphora Guesthouse
A variety of cutely furnished self-catering studios in a charming old stone villa with stunning sea vistas from the terrace.

Ⓐ D6 Ⓐ Off SH8, Himarë Old Town Ⓣ 67 514 6685

13 Himarë

Ⓐ D6 Ⓐ 52 km (32 miles) N of Sarandë Ⓑ Himarë Bus Stop, SH8

Himarë was founded over 2,000 years ago, and you can still see evidence of its ancient past dotted throughout town, most notably Himarë Castle, perched on a hilltop over-looking the sea. Himarë is divided into two distinct neighbourhoods: the old town, on the hillside above the sea; and the modern town down by the beach.

Himarë's old town dates back to the Illyrians, who settled in the area around the 3rd century BCE, before the ancient Greek Chaonians built their first fortification here to protect it as a trading post, naming it Chimaira. Strolling through the narrow, cobbled streets today, you can almost feel the history radiating from every ancient stone up here. Orthodox churches nestle between the old stone houses and accommodation comes in the form of family-run guesthouses and rustic apartments. The ruins of the 4th-century CE **Himarë Castle** offer a fascinating insight into Himarë's past, not to mention a beautiful hilltop spot with views across the mountains and sea. Many churches were built within the castle complex during the 8th century, some of which remain relatively intact. The Kisha e Episkopisë (**Episcopal Church**) is particularly well kept and features the double-headed Albanian eagle on its gates.

Down on the seafront, the majority of Himarë's modern centre was built in the 1960s. A long stretch of coarse-sanded beach fringes the new town, attracting large crowds in summer.

Himarë Castle
Ⓐ Off SH8, Himarë Old Town
Ⓑ Himarë Fshat Bus Stop

Episcopal Church
Ⓐ Off SH8, Himarë Old Town
Ⓑ Himarë Fshat Bus Stop

14 Porto Palermo Castle

Ⓐ D7 Ⓐ Porto Palermo Ⓑ Qeparo Bus Stop Ⓞ 9am-6pm daily Ⓦ porto-palermo.milinevsky.com

Porto Palermo Castle is cast out at the tip of a peninsula in a bay 8 km (5 miles) south of Himarë. This imposing fortress's triangular shape and round towers have led some historians to believe the Venetians may have built it. However, a plaque declares this castle to be the brainchild of Ottoman radical Ali Pasha, built with assistance from the French in the early 19th century. During World War II and into the communist era

Porto Palermo Castle, crowning the tip of a peninsula south of Himarë

ALI PASHA

Born in Tepelenë in 1744, Ali Pasha was the most famous pasha (feudal lord) in Ottoman Albania. He ruled a kingdom that spanned parts of Albania, Macedonia, Epirus, Thessaly and the Morea, using murder and brigandry to maintain his power. In 1819, Sultan Mahmud II ordered his assassination: with his sons and allies having deserted him, Ali Pasha was finally captured and killed in 1822.

of the 1970s and 80s, it was used as a prison. There's still a dark and imposing feel to each windowless room inside, especially the former cells on the ground floor. Up on the rooftop, old stone gun towers give way to a stunning view of the bay. You can even catch a glimpse of a nearby abandoned submarine base hewn into the rocks on the other side of the bay. The castle originally occupied an island, but a strip of reclaimed land (Palermo Beach) now connects it to the mainland.

15

Borsh Castle

D7 Off SH8, Borsh
Borsh Bus Stop

Don't let the final climb up a steep, dirt hillside track to Borsh Castle put you off. The hike to the top of the hill on which the castle sits rewards with beautiful views of the surrounding rugged Cerunian Mountains and the chance to explore ruins that are rich with intrigue. Large portions of this Byzantine stronghold have been destroyed, but its thick, fortified walls remain, alongside the dramatic ruins of the 17th-century Haxhi Bendo Mosque. During the Ottoman era, Borsh Castle came under the control of Ali Pasha; the mosque is named after a local man who served under him. Today, the castle is not maintained at all and there is no entry fee, but it is open to the public to freely wander. Often the only sign of life up here is a herd of roaming goats.

16

Borsh Beach

D7 Off SH8, Borsh
Borsh Bus Stop

Despite being one of the longest beaches on the Albanian Riviera, Borsh Beach is not as built up as the rest of the coast. Development is coming, however, with a glut of luxury hotels and glamping sites being constructed along the waterfront. For now, parasols and loungers spill onto the pebbles from bars and hotels. People are drawn to the inviting waters and shores; without the buzz of jet skis or outboard motors, it's one of the Riviera's quieter stretches.

TOP 3 RIVIERA SUNSET SPOTS

Upper Qeparo
From a terrace within Qeparo Castle, you can watch the sea reflecting gold rays against the mountains all around.

Lëkurësi Castle
High above Sarandë *(p124)*, this castle enjoys far-reaching views from its terrace.

The Last Bay
Soak up the fabulous panorama of the sun dipping behind the islets off Ksamil *(p118)*.

→ Gjipe Beach, reached along a dirt path or on a hike through Gjipe Gorge

Upper Qeparo and Lower Qeparo

D7 39 km (24 miles) N of Sarandë From Vlorë and Sarandë (on request)

In the Middle Ages, fearing smuggler raids and attacks by pirates, the people of Qeparo needed to put some distance between their village and the sea, so they settled halfway up Mount Gjivlash. By the 1950s, the threat from the sea had long vanished, and the construction of a coastal road brought the promise of well-connected land prime for agriculture and, eventually, tourism. Apart from a few stalwart families who still remain in the medieval stone houses of what is now known as Upper Qeparo, the entire population relocated to a new village down by the seaside.

↑ Old houses in the pretty village of Upper Qeparo

From the new village of Lower Qeparo, a twisting, 2.5-km- (1.5-mile-) long dirt road leads to pretty Upper Qeparo. Up here, cobbled streets weave to the ruins (and fine coastal views) of Qeparo Castle, flowering bougainvillea creeps up the village's old stone walls, and olive trees grow through the cracks of abandoned buildings.

Lower Qeparo has a few guesthouses and restaurants, all backing onto one of the most beautiful sections of the Albanian Riviera, where the sand is soft underfoot and there are fewer people than in some of the coast's more popular beaches.

Gjipe Beach

C6 Off SH8, near Illias From Vlorë and Sarandë (on request)

Quiet, undeveloped Gjipe Beach is a bit of a hike to get to – and is all the better for it. A few entrepreneurial locals set up ramshackle beach bars during the peak season, but you can usually find some lounger-free space. There are some small secluded sections of sand that can be accessed by clambering over the rocks that bookend the beach.

Gjipe Beach is a 20-minute walk along a dirt path from the nearest car park. Alternatively, you can follow the 3-km- (1.8-mile-) long Gjipe Gorge Trail from the main road, the SH8. The gorge's towering, tree-lined cliffs are home to a huge amount of biodiversity, and its shallow, saline waters attract loggerhead turtles and bottlenose dolphins. Spotting these beautiful creatures is a

joy, but always keep your distance, especially when the turtles are nesting.

19 Lukovë

D7 Lukovë Bus Stop, SH8

A smattering of houses 150 m (500 ft) above the coastline marks Lukovë village, a peaceful place where a handful of restaurants make the most of the vantage point. Several hiking trails snake into the mountains from the village, including an easy walk that leads to a small waterfall – follow the marked path from the mini market in Lukovë to the 14th-century Byzantine church of Shën e Premtes (St Friday) and a trickle of water in the rocks. A ten-minute walk along a narrow road from the village leads to Lukovë Beach.

20 Lukovë Beach

D7 Lukovë-Shpellë Lukovë Bus Stop, SH8

Known locally as Lukovë Cave, this horseshoe-shaped bay is fringed with marble-like white rocks that are pocked with sea caves. You can hire kayaks and stand-up paddleboards from beach bars to explore the caves. At one end of the beach, a Cold War bunker has been turned into a restaurant and bar: people jump into the sea from platforms here.

DRINK

No Name Bar

Spread across two floors on the beachfront, this popular bar has a chilled vibe. Woven egg chairs and wooden swings provide fun spots to sip cocktails against an idyllic sea backdrop.

D7 Lukovë Beach May-Oct: 7am-7pm daily 69 531 3856

Taverna Dashi

This taverna is tucked away in an olive grove, far from the madding beach crowds, but you can still see the Ionian between the trees. It serves a menu of Italian-influenced fresh seafood and salads, and the shaded terrace is ideal for a cold beer.

D7 Lukovë-Shpellë 8am-10pm daily 69 440 5233

→ The idyllic, curving bay of Lukovë Beach

21   

Blue Eye

D7 20 km (12 miles) E of Sarandë via the SH99 visitsaranda.net/see/blue-eye

Nestled inland from the southern Albanian coast, Syri i Kaltër, or the Blue Eye, is a natural wonder tucked away in lush forest near the Gjirokastër County border. Its name derives from the deep-blue colour of the water, which fills this natural spring; the source of these waters is the Bistricë River, which flows nearby. It's thought that the spring reaches depths of up to 50 m (160 ft), its ice-cold waters pouring out into the river at an estimated 18,400 litres (4,000 gallons) per second at high water. There are 17 other springs dotted around the area, while another similarly impressive Blue Eye can be found in Northern Albania, near Theth *(p92)*.

Once a hidden gem, today this natural phenomenon is one of Albania's most popular tourist sights and can be visited either by car, on an organized tour or (less frequently) by bus.

The nearest city on the Albanian Riviera is Sarandë; tours to the Blue Eye are available from this city, as well as from Gjirokastër and Tirana. The closest car park is located just off the SH99, the main road between Sarandë and Gjirokastër,

THE MAKINGS OF SARANDË'S BLUE EYE

The waters of the Blue Eye come from a deep, almost vertical cave, making it a Vauclusian, or karst, spring. Water gushes up from the underwater cave beneath the centre with great force, before dispersing across the rest of the spring. Thanks to this, the Blue Eye has a deep, dark centre and a shallow, light-blue outer edge, creating the appearance of a "blue eye". It's not certain how deep the Blue Eye actually is. In 1984, divers managed to reach a depth of 50 m (160 ft) in an attempt to find the bottom, but they were prevented from getting any further due to the pressure at which the water is pushed out.

↓ Blue waters of the Blue Eye and *(inset)* the forested area around the spring

which is why the Blue Eye is a popular stopping-off point when travelling between the two areas.

Whichever way you arrive, it's a 2-km (1-mile) walk from the car park to the Blue Eye, which takes approximately 20 minutes. The route follows a scenic forest trail, passing a hydroelectric dam and reservoir along the way. (There are a number of other hiking trails that can be explored in the area around the spring.)

There's no missing the spring once you arrive: the expanse of gurgling, clear water spreads out before you as you emerge from the forest path.

There are plenty of scenic viewpoints around the Blue Eye, but for one of the best perspectives, head to the wooden viewing platform set up above the spring and gaze down into the waters. The two restaurants next to the Blue Eye are pleasant spots for a cold drink and a view of the picturesque Bistricë River nearby.

As a hugely popular tourist spot, the Blue Eye can get busy in the summer months. To experience the spring in tranquillity, plan to arrive at the start or end of the day – you'll likely have the area (almost) to yourself.

↑ Enjoying one of the restaurants found on the Blue Eye, surrounded by its bright waters

INSIDER TIP
Swimming Spots

Swimming in the Blue Eye is not allowed. Instead, head to the river bank downstream, where you can dip your feet in the cool river.

A DRIVING TOUR

THE NORTHERN RIVIERA

Length 215 km (134 miles) **Stopping-off points** Golem and Gjipe beaches, Vlorë for overnight stays **Terrain** Twisting mountain roads with sharp turns

This long drive leads south from the bustling port city of Durrës to the idyllic hilltop village of Lukovë, showing off the northern Riviera's glitzy beach resorts and its slow-paced coastal village life all in one day. The route passes through some of the coastal road's most scenic sections – the forested mountain pass of Llogara National Park and the many twisting hillside roads that reveal far-reaching views of the Adriatic and Ionian seas at every turn. Stops include white beaches, ancient ruins and a dramatic fortress cast out in the sea.

Begin the drive in **Durrës** *(p126), home to a well-preserved amphitheatre and an ancient castle.*

Golem Beach *(p128) stretches for miles along the coast. There are plenty of places to grab a cold drink with a view of the sea and to dip your toes in the coarse white sand.*

Highlights at the ancient site of **Apollonia** *(p134) include the restored columned façade of a Roman building and an informative archaeological museum housed within a Byzantine church.*

The mountain pass through **Llogara National Park** *is one of the most scenic sections of road in all of Albania. The steep route climbs above the cloud cover, and is enclosed on all sides by fragrant pine forest.*

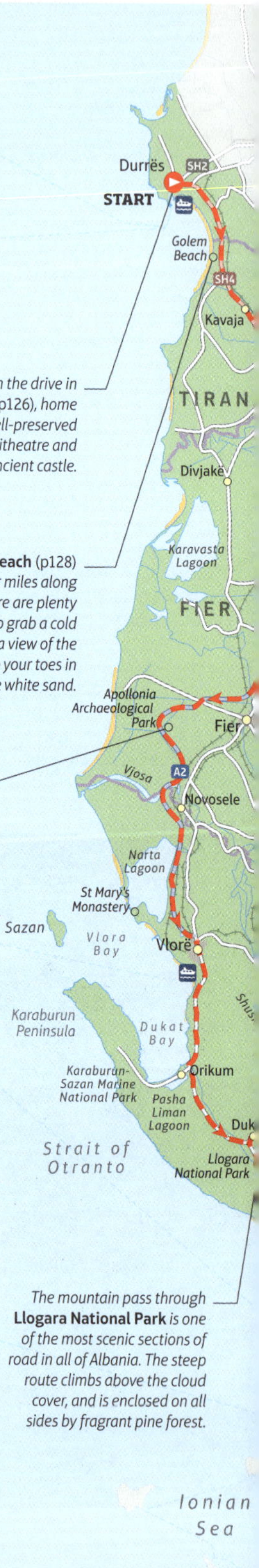

Restored Roman ruins at Apollonia ↑

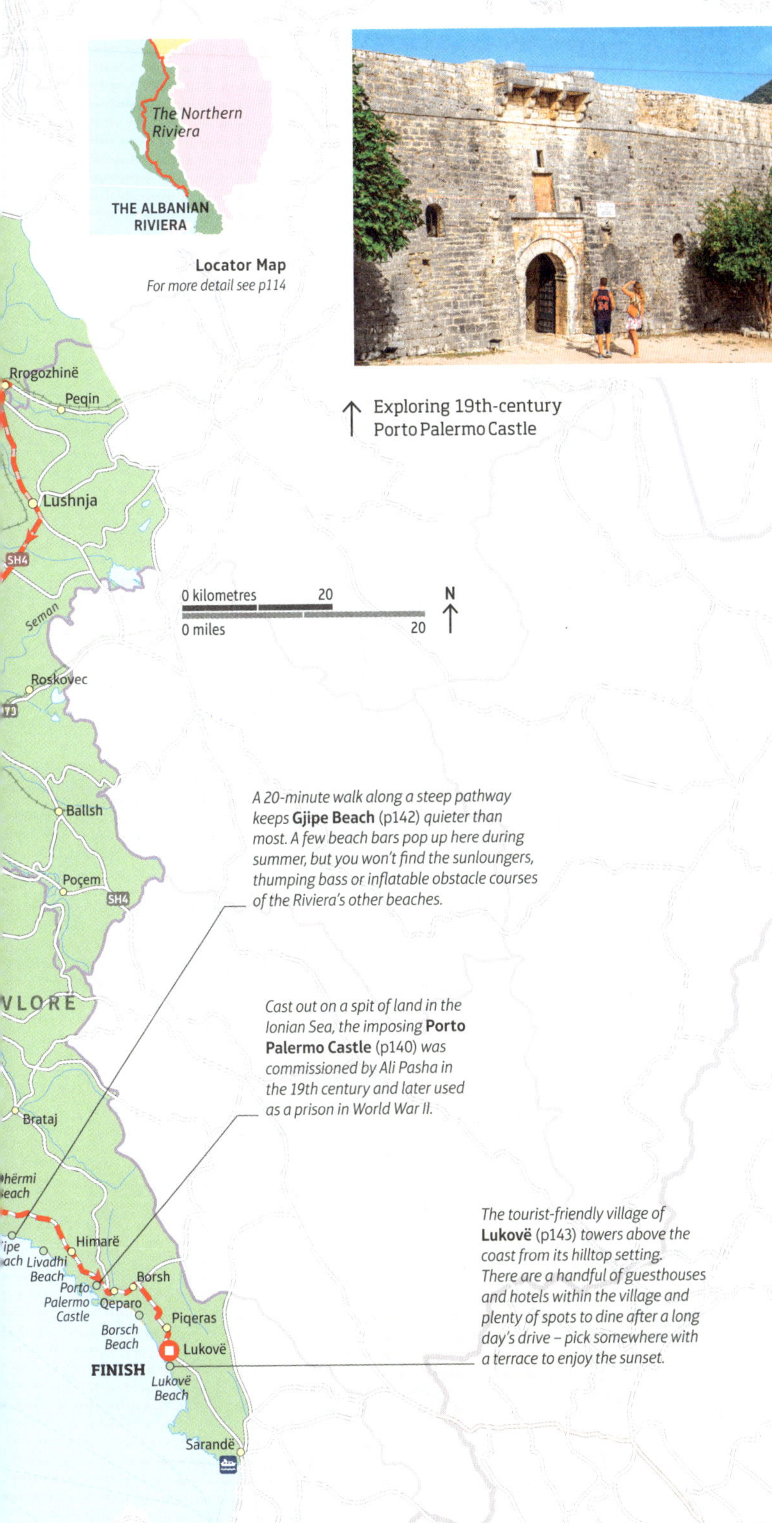

↑ Exploring 19th-century Porto Palermo Castle

*A 20-minute walk along a steep pathway keeps **Gjipe Beach** (p142) quieter than most. A few beach bars pop up here during summer, but you won't find the sunloungers, thumping bass or inflatable obstacle courses of the Riviera's other beaches.*

*Cast out on a spit of land in the Ionian Sea, the imposing **Porto Palermo Castle** (p140) was commissioned by Ali Pasha in the 19th century and later used as a prison in World War II.*

*The tourist-friendly village of **Lukovë** (p143) towers above the coast from its hilltop setting. There are a handful of guesthouses and hotels within the village and plenty of spots to dine after a long day's drive – pick somewhere with a terrace to enjoy the sunset.*

A BOAT TRIP SARANDË TO BUTRINT

Length 7-8 hours **Stopping-off points** The deserted beaches of Kroreza and Kokoma, the castle of Ali Pasha at the entrance to Butrint National Park

Chartering a boat and skipper from the marina in Sarandë, you can follow this route on the Ionian Sea north to the deserted beaches of Krorëza and Kakoma – accessible only by boat or a long hike. Hopping between hidden snorkelling spots and uninhabited islands, it takes in a rugged coastline where mountains plummet to teal waters, ending with the historical intrigue of Ali Pasha's isolated castle in the Vivari Channel in Butrint National Park.

Accessible only by sea or a hike, ***Krorëza Bay*** *still has several pop-up beach bars to enjoy on its white pebble shores.*

A horseshoe of ivory-white sand, ***Kakoma Beach*** *is completely undeveloped. It is another bay that's accessible only by boat or on foot, and without any amenities. A hike leads from here to Manastiri i Shën Merisë, a Byzantine monastery on a forested hill.*

With clear waters and a rocky seabed, the inlet at ***Plazhi i Ushtari*** *is an excellent snorkelling spot. It is locally known as Soldier's Bay for its resemblance to a man's profile when viewed from on high. There's also a small slip of beach, which you can swim to from an anchored boat.*

↑ Ali Pasha Castle, perched at the end of an islet in Butrint National Park

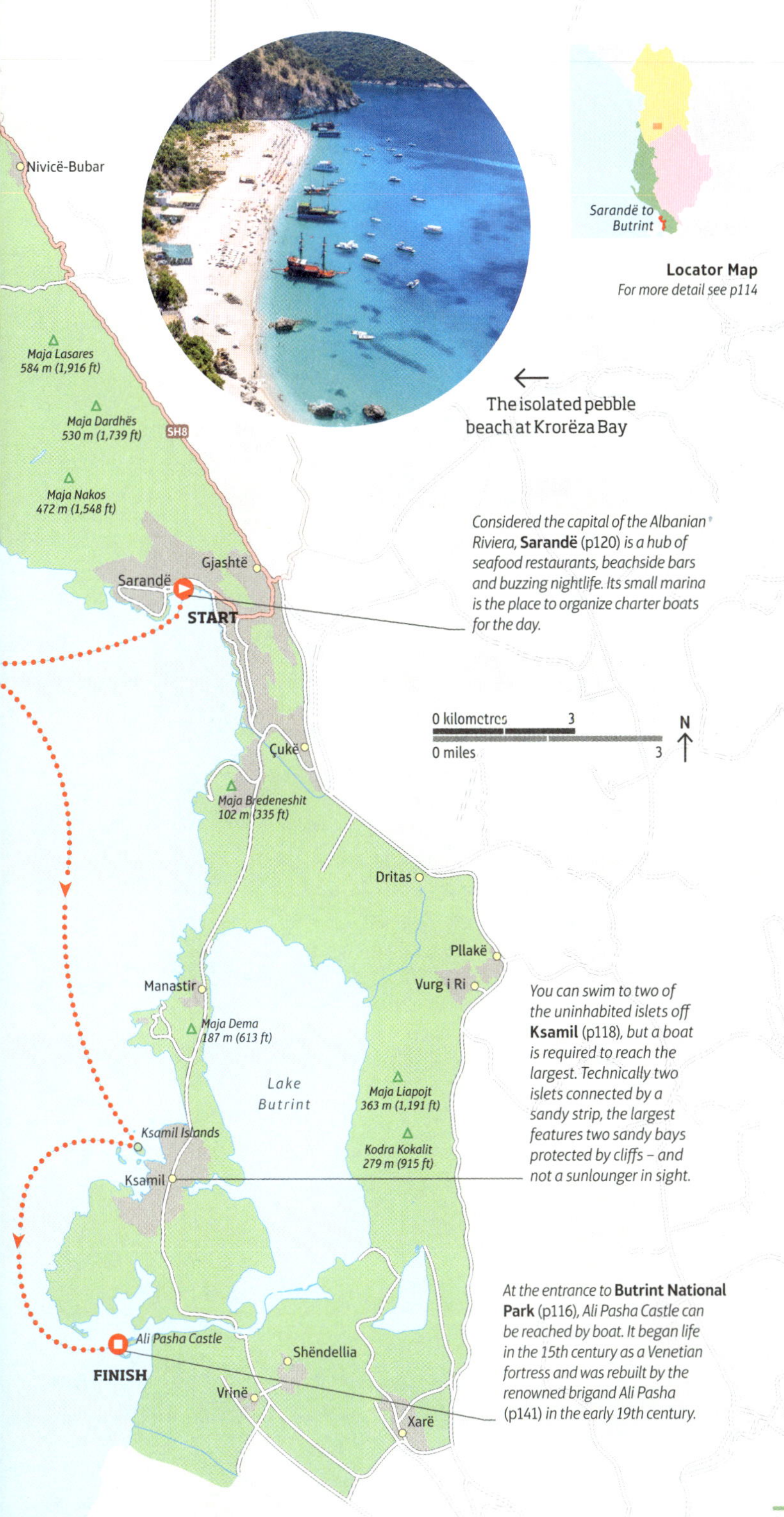

The isolated pebble beach at Krorëza Bay

Considered the capital of the Albanian Riviera, **Sarandë** *(p120) is a hub of seafood restaurants, beachside bars and buzzing nightlife. Its small marina is the place to organize charter boats for the day.*

You can swim to two of the uninhabited islets off **Ksamil** *(p118), but a boat is required to reach the largest. Technically two islets connected by a sandy strip, the largest features two sandy bays protected by cliffs – and not a sunlounger in sight.*

At the entrance to **Butrint National Park** *(p116), Ali Pasha Castle can be reached by boat. It began life in the 15th century as a Venetian fortress and was rebuilt by the renowned brigand Ali Pasha (p141) in the early 19th century.*

The Osumi River passing through the Osumi River Canyon

SOUTHERN ALBANIA

The first visible traces of Southern Albania's history are found in the remains of ancient Greek settlements like Antigonea, where the city's ruler, Pyrrhus of Epirus, stalled the rising power of Rome in a series of exhausting battles in the 3rd century BCE. The region eventually fell to the Romans, who built a section of the Via Egnatia trading route here, through which goods and ideas were carried across Southern Albania.

In the 14th century, Eastern Orthodox priests left behind an impressive collection of icons in Berat and monasteries around Lake Ohrid. From the 15th century, the Ottoman Empire instigated a change in religious practices and oversaw the building of many new structures. During this period, places like Gjirokastër and Korçë were transformed from rocky redoubts into thriving cities. Thanks to the south's dizzying topography, destinations deep in the wild were never truly conquered during this time. Nature spots including Hotovë-Dangëlli, Tomorr Mountain, Shebenik and Jabllanicë remained remote, and have since become national parks.

Southern Albania was also once the birthplace of two key figures of 20th-century Albania: the politician Enver Hoxha, who led the communist government in the second half of the century, and the prolific author Ismail Kadare, who commented on this regime in his novels.

SOUTHERN ALBANIA
Must Sees
1 Gjirokastër
2 Berat
3 Vjosa Wild River National Park
4 Korçë
Experience More
5 Osumi River Canyon
6 Archaeological Park of Antigonea
7 Fir of Hotovë-Dangëlli National Park
8 Çobo Winery
9 Holta Canyon
10 Tomorr Mountain National Park
11 Elbasan
12 Shebenik-Jabllanicë National Park
13 Voskopojë
14 Lake Ohrid
Tirana
TIRANA
NORTHERN ALBANIA
p84
TIRANA
p62
Krrab Mountain
SH3
SH3
A3
ELBASAN
SH7
SH7
Peqin
Shkumbin
SH70
Cërrik
SH88
SH59
Belsh
Devoll
KANIONI I HOLTËS
Rezervuar i Murizit
Gramsh
Devoll
SH72
Kuçovë
Dimal
ÇOBO WINERY
Osumi
Çuka Partizane
2, 416 m (7,926 ft)
BERAT
TOMORR MOUNTAIN NATIONAL PARK
SH72
Tomorr
FIER
BERAT
Poliçan
Ballsh
Selenicë
THE ALBANIAN RIVIERA
p112
Çorovodë
Gllave
OSUMI RIVER CANYON
Trebeshina
VJOSA WILD RIVER NATIONAL PARK
Kotë
Sukë
SH4
Memaliaj
Gribe Mountain
Shushica
Këlcyrë
Tepelenë
Nemerçke
Maja e Këndrevicës
2, 121 m (6,959 ft)
Drino
Brataj
Çikë
GJIROKASTËR
Dhërmi
VLORË
ARCHAEOLOGICAL PARK OF ANTIGONEA
SH83
Himarë
GJIROKASTËR
Borsh
Gjerë
Qeparo
SH4
Adriatic Sea
Piqeras
Lukovë
Ancient Theatre of Hadrianopolis
Delvinë
Ereikoussa
Muzinë
Othonoi
Sarandë
Sarandë Bay
0 kilometres 20
0 miles 20
N
Corfu
Lake Butrint

DIBËR
NORTH MACEDONIA
SHEBENIK-JABLLANICË NATIONAL PARK
12
Dorëz
Librazhd
Shebenik
Hotolisht
Shkumbini
SH3
Black Drin
R1201
Сатеска Река
Mešeišta
A2
Airoporti i Gjakovës
A3
Struga
A2
Ohrid
Resen
Qafë Thanë
LBASAN
Prrenjas
Lake Ohrid
Golik i Poshtëm
SH3
National Park Galichica
LAKE OHRID
14
Holtas
Pogradec
Pllaja e Pusit 2,287 m (7,503 ft)
Shkumbin
Leshnicë
Lake Big Prespa
Valamarë
Bratilë
SH79
Sovjan
Lozhan i Ri
Maliq
Plasë
Moglicë
SH71
SH3
SH3
VOSKOPOJË
13
SH63
4
KORÇË
Bilisht
KORÇË
Boboshticë
Pindus Mountain
Ujëbardhë
SH72
Vithkuo
Miras
Devoll
Ostrovicë
Osumi
SH75
Gramos
7
FIR OF HOTOVË-DANGËLLI NATIONAL PARK
Ersekë
Përmet
Gozhdarazhde
SH75
Vjosa
untain
Leskovik
Maja e Papingut 2,485 m (8,153 ft)
SOUTHERN ALBANIA
Bitola
Pelister 2,601 m (8,533 ft)
Pelister National Park
E015
Lake Small Prespa
E02
Vigla
Florina
Macedonia Mountain
A29
Chloi
Mesopotamia
Maniaki
Haliacmon
Argos Orestiko
Nestorio
Gramos Mountain 2,523 m (8,278 ft)
A29
Neapoli
Aetomilitsa
GREECE
Tsotyli
Eptachori
E020
Pentalofos
Smolikas 2,637 m (8,652 ft)
Grevena
Konitsa
Distrato
Zakas
E020
Vikos Gorge National Park
Kipoureio
Vovousa
kavijë
E022
Kranea
A2
Kalpaki
Koukouli
E06

GJIROKASTËR

D6 Bulevardi 18 Shtator Rruga Alqi Kondi; www.gjirokastra.org

Gjirokastër's name draws from the Greek word *kástron* (castle), a nod to the 12th-century fortifications that still dominate the city. Cobbled streets wind through its Old Town, a UNESCO World Heritage Site containing 15th-century neighbourhoods and 19th-century Ottoman mansions. It's also a centre for traditional iso-polyphony group singing, and was the birthplace of two key figures of modern Albania: the former leader Enver Hoxha and the celebrated writer Ismail Kadare.

①

Gjirokastër Bazaar

Rruga Gjin Bue Shpata
10am-10pm daily

For over four centuries, the market-lined streets below Gjirokastër Castle have together made up the Gjirokastër Bazaar. Originally built during Ottoman rule, the city's first bazaar was destroyed during a fire in the 19th century; it was rebuilt again soon after. The area was once filled with the sounds of traditional metalwork being shaped, looms sliding and coffee grinding. One of the few times the bazaar was quiet was during the post-communist crisis of the 1990s, when many stores were abandoned and historic townhouses changed hands for low sums.

Today, it's a different story, and the bazaar is bustling once again. Locals flock here for the many shops, cafés and restaurants that line the streets. By day, there's an endless hubbub of shoppers; at night, locals make their way to the busy wine bars and rooftop restaurants.

Walking through the bazaar area is one of the best ways to take in its distinctive architecture. Two- and three-storey townhouses, dating back to the 19th century, get wider as they rise upwards. The main streets – including Rruga Gjin Zenebishti, Rruga Zejtarëve and Rruga Ismail Kadare – are steep but cobblestoned, making for a scenic stroll.

The compact district is anchored by the **Bazaar Mosque** (Xhamia e Pazarit). Built in 1757 during Ottoman rule, it's one of the only mosques to survive the communist era's destruction of religious sites in the whole of Albania and remains hugely important to the city. Under communism, a secret military bunker was built underneath the structure.

Bazaar Mosque
Rruga Ismail Kadare
9am-9pm daily

Steep, cobbled streets of Gjirokastër's UNESCO-listed Old Town

Cold War Tunnel

Sheshi Çerçiz Topulli
9am-6pm daily; Tours: every 90 minutes from 10am Sat & Sun

The largest of the 99 bunkers that burrow below Gjirokastër, the Cold War Tunnel was constructed during the government-led nuclear paranoia of the 1970s. According to plans at the time, only 300 Communist Party members and their families would have access to the 59 concrete rooms spread across the 800-m- (2,600-ft-) long tunnel in the event of nuclear war. The project was completed in total secrecy, meaning that most locals only found out about the tunnel's existence once the regime changed in 1991. Today, there are only a few original furnishings left inside the bunker spaces, including telephones and a rusting Czechoslovakian filtration system, among the low vaulted ceilings.

The best way to see the deserted bunkers today is on a guided tour, which begins at the entrance next to the city's Municipality building. On the tour, visitors will first descend into the cold, grey entrance chamber before heading into the tunnels. Inside, displays shed light on plans to continue party rule from the bunkers: the space includes a decontamination room (in the event of nuclear war), a school, a law court and an interrogation cell.

Did You Know?

Most of its furnishings were looted when the Cold War Tunnel was discovered in the 1990s.

TOP 4 DISHES IN GJIROKASTËR

Qifqi
A specialized metal pan with indents is used to sear these egg- and mint-loaded rice balls.

Oshaf
Gjirokastër's panna-cotta-style dessert is made with fresh, crushed figs mixed with sheep's milk and cinnamon.

Petulla
These rounded, deep-fried pancakes are served with jams made with local fruits like plums or figs.

Shapkati
An eat-on-the-go traybake made from local ingredients, like cornflour, milk, spinach and dill.

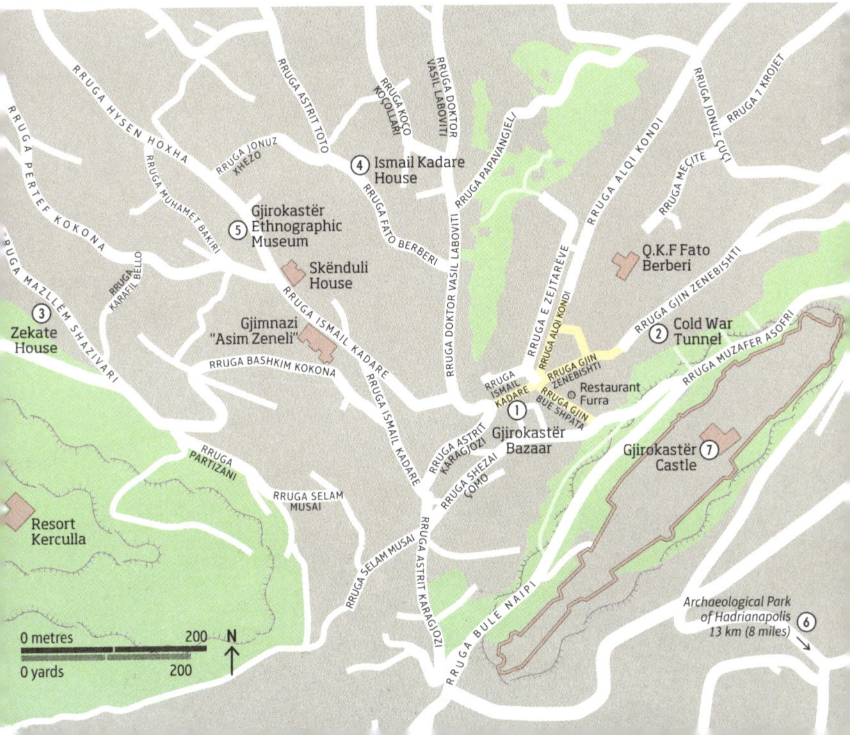

EAT

Restaurant Furra

Opened on the site of a historic bakery with an oven that dates from 1720, this restaurant is run by Gjirokastër-born chef Alban Veliu. Expect delicious local dishes like *qifqi* (rice balls) and the dessert *oshaf*.

Rruga Gjin Bue Shpata, Gjirokastër
furra-rooms.al

Zekate House

Rruga Bashkim Kokona
69 409 8988 11:30am-11:30pm daily

Only the richest Ottoman-era merchants and administrators could afford to build fortified tower houses, known as *kullë*, in Gjirokastër. Castle-like Zekate House is one such *kullë*, built around 1812 by Beqir Zeko, a local administrator in Ali Pasha's government.

Zekate House's interior can be explored on a self-guided visit, starting with a climb up the broad stone staircase to the top floor. Guest galleries on either wing of the house remain largely unchanged since Ottoman times, with original low sofas lining the edges of the rooms.

On the next floor below are family rooms that also doubled as entertainment spaces. Their wooden ceiling roses and ornate fireplaces hint at the former owners' wealth. On the ground floor, explore the kitchen and storage room, with its meat hooks and coffee-grinding stone. An old fire-escape passage leads from here to the floor above.

Today, the family that manages Zekate House has built an Ibiza-style terrace bar in the compound. After exploring the historic home, visitors can enjoy a refreshing drink while lounging on a swing chair under an arbour of vines. Zekate House only closes its doors when the adjoining bar pours its last drink, making it possible to enjoy exploring one of Gjirokastër's grandest houses well into the evening.

Ismail Kadare House

Rruga Fato Berberi 16
69 698 7970 9am-6pm daily

Ismail Kadare *(p159)* was one of Albania's most internationally celebrated writers who worked in the 20th and 21st centuries. His former family home is preserved as Ismail Kadare House, a historic jewel in Gjirokastër. The author described growing up in this townhouse in his 1971 novel, *Chronicle in Stone*.

Originally built at the end of the 18th century, the house was later renovated after a fire in the 1990s caused damage to the building; it eventually reopened to the public in 2018. Historic features include the water cistern, typical of many Gjirokastër homes of this era, where rainwater from the mansion's slate roof collects.

Inside, a modernized white interior awaits, where signage leads visitors to the top floor. The *oda*, or grand living room, here would have once welcomed neighbourhood guests and is where, writes Kadare, "women would sit when they came to visit, sipping their coffee and making sage pronouncements". On the middle floor, televised projections bring Kadare's texts to life alongside decorative quotes from the writer's works. Found all over the walls, these quotes shed further light on day-to-day life in mid-20th-century Gjirokastër.

Exploring the ruins of the Archaeological Park of Hadrianopolis near Gjirokastër

5 

Gjirokastër Ethnographic Museum

Rruga Hysen Hoxha
9am-6pm daily
gjirokastër.org

The city's cultural history is brought to life inside the Gjirokastër Ethnographic Museum. Located inside a stone mansion, the museum is home to displays of folk textiles, kitchenware and metalwork, shown across three floors. Throughout the museum space, displays shed light on local traditions – like celebratory raki dancing – Gjirokastër food specialities, and the architectural styles of the region.

The museum building itself is also of historical significance: it was built on the site of former communist leader Enver Hoxha's childhood home.

6 

Archaeological Park of Hadrianopolis

Sofratikë

A walk around the open-air Archaeological Park (Parku Arkeologjik) of Hadrianopolis, located around a 20-minute drive from Gjirokastër, is like stepping back in time. Although the original settlement was Greek, the Roman Emperor Hadrian refounded the city and named it after himself.

Explore the few excavated zones of the park, including the ruins of a bath complex. The highlight is the Roman theatre, which was uncovered by local farmers in the 1980s following a landslide; its hundreds of benches are built into the curving hill.

A room in the Gjirokastër Ethnographic Museum and *(inset)* the façade of the museum

ALBANIAN LITERATURE

Albanian literature grew from oral storytelling traditions. Folktales were captured and spread across the region through song, often in styles like iso-polyphony chanting *(p36)*. Fast-forward to the modern day, and many authors have continued these past traditions while also creating new styles. From poetry addressing Ottoman rule to novels reflecting on the communist regime, Albanian texts are nothing short of ground-breaking.

REVOLUTIONARY TEXTS

After Ottoman rule was established in the 14th century, the official use of the Albanian language was reduced and eventually banned until 1909. Literature in the Albanian language became scarce, until a cultural revolution known as the Albanian National Awakening (Rilindja Kombëtare) against Ottoman rule began to take hold at the end of the 19th century.

One pioneer of this movement was Naim Frashëri (1846–1900), a historian and writer whose poems invoked legends like resistance warrior Gjergj Kastrioti, better known as Skanderbeg *(p73)*. During the late 19th century, Frashëri also wrote textbooks for the first ever Albanian language school in Korçë, which is now a museum *(p171)*.

Other writers of the period produced the literary building blocks of this cultural renaissance. In the mid-19th century,

NAIM FRASHËRI

The Albanian writer, historian and translator Naim Frashëri (1846–1900) was a key figure in Albanian literary history. Through his education and translation work, he sought to awaken Albania's literary consciousness and support a cultural revolution in the region as part of the Albanian National Awakening. In addition to this, Frashëri was a prolific poet of international renown; he was regarded as the national poet of Albania.

Korçe's Teatri Andon Zako Çajupi, named after the playwright and lawyer

A selection of Albanian books for sale at a kiosk, including a Kadare title

Pashko Vasa (1825-92) used his experience while working at the British Consulate in Shkodër to author Albania's first national phrase book, allowing non-native speakers to understand Albanian prose. Playwright and lawyer Andon Zako Çajupi (1866-1930), meanwhile, advocated for the Albanian alphabet to be in Latin script, rather than Arabic or Greek.

WRITING IN THE COMMUNIST ERA

The communist regime of the late 20th century led to folk traditions being revisited in Albanian literature. The writer Mitrush Kuteli (1907-67), who grew up near the tranquil shores of Lake Ohrid *(p180)*, wrote a collection of stories published as *Albanian Nights* in 1938, which brought life to local tales from the city of Pogradec *(p180)*.

Writers also reflected on the communist regime in their works. The journalist Musine Kokalari (1917-83) was one of the first female writers to be published in Albania. She fell foul of communist authorities and spent 18 years in prison, followed by a 19-year internment in the quiet northern town of Rrëshen.

A literary giant who skirted the censors was Gjirokastër-born Ismail Kadare (1936-2024). He used literary devices to explore themes of totalitarianism and oppression in his works. His acclaimed novel *The Palace of Dreams* (1981) is set in the dictatorial Ottoman Empire, which readers could understand as a metaphor for the 20th-century communist rule. He was nominated for the Nobel Prize in Literature 15 times before his death in 2024.

CONTEMPORARY WRITERS

After the fall of the communist government in the 1990s, the works of many Albanian writers gained a bigger international reach. Both the works of Ag Apolloni (b 1982), who published the novel *The Howl of the Wolf* (2013), and the award-winning poet Luljeta Lleshanaku (b 1968), have been translated into a number of languages. The writer and academic Lea Ypi (b 1979) wrote the memoir *Free: Coming of Age at the End of History* (2021), which chronicles the writer's experience growing up and living in Albania before, during and following the communist government's rule.

The journalist Musine Kokalari, who criticized communist rule

7

GJIROKASTËR CASTLE

Rruga Elvia Celebi Apr-Sep: 9am-7pm daily; Oct-Mar: 9am-5pm daily

Located on a towering precipice, Gjirokastër Castle (Kalaja e Gjirokastrës) is the city's most popular sight. It's one of the oldest castles in the Balkans, offering insight into the region's far-reaching past as well as stunning views from its hilltop location.

Gjirokastër Castle has overlooked the Drinos Valley since the 12th century. The settlement inside the fortress walls was added by Ottomans in the 15th century and, in the early 19th century, the castle was fortified further by the regional ruler Ali Pasha *(p141)*.

Accessed via steep steps up from Gjirokastër Bazaar *(p154)*, Gjirokastër Castle holds displays of historic weapons, folk dress and instruments. While exploring its grounds, visitors can also enjoy sweeping panoramic views of the old city below.

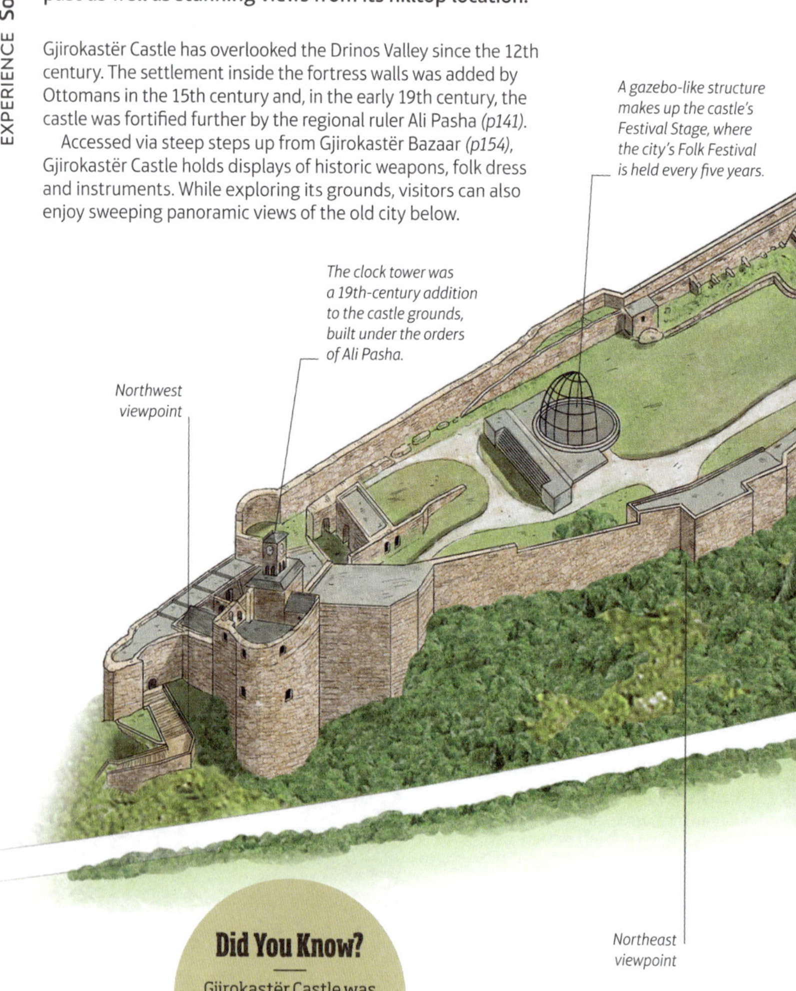

Did You Know?

Gjirokastër Castle was temporarily used as a prison during communist rule.

The Bektashi Tomb is where the remains of two religious figures of the Islamic Bektashi Order were laid to rest.

The castle is home to an American aeroplane. After being abandoned in 1957, the plane was moved to the castle grounds in 1970.

←

Illustration showing the grounds of Gjirokastër Castle

1 The extensive grounds of Gjirokastër Castle loom over the city.

2 A clock tower was added to Gjirokastër Castle in the 19th century.

3 Tunnels and stone corridors can be found inside Gjirokastër Castle.

2

BERAT

D5 Rruga Antipatrea Teodor Muzaka; www.berat.al

Romans, Byzantines, Bulgarians and Ottomans all took turns to build Berat into a city worthy of UNESCO World Heritage status. The latter empire, which took control in 1417, left the most visible legacy. Metalwork, leatherwork and other artisanal industries paid for the pretty white houses that line the streets towards the banks of the Osumi River, which give this "City of a Thousand Windows" its historic charm.

Berat Castle

Sheshi Sallabanda
9am-6pm daily
berat.al

The area around Berat Castle (Kalaja e Beratit) is made up of many sites within a large, historic citadel district. Found above Berat's city centre, it has been fortified in some capacity for centuries, and was fought over by Romans, Goths and early Byzantines. The current Berat Castle took its present shape during the 14th century, when it hosted homes, artisan workshops and a dozen or more churches. However, when the Ottoman Empire invaded Berat in the same century, the castle was partially destroyed.

Today, all that's left of the original castle structure itself are the crumbling stone walls lining the cliff edge. Just as there was when it was built, a busy neighbourhood remains within the castle grounds, although many of the buildings have changed since then. Here, there are numerous stalls selling handmade crafts, food spots nestled into hidden courtyards and countless bars serving up delicious drinks.

There are many other historic sights within the castle grounds, including the striking remains of the **Red Mosque**. One of the oldest mosques in Albania, this red-brick religious site was constructed during the early 15th century to create a prayer space for Ottoman soldiers in the area. Its original timber roof has long since disappeared, and today only the picturesque ruins of the minaret remain. Walk up the stone steps of the minaret to take in wonderful views over the Osumi River and mountains beyond.

Tucked into the hillside within the historic Berat Castle district is the **Holy Trinity Church**, a masterpiece of Byzantine architecture; its distinctive cross-shaped structure and looming octagonal dome are both hard to miss. The church was originally constructed in the early 14th century and decorated with typical Byzantine frescoes depicting biblical scenes. Although a

Historic houses beside the Osumi River in Berat

guardian has been appointed to show visitors around the building, they're not always available; it's always possible to take in the building's exterior, though, as well as the stunning views across the Osumi floodplain.

Another key sight within the castle grounds is the **Onufri Iconography Museum** (Muzeu Kombëtar Ikonografik Onufri), located inside the Byzantine Church of the Dormition of St Mary. This unique museum houses one of the greatest collections of Albanian religious paintings in the region. The museum was named after a 16th-century Orthodox priest-turned-painter known as Onufri, who had first trained in Venice before returning to Southern Albania to create his celebrated icons and murals. His works are the highlight of this collection, which comprises over 200 icons and religious artifacts.

Take in the sight of the many Byzantine icons, stunning golden pulpits and an intricate iconostasis (altar screen) that fills an entire wall of the old church. Some of Onufri's most famous icons are also on display here, including the icon known as *Johan the Baptist*, which was taken from its original place inside a Berat church; this work is a key example of the artist's legendary hand and bold, contrasting colours. Another striking work by Onufri on display here is known as *Jesus Appearance in Temple*, featuring Onufri's distinctive use of bold red tones in his icons.

Red Mosque
Rrugica Mbrica
Minaret: 9am–6pm daily

Holy Trinity Church
Kalaja 10am–4pm daily

Onufri Iconography Museum
9am–6pm daily
muzeumet-berat.al/en/onufri-iconographic-museum

Did You Know?

As well as producing icons, the 16th-century priest and artist Onufri founded a painting school in Berat.

GREAT VIEW
A Castle Tower

Just a five-minute walk from the Holy Trinity Church, the observation deck built on top of a former Berat Castle tower offers the best views of Berat below.

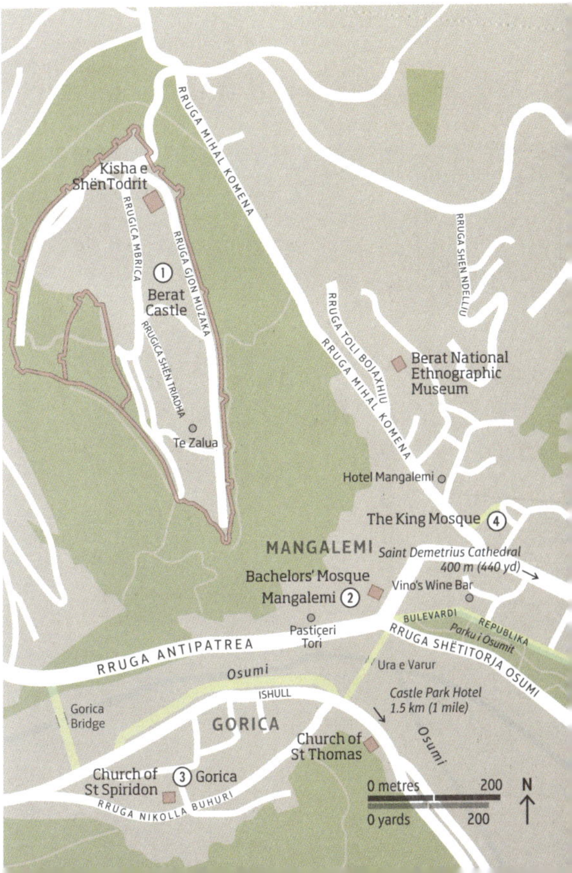

Rruga Mihal Komena
Kisha e Shën Todrit
Rrugica Mbrica
Rruga Gjon Muzaka
① Berat Castle
Rrugica Shën Triadha
Te Zalua
Rruga Shen Ndelliu
Rruga Toli Bojaxhiu
Rruga Mihal Komena
Berat National Ethnographic Museum
Hotel Mangalemi
The King Mosque ④
MANGALEMI
Saint Demetrius Cathedral 400 m (440 yd)
Bachelors' Mosque
Mangalemi ②
Vino's Wine Bar
Pastiçeri Tori
Rruga Antipatrea
Bulevardi Republika
Parku i Osumit
Rruga Shëtitorja Osumi
Ura e Varur
Osumi
Ishull
Gorica Bridge
GORICA
Castle Park Hotel 1.5 km (1 mile)
Osumi
Church of St Thomas
Church of St Spiridon
③ Gorica
Rruga Nikolla Buhuri
0 metres 200
0 yards 200
N

Mangalemi

Mangalemi is one of Berat's historic quarters, located near the Osumi River. Mangalemi was originally part of Berat's Islamic old town; at the time, Christians historically lived across the river in the Gorica area. Although it was built during the 15th century, the old neighbourhood owes its current charm to Ahmet Kurt Pasha, Berat's productive 18th-century ruler. As well as overseeing the building of many sights found within this neighbourhood, the pasha renovated the King Mosque, built the nearby Gorica Bridge and constructed a harem in the piazza, where today summer concerts take place. The stunning Hotel Mangalemi was later built over his former home.

A stroll through here is the best way to see this compact, but bustling, quarter. Head from the castle hill's historic houses to the tree-lined boulevard of Rruga Antipatrea to enjoy one of the many cafés here serving raki and black coffee. Over on the Bulevardi Republika, located next to a busy riverside park, are plenty of restaurants with outdoor terraces. Throughout the quarter, former artisans' shops are now home to popular bars, busy galleries and art studios.

Just beyond the Mangalemi area lie a number of other historic sights. Highlights include **St Demetrius Cathedral** (Katedralja e Shën Dhimitrit), with its immersive interior filled with a lot of gold, incense and candlelight, and the **Bachelors' Mosque** (Xhamia e Beqarëve), which was first built for the unmarried tradesmen of Berat.

St Demetrius Cathedral
Rruga Rilindja
7am-6pm daily

Bachelors' Mosque
Rruga Antipatrea
During prayer times

Inside the prayer hall of Berat's 15th-century King Mosque ↑

Gorica

The other of Berat's two historic quarters, the pretty Gorica neighbourhood sprang up on the southern bank of the Osumi River, opposite Mangalemi. The two quarters were connected by the picturesque 18th-century Gorica Bridge, which was later replaced in the 20th century.

Gorica is a cobblestoned maze of churches and stone houses. Many of the area's grander homes were built closer to the river bank, while

PICTURE PERFECT
Gorica Bridge

After the original bridge over the Osumi River washed away in a flood, the Gorica Bridge was rebuilt in the 1930s. Take a snap of it from either the Mangalemi or Gorica banks.

A cobblestoned street in Berat's historic Gorica neighbourhood

more modest apartments were built higher uphill. Today, a few of these historic mansions stand derelict, while others have been maintained and converted into traditional guesthouses or art studios.

Two notable 14th-century Orthodox churches can be found in Gorica: the small **Church of St Thomas** (Kisha e Shën Thomait), accessed via a rosemary-lined path, and the **Church of St Spyridon** (Kisha e Shën Spiridhonit), a five-minute walk away from the first. The latter is the grander of the two, complete with a gilded interior home to many impressive icons and decorated with a striking fresco.

The ruins of the 4th-century CE Gorica Castle are also found in this neighbourhood. The ruins can be accessed via a short network of trails, which lead uphill to the site from the Gorica Bridge.

Church of St Thomas
Rruga Kristaq Tutulani
8-10am & 5-7pm daily

Church of St Spyridon
Rruga Nikolla Buhuri
8-10am & 5-6pm daily

④

The King Mosque

Rruga Kurt Pasha
8am-noon & 3-8pm daily

One of Berat's main mosques, the King Mosque (Xhamia Mbret) is an impressive 15th-century structure. The building was renovated by Ahmet Kurt Pasha during his rule in the 18th century, when its conspicuously colourful interiors had further additions made to them.

Despite its status as a Cultural Monument, the mosque suffered damage during Albania's cultural revolution in the 1960s, when its stone minaret was toppled. Both the historic minaret and the rest of the site have since been restored.

Today, highlights include the red-ceilinged prayer hall, decorated with Quranic inscriptions and an intricate calligraphic frieze. Elsewhere, there are a number of whitewashed porticoes and many intricate domed ceilings. The mosque complex also contains two historic *tekkes* (Islamic lodges) and a well.

DRINK

Vino's Wine Bar
A welcoming wine bar is the place to go to enjoy an excellent Albanian wine list.
Rruga Antipatrea
67 527 0952

Te Zalua
This bar, located above the Mangalemi quarter, serves delicious Albanian small plates alongside Korça beer.
Rruga Gjon Muzaka

Pastiçeri Tori
Queue up at this coffee and pastry shop to try *tortë tabosh*, a local cake laced with walnuts and lemon zest.
Rruga Antipatrea
68 232 1073

STAY

Hotel Mangalemi
Built over the mansion of the former Berat ruler Ahmet Kurt Pasha, this hotel is decorated with stunning stone floors and gorgeous room furnishings.
Rruga Mihal Komneno
mangalemihotel.com
ⓁⓁⓁ

Castle Park Hotel
This historic hotel has charming and spacious rooms, as well as a gourmet, slow-food restaurant. Rafting, eBiking and kayaking tours are on offer here.
Rruga Berat-Përmet
castle-park.com
ⓁⓁⓁ

3

VJOSA WILD RIVER NATIONAL PARK

A D6 W vjosanationalpark.al

One of Europe's only wild rivers, the Vjosa is at the heart of the Vjosa Wild River National Park (Parku Kombëtar i Lumit të Egër Vjosa), established in 2023. Its pristine nature makes it an ideal home for many bird and animal species – including flamingos and European otters – and draws those seeking a dose of unadulterated nature.

The mighty waters of the Vjosa River careen through most of Southern Albania. Its source, though, is found in the Pindus Mountains of Greece. The river courses through Albania for 190 km (120 miles), past towns and cities, before pouring out into the Adriatic Sea.

Wild and protected, the Vjosa River and its surrouding areas are where over 1,000 species thrive. Among them are around 250 bird species, including Egyptian vultures and stone curlews, making it a twitcher's paradise. At the mouth of the Vjosa, the river becomes part of a wetland delta near the Narta Lagoon, an area rich in birds such as kingfishers and flamingos. Aside from bird-watching, visitors head to the Vjosa for rafting, kayaking and hiking in the summer months.

INSIDER TIP
Water Sports on the Vjosa River

The best way to enjoy a water-based adventure on the Vjosa is on an organized tour. Try rafting, canyoning and hiking with the likes of Exploring Përmet *(www.exploringpermet.com)*.

EAT

Lord Byron

This restaurant serves dishes made with over 30 years of organic know-how. Expect sharing plates of grilled meats and local cheeses.

Rruga Tepelenë KM1
W lordbyron.al

Restaurant Gryka e Kelcyres

This hotel restaurant on the banks of the Vjosa serves traditional Albanian cuisine.

Kelcyre-Permet
W gryka-e-kelcyres-hotel.al

ⓛⓛⓛ

1 The Vjosa River flows through a number of towns in Southern Albania, including Përmet.

2 Bright flamingos flock into the waters of the Narta Lagoon, a wetland reserve that is also part of the Vjosa Wild River National Park.

3 The waters of the Vjosa River are so pristine that they take on a stunning blue-green hue along some parts of the waterway.

↑ A group rafting in the Vjosa Wild River National Park

WILDLIFE IN ALBANIA

Albania is a small country with a huge range of landscapes, within which plenty of local wildlife thrives. With so much variety, there is a wealth of biodiversity to uncover: expect everything from small endemic insects to rare forest mammals in the protected national parks and nature reserves found across mountains, wild rivers and open waters.

↑ Spotting marine life in the waters off Albania's coast

UNDER THE SEAS

Common dolphins dart through the waters all along Albania's coast, but cetaceans and three different species of turtles are especially drawn to the nutrient-rich area where the Adriatic and Ionian seas meet close to Vlorë *(p130)*.

Larger species inhabit the waters of the Karaburun-Sazan National Marine Park, home to some of the greatest aquatic biodiversity in the area. Sperm whales and the endangered Mediterranean monk seal have both been spotted here; camera traps on the Karaburun Peninsula have documented a promising recovery in numbers of the latter.

BROWN BEARS

There are thought to be around 200 brown bears roaming throughout the forests of Albania. While attacks on humans are extremely rare, sightings of the bears are not. In many of Albania's 15 national parks - including Shebenik-Jabllanicë *(p178)* - it's easy to notice indications of the presence of bears, from scratch markings on trees to huge paw prints on the ground. The diet of brown bears includes forest fruits, roots and berries, which are plentiful here.

←

Flamingos and Dalmatian pelicans roaming the wetlands of Albania's Adriatic shores

LAND OF BIRDS

The eagle is the national symbol of Albania. Short-toed eagles keep to open plains and forests, while white-tailed eagles populate areas near the sea. To see a golden eagle, though, is a rarity, as these birds nest on cliffs in the highest peaks. It's thought that as few as 50 to 100 breeding pairs remain in these parts.

As well as eagles, there are over 300 other avian species that thrive across Albania. Around ten of these - including Dalmatian pelicans and Egyptian vultures - are globally threatened. The wetlands of the Narta Lagoon *(p166)* are home to many birds, including flamingos, zitting cisticolas and Dalmatian pelicans. Over in the Albanian Alps near Theth *(p92)*, species including goshawks, pallid harriers and merlins regularly glide over the foothills.

RARE WILDCATS

One of Europe's largest predators, the critically endangered Balkan lynx can be found in Albania. Between Albania and North Macedonia, the number of Balkan lynx may be down to as few as 50 cats. A cross-border Balkan Lynx Recovery Programme is raising awareness around the protection of this long-eared wildcat on both sides of the border.

1

2

3

1 The Balkan lynx is a rare and critically endangered species.

2 Brown bears roam through the forests of Albania.

3 Spotting a golden eagle in this region is a rare delight.

4

KORÇË

F5 Qemal Stafa Stadium, Qytet Studenti discoverkorca.al

Unlike its Roman and Byzantine neighbours, Korçë was founded under Ottoman governance in the 15th century. Named after the word its hilly terrain, the city is located at an altitude of 850 m (2,790 ft), with Albania's main organized ski slope just 15 km (9 miles) away. It's home to incomparable religious icons, several national museums and the first Albanian language school, but its biggest draw today is the vibrant and friendly atmosphere of the city.

Old Bazaar

Five centuries ago, Korçë's Old Bazaar (Pazari i Korçës) teemed with traders shopping and trading from hundreds of market stalls. Since then, it has been destroyed and rebuilt several times, always in its original form. What can be seen today is the result of these renovations.

The indoor section of the Old Bazaar is still a place to pick up produce like mountain honey and herbs, as well as antiques. Come evening, it transforms into Korçë's nightlife hub, with cafés and bars at every turn.

National Museum of Medieval Art

Bulevardi Fan Noli 59 9am-7pm daily muzeumesjetar.gov.al

Korçë's National Museum of Medieval Art (Muzeu Kombëtar i Artit Mesjetar) holds one of the world's best assemblages of icons. These religious portraits, usually associated with Orthodox and Catholic faiths, were created during the last centuries of the Byzantine Empire and the Renaissance period.

The double-floored first room, painted entirely in gold, showcases a display of hundreds of rare icons. Look out for celebrated icons painted by Onufri, Berat's priest-turned-artist *(p163)*. The museum's other medieval exhibits include silver Bible covers and stone carvings.

Resurrection of Christ Cathedral of Korçë

Bulevardi Republika 7am-7pm daily 82 24 28 76

Under communism, the city's only Orthodox cathedral was

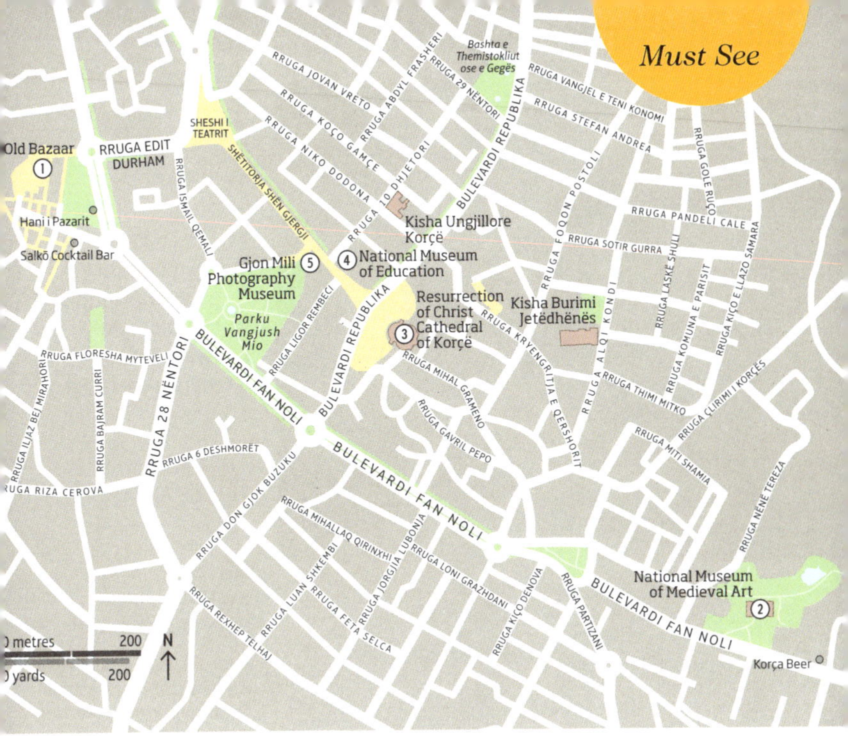

Old Bazaar ①
Hani i Pazarit
Salkō Cocktail Bar
Rruga Edit Durham
Sheshi i Teatrit
Gjon Mili ⑤ Photography Museum
Parku Vangjush Mio
④ National Museum of Education
Kisha Ungjillore Korçë
Resurrection of Christ ③ Cathedral of Korçë
Kisha Burimi Jetëdhënës
Bashta e Themistokliut ose e Gegës
National Museum of Medieval Art ②
Korça Beer
Bulevardi Fan Noli
Bulevardi Republika
Rruga 28 Nëntori
Rruga 29 Nëntori
Rruga Jovan Vreto
Rruga Koço Gamçe
Rruga Niko Dodona
Rruga Abdyl Frashëri
Rruga 10 Dhjetori
Rruga Vangjel e Teni Konomi
Rruga Stefan Andrea
Rruga Gole Ruço
Rruga Pandeli Cale
Rruga Sotir Gurra
Rruga Foqon Postoli
Rruga Ismail Qemali
Shëtitorja Shën Gjergji
Rruga Ligor Rembeci
Rruga Kryengritja e Qershorit
Rruga Mihal Grameno
Rruga Gavril Pepo
Rruga Floresha Myteveli
Rruga Iljaz Bej Mirahori
Rruga Bajram Curri
Rruga Riza Cerova
Rruga 6 Deshmorët
Rruga Don Gjok Buzuku
Rruga Mihallaq Qirinxhi
Rruga Jorgjia Lubonja
Rruga Loni Grazhdani
Rruga Luan Shkembi
Rruga Feta Selca
Rruga Rexhep Telhaj
Rruga Kiço Denova
Rruga Partizani
Rruga Alqi Kondi
Rruga Thimi Mitko
Rruga Miti Shamia
Rruga Çlirimi i Korçës
Rruga Nënë Tereza
Rruga Laskë Shuli
Rruga Komuna e Parisit
Rruga Kiço e Llazo Samara
0 metres 200
0 yards 200
N

destroyed in the 1950s. By 1992, the Resurrection of Christ Cathedral of Korçë (Katedralja Ortodokse Ringjallja e Krishtit) was built in its place. The present cathedral is a grand example of Byzantine Revival architecture, with its soaring domes, gilded interiors and glittering iconography.

National Museum of Education

Bulevardi Shën Gjergji
9am-7pm daily

The National Museum of Education (Muzeu Kombëtar i Arsimit) is of great importance, as in 1887 it was the site of the first school to conduct lessons in Albanian. Teaching had to be carried out in secrecy: writing and teaching in the Albanian language was banned under the Ottoman Empire until 1909. Head up the stairs to see the classroom filled with school bench seats where, for the first time in Albanian history, boys and girls shared a classroom.

Snow-covered buildings in the mountainous city of Korçë

Gjon Mili Photography Museum

Rruga Konferenca e Pezës
9am-2pm Tue-Sat

Gjon Mili (1904–94) was a Korçë-born photographer who emigrated to America, where he worked for *Life* magazine for over 40 years as a photographer. This museum showcases his finest photos of famous figures, including Pablo Picasso and Enver Hoxha. Displays explain Mili's use of strobe lights and electronic flashes to capture fast-moving scenes from a distance, techniques he picked up as a technical photographer in the American military.

DRINK

Hani i Pazarit

A historic inn serving Albanian wine, where traditional local music can also be enjoyed.

Rruga Kiço Greço, Korçë **hanipazarit.com**

Korça Beer

Part of one of Korçë's best breweries, this spot pours pints at source until midnight.

Bulevardi Fan Noli, Korçë **birrakorca.com.al/en/restaurant**

Sa!kō Cocktail Bar

This bar is the place to go for raki cocktails.

Rrugica Jovan Spiro Kosturi 8, Korçë **68 9076 400**

Exploring one of the leafy sections of Osumi River Canyon

The 26-km- (16-mile-) long gorge was formed approximately two to three million years ago.

EXPERIENCE MORE

Osumi River Canyon

E6 Near Çorovodë From early spring to late summer for rafting

With steep cliffs and fragrant vegetation, the Osumi River Canyon (Kanionet e Osumit) is a scenic nature spot full of breathtaking viewpoints from top to bottom. The 26-km- (16-mile-) long gorge was formed approximately two to three million years ago, as the result of land erosion from searing currents of meltwater.

Today, the Osumi River Canyon has become one of the most important canyons of Southern Albania. Water fills the gorge every spring, transforming it into a popular whitewater-rafting spot. To take in some of the best views from within the canyon, join an organized rafting tour.

Tours starting from nearby Berat *(p162)* can be booked via one of the city's many adventure agencies, like Berat City Tours *(www.beratcitytours.com)*. It's also possible to arrange trips that start closer to the canyon through agencies like Albania Adventure Resort *(www.aar.al)* in Çorovodë, which offers challenging canyoning experiences, too. Rafting trips typically include transport from a hotel in Berat, as well as the provision of safety equipment, wetsuits and a picnic lunch.

The Osumi River Canyon is also a popular spot for hiking and wild swimming. From later summer, the river creates a series of natural swimming pools, making it possible to walk or wade in the cold waters most of the way along the gorge.

Nearby, in the small town of Bogovë, is the especially stunning Bogovë Waterfall (Ujëvara e Bogovës). Many tours to Osumi River Canyon make a detour to this lovely waterfall, which can be seen following a short hike from the town of Bogovë.

Did You Know?

The width of Osumi River Canyon varies between 1.5 m (5 ft) and 35 m (115 ft).

Archaeological Park of Antigonea

E6-7 Rruga Kryepiskopi Anastas Summer: 9am-6pm daily; Winter: hours vary, check ahead

A circuit road leads from the city of Gjirokastër *(p154)* all the way to the remotely located Archaeological Park of Antigonea. Just 17 km (10 miles) from the Greek border, this park is the site of the ancient Greek city of the same name. Antigonea was originally founded by Pyrrhus of Epirus in the 3rd century BCE, whose

forces fought valiantly against the unstoppable rise of the Roman Empire.

After significant fighting over the city, Roman troops eventually had Antigonea burnt to the ground, an event from which the ancient city never fully recovered. It remained lost to antiquity from then on, and was only uncovered in the 1960s, when archaeological excavations revealed the settlement's footprint. Antigonea is a significantly older archaeological site than others in the region which also explains the greater deterioration of the ancient site.

Today, visitors can make their way through the archaeological park to see ancient remains of the city, following routes indicated by the signs from the park's entrance booth.

Some of Antigonea's highlights include the foundations of a leather workshop found in the plateau – shaded by looming oak trees nearby – and the stone ruins of the once-thriving ancient agora of the city. Other discoveries made on the site include historic kitchen implements, bronze dishes and numerous storage containers. There are also remains of what is thought to be a 5th- or 6th-century Christian church, indicating that the site may not have been entirely abandoned after its Roman assault. Among it all, there are also impressive viewpoints to enjoy.

The whole recommended circuit would take a few hours to complete, although it's possible to tackle sections of it instead. The first raised part of the trail is very steep but rewarding, as it leads to a stunning panoramic view of the surrounding landscape. There's little by way of amenities throughout the park, so it's recommended that visitors arrive with enough provisions for their time here.

A PYRRHIC VICTORY

Pyrrhus of Epirus (d 272 BCE) was a tireless opponent of Rome, as demonstrated by his efforts in Antigonea. The regional Greek ruler crossed the Adriatic Sea to defeat the Romans at Heraclea and Asculum. Although both sides' losses were similar, Pyrrhus lost veteran troops which could not easily be replaced. As a result, the phrase "Pyrrhic victory" has been used to describe victories that come at an unmanageable cost.

↑ Ruins at the Archaeological Park of Antigonea

Kadiut Bridge in the Fir of Hotovë-Dangëlli National Park

Fir of Hotovë-Dangëlli National Park

E6 Frashër

The largest of Albania's national parks, the Fir of Hotovë-Dangëlli National Park (Parku Kombëtar Bredhi i Hotovës-Dangëlli) is one of the region's greenest landscapes. It takes its name from its dense spread of fir trees, which grow here alongside maple and juniper. The best way to access it is along the forested backroads between the cities of Përmet and Korçë *(p170)*.

The park is home to some stunning vistas thanks to its dramatic topography. These include sweeping sandstone cliffs, limestone escarpments, deep caves and, near the village of Bënjë, six thermal springs. Not far from Bënjë is Lëngarica Canyon, another highlight of the park, offering gasp-worthy vistas. A number of rare species thrive within this rural setting, including Eurasian otters, red squirrels, lanner falcons and eagle owls.

As well as the abundant nature, visitors are drawn to Fir of Hotovë-Dangëlli National Park for its remote tranquillity. There isn't much by way of information points once inside the park, but there are official campsites within its bounds, allowing visitors to get really close to nature.

Also within the park is the commemorative **Frashëri Brothers Museum**, which can be found in the northern zone. Three stone busts mark the entrance to this small museum dedicated to the locally born Frashëri Brothers: statesman Abdyl, playwright Sami and journalist-translator Naim. The trio were key figures in the Albanian National Awakening (Rilindja Kombëtare), and are considered some of the founding fathers of modern Albania *(p158)*. Their sacred burial spot is a 15-minute walk away from the museum. Using photographs and documents, the museum details the lives of these brothers in an insightful display set across ten small rooms.

TOP 4 ANIMALS IN FIR OF HOTOVË-DANGËLLI

Lanner Falcons
These large falcons hunt cooperatively, swooping down on bats and rabbits in the park.

Eurasian Otters
Spot playful pups hunting around the lakes of the national park by night.

Brown Bears
Deep within the forested sections of the park roam Eurasian brown bears.

Red Squirrels
Smaller than their grey cousins, red squirrels enjoy the park's varied flora year-round.

STAY

Farma Sotira

Located between the Fir of Hotovë-Dangëlli National Park and Korçë is this friendly log-cabin hotel and campsite. As well as accommodation, Farma Sotira offers riding, beekeeping and hiking experiences.

E6 7401 Ersekë
farmasotira.com

Frashëri Brothers Museum

Frashër

8 Çobo Winery

D5 Ura Vajgurore
9am-7pm daily
cobowine.com

The historic Çobo Winery is among the most famous wine producers in Albania. Its history goes back around a century, when the Çobo family first started to grow grapes on Berat's cool slopes. This continued for generations, until the wine industry was collectivized under communism; the winery moved back into family ownership in 1994.

Since then, the winery has been credited with pioneering a rebirth in Albanian wine and saving the white wine grape Puls i Bardhë, which was down to a single vine. Çobo was also one of the first wineries in the region to introduce sparkling wines.

Visits to the winery must be arranged in advance. On a tour, explore the well-maintained vineyard, which is also home to a centuries-old olive tree. The wine-cellar experience includes a tour around the winery's many oak barrels, where 100,000 bottles are aged each year. Visitors can see the micro-fermentations and blends which will create new styles of wine. There are also outdoor tastings, served with Berat's famous olives and cheeses.

> **Çobo Winery's history goes back around a century, when the Çobo family first started to grow grapes on Berat's cool slopes.**

Holta Canyon

D5 Near Gramsh

Covering a stretch of around 3 km (2 miles) near the town of Gramsh, the Holta Canyon (Kanioni i Holtës) is a hot spot for many outdoor activities, particularly canyoning. There is little by way of organization around the area, but experienced canyoners regularly arrive here from spring to late summer to hop, wade and swim through the current between rocky islands in the river.

In the vicinity of the Holta Canyon are a few busier nature spots, including the popular Kalaja e Tërvolit hiking area and the impressive Shpella e Kabashit caves.

Visiting the Çobo Winery and *(inset)* a bottle of Çobo wine ↓

Tomorr Mountain National Park

D5 Near Vodicë
akzm.gov.al

With its diverse landscapes and epic waterways, Tomorr Mountain National Park (Parku Kombëtar Mali i Tomorrit) showcases some of the best of Albanian nature. The park rises from the white water of the Osumi River in the west up to the Tomorr Massif, which peaks at just over 2,400 m (7,900 ft). Among these wild landscapes, plenty of beautiful local flora – from evergreen mistletoe and Bosnian pine to deciduous whitebeam and Turkish hazel – thrives.

While it's possible to drive through some sections of the national park, the best way to explore Tomorr is on a hike, using the city of Berat *(p162)* as a base. From there, it's possible to set out to see highlights like the gushing Sotirë waterfall, which tumbles from limestone cliffs. A six-hour hike from Berat is the park's 2,500-m- (8,100-ft-) high Maja e Partizanit peak, which is known as the "Olympus of Albania". The eponymous Mount Tomorr itself is frequented by hikers and pilgrims alike, thanks to its association with a number of key figures: the Virgin Mary, an Islamic caliph and Albanian lightning god, Zojz.

Elbasan

D4 elbasani.gov.al

Albania's fourth-most populous city, Elbasan has long been an important centre and commercial hub in Southern Albania. During the Roman era, the city was positioned on a key junction along the Via Egnatia, an important Roman highway; a stroll through the old town will take you along remains of this historic route.

Elbasan's old centre today bears the marks of its varied past. In addition to the Roman road, Byzantine rulers also expanded the city walls in the 6th century. Later, Ottomans reused old Roman and Byzantine bricks for new structures like **Elbasan Castle**.

The site of the castle dates back to the Roman era. Under Ottoman rule, it was further fortified, as 9-m- (30-ft-) high towers were built onto the castle and a river was redirected to serve as a moat. Sinan Pasha, one of the Ottoman Empire's Albanian-born Grand Viziers in the 16th century, funded a hammam, the ruins of

EAT

Real Scampis
Carved into Elbasan Castle, this restaurant serves local dishes.

D4 Rruga Xhaferr Kongoli, Elbasan
realscampis.com

Taverna Kala
Enjoy local dishes like beans and stuffed peppers at this taverna.
D4 Porta e Kalase, Elbasan 69 455 2951

Elbasan's 19th-century clock tower at dusk

which can still be seen inside the walls of the castle. By the 17th century, both the castle and city centre resembled a citadel, with nearly 1,000 leather-, metal- and silver-crafting workshops found within its grounds. Today, the castle is the beating heart of Elbasan and a favourite spot for a stroll, with green spaces, shops and venues dotted throughout. To explore the remains of the historic structure's grounds, follow the path from the main gate by the 19th-century clock tower – something of a city landmark – past alleys and shopfronts shaded by grapevines and pomegranate trees. Summer festivals, including a carnival, draw crowds to the city centre, transforming it into one big pavement café.

The streets surrounding and within the site of the castle are home to a number of notable historic buildings. The 16th-century Orthodox Church of St Mary is a mini architectural masterpiece, decorated with nearly 100 icons and a stunning ceiling fresco inside. On the same street stands the King's Mosque, built in the 15th century, with a Catholic church also nearby. These religious buildings are located around the same small area, a sign of the region's historic tolerance and pluralism in the face of changing empires.

Enjoying a café within Elbasan Castle and *(inset)* one of the castle's remaining old walls ↑

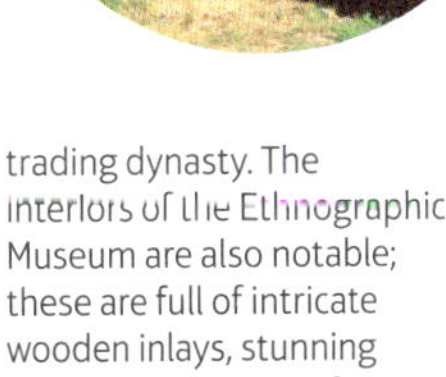

Inside an 18th-century mansion close by lies the **Elbasan Ethnographic Museum** (Muzeu Etnografik i Elbasanit). The museum is home to a collection of over 800 artifacts related to Elbasan's commercial and crafting history. The exhibition space includes displays of carpets woven during the Ottoman era and black-and-white photographs, as well as objects like historic coffee pots, furs and metals. Upstairs, there are multiple receiving rooms ringed by low benches, while a former workroom showcases a weaving loom once owned by the Sejdin family, a wealthy Elbasan trading dynasty. The interiors of the Ethnographic Museum are also notable; these are full of intricate wooden inlays, stunning frescoes, ceiling motifs and vintage shutters.

Elbasan Castle
Rruga Xhaferr Kongoli

Elbasan Ethnographic Museum
Rruga 11 Nëntori
8am-4pm Mon-Fri, 9:15am-1:45pm Sat-Sun
mee.al

EDWARD LEAR IN ELBASAN

During the autumn of 1848, English poet and artist Edward Lear (1812-88) spent time in Elbasan as he journeyed through Albania. Lear produced many paintings and sketches during his travels through the region, capturing views of Elbasan and the neighbouring Tomorr Mountain National Park, as well as scenes of migrant shepherds against the purple hills of Elbasan's Shkumbin River. These works were published alongside his writings about the country in his *Journal of a Landscape Painter in Greece and Albania*, published in 1851. In this publication, he made note of the city views he enjoyed from Elbasan Castle, as well as its flourishing vegetation.

Mountain peaks dotted with greenery in Shebenik-Jabllanicë National Park

Shebenik-Jabllanicë National Park

E4 Qarrishtë

Remote and tranquil, Shebenik-Jabllanicë National Park (Parku Kombëtar Shebenik-Jabllanicë) is Albania at its wildest. This high-altitude park was carved by glaciers, which left behind wildflower meadows, elevated lakes and sheer cliffs. These dramatic landscapes are among the greenest of Southern Albania's national parks; hiding within the dense forests are brown bears, grey wolves, golden eagles and Balkan whip snakes.

Although the park has a few roads, it's best explored on foot. Part of the High Scardus Trail *(p184)* runs through the area, but otherwise marked paths are few; using local guides or suggested routes is recommended.

The best time to explore Shebenik-Jabllanicë is between April and October, when any ice has melted from most of the routes, apart from those leading to the highest peaks like Mali i Shebenikut. Nearby villages – including Stëblevë, Fushë Studë and Qarrishtë – have a few campsites and homestays, while there are some rural restaurants and places to stay within the park.

Voskopojë

E5

In the 18th century, the town of Voskopojë was the heart of Albania's Aromanian community. From 1788, ethnic discrimination scattered the inhabitants, who left five churches behind. The Church of St Athanasius features martyr scenes painted by the Albanian artists Kostandin and Athanas Zografi. The Aromanian community also created the frescoes of the Church of St-Kolli. Icons from many of the churches were saved from socialist-era destruction and are now housed inside Korçë's National Museum of Medieval Art *(p170)*.

INSIDER TIP
Spring Water

Voskopojë's claim to fame isn't just its beautiful historic churches; the town is also known for its fresh mountain spring water. Locals here will often fill their water bottles directly from the source.

Frescoes lining the historic walkways of the Church of St-Kolli in Voskopojë

A bird's-eye view over one of the bends of the winding Vjosa River

CONSERVATION EFFORTS IN ALBANIA

Albania has long been home to impressive natural landscapes, from its legendary Accursed Mountains in the north to the Vjosa River in the south. Efforts are being made to conserve this nature: many parks were made nature reserves in the late 20th century, and Albania became one of the newest members of the International Union for Conservation of Nature (IUCN) in June 2024.

SUCCESSFUL PROJECTS

Conservation efforts across the region are ongoing, and there have already been plenty of successful projects. Rewilding work along the Vjosa River *(p166)* since 2014 has helped support the natural biodiversity of the area. The over 250 bird species of Divjaka-Karavasta National Park, meanwhile, have been protected from tourism developments along the coast here.

One of the wetlands of Divjaka-Karavasta National Park

LOOKING TO THE FUTURE

Conservation work is underway to protect areas like the stunning Shebenik-Jabllanicë National Park, one of Europe's most biodiverse areas, which currently remains under threat from pollution and deforestation. The Albanian Development Fund has planned a further roadmap to biosecurity in the area, including the planting of indigenous trees and support for ecotourism in the area.

A wild horse in Shebenik-Jabllanicë National Park

LAKE OHRID

E4 Between Lin and Pogradec albania.al/destinations/pogradec

Formed over four million years ago, Lake Ohrid is one of the world's oldest and deepest lakes. Its crystalline waters stretch across an expanse of 350 sq km (130 sq miles) and draw visitors seeking out the abundant nature and waterside adventures here. Today a UNESCO World Heritage Site, Lake Ohrid falls across the borders of Albania and the Republic of North Macedonia; 64 per cent of its shoreline belongs to the latter.

Nestled into the peaks at an altitude of over 690 m (2,200 ft), Lake Ohrid is something of a mountain oasis. Its sweeping expanse of tranquil waters is sourced by many underground springs and reaches depths of over 280 m (940 ft). Both the lake and its surrounding area are home to plenty of unique nature; over 200 endemic species, including sponge and trout, thrive in and around these waters. Lake Ohrid is a bird-watcher's paradise, too: swathes of reedbeds and flooded meadows shelter the likes of rare nightingales, reed warblers and golden orioles.

The area around Lake Ohrid has been inhabited since Neolithic times, but the most lasting legacy has been left by the Byzantine monks who used the tranquil setting to build several monasteries overlooking the lake; beautiful examples of these still remain over the border, on the North Macedonian shores.

The Albanian section of the lake's shoreline starts from the historic Lin peninsula and ends at the quiet beach of Drilon. Bathers, snorkellers, paragliders and experienced scuba divers – there are no diving schools on the Albanian shore – head here to enjoy the water, which remains bracingly cool all year long.

TOP 3 ALBANIAN SPOTS ON LAKE OHRID

Lin
A town with ancient roots, Lin is home to the old foundations of a Byzantine church.

Pogradec
This small city is perfect for a tranquil lakeside holiday, with many historic sights to explore.

Drilon
Peaceful Drilon is full of scenic alleys and charming teashops under weeping willows. Rowing boat hires are also available from here.

→ The expansive waters of Lake Ohrid, with the city of Pogradec

↑ A café terrace in the town of Lin, overlooking the waters of Lake Ohrid

CROSSING INTO NORTH MACEDONIA

Qafë Thanë is a scenic border crossing which overlooks Lake Ohrid. Buses from Tirana to Pogradec and Korçë pass within 2 km (1.25 miles) of it, where travellers can easily tackle the final short distance across the border on foot. Taxis (and the occasional bus service) wait on the other side, ready to help travellers complete the short 30-minute drive to the town of Ohrid in the Republic of North Macedonia.

← Enjoying Lake Ohrid's waters near the town of Drilon

CYCLE TOUR
TRANS DINARICA

Distance 75 km (45 miles) **Stopping-off points** Gramsh has many restaurants serving up delicious local fare **Terrain** Paved, undulating roads

Since 2024, the long-distance Trans Dinarica trail has charted a huge 5,500 km (3,400 miles) across the western Balkans, with the longest sections of the trail passing through Albania. Starting in the city of Elbasan, this scenic southern section takes cyclists past a socialist industrial experiment and an artificial lake, before ending in the timeless village of Moglicë.

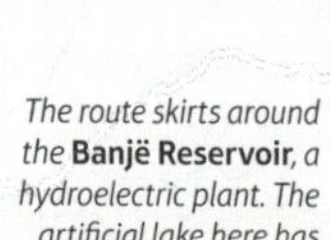

Just outside of Elbasan, pass the ***Kombinati Metalurgjik*** *factory to see remnants of the city's industrial history.*

Pedal out of ***Elbasan*** *(p176) from the city's main street, the Via Egnatia, which has been used by travellers for over 2,000 years.*

The route skirts around the ***Banjë Reservoir****, a hydroelectric plant. The artificial lake here has scenic bridges and hills.*

↑ Taking in the mountain and river views along the Trans Dinarica Trail

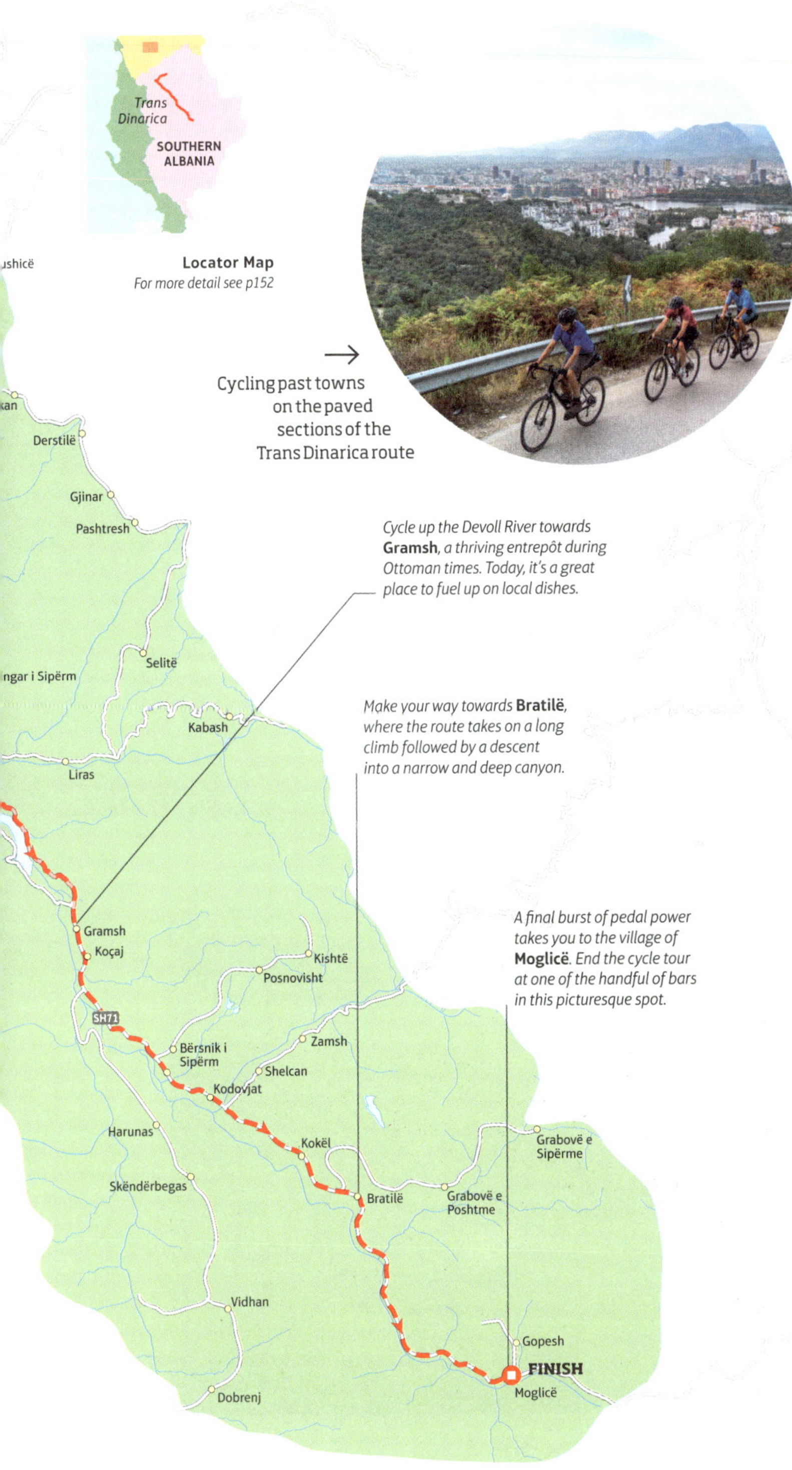

→ Cycling past towns on the paved sections of the Trans Dinarica route

Cycle up the Devoll River towards **Gramsh**, *a thriving entrepôt during Ottoman times. Today, it's a great place to fuel up on local dishes.*

Make your way towards **Bratilë**, *where the route takes on a long climb followed by a descent into a narrow and deep canyon.*

A final burst of pedal power takes you to the village of **Moglicë**. *End the cycle tour at one of the handful of bars in this picturesque spot.*

HIKING TOUR

THE HIGH SCARDUS TRAIL

Distance 17 km (10.5 miles) **Walking time** Approx six hours **Terrain** Hilly, at an altitude of over 1,100 m (3,600 ft)

The 360-km- (220-mile-) long High Scardus Trail – around one third of which lies within Albania – is a historic route across the Balkans. This short section of the trail leads experienced hikers through the breathtaking nature of Shebenik-Jabllanicë National Park *(p178)*, passing glacial lakes and wildflower meadows along the way. Due to high winds and snowfall in the area, the route can only be accessed from late May through to October; for exact routes and guidance, check the High Scardus Trail website *(www.high-scardus-trail.com)*.

START
Stëblevë

ALBANIA

Start from the picturesque village of **Stëblevë**, *located at an altitude of 1,130 m (3,700 ft), taking in views of the surrounding wildflower meadows.*

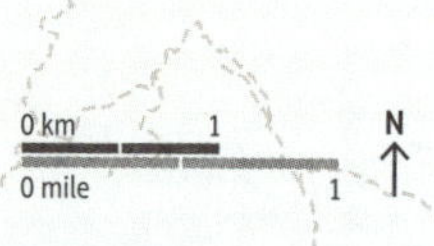

Strapit 1,975 m (6,480 ft)

Jabllanicë 2,257 m (7,405 ft)

↑ Enjoying epic mountain vistas along the High Scardus Trail

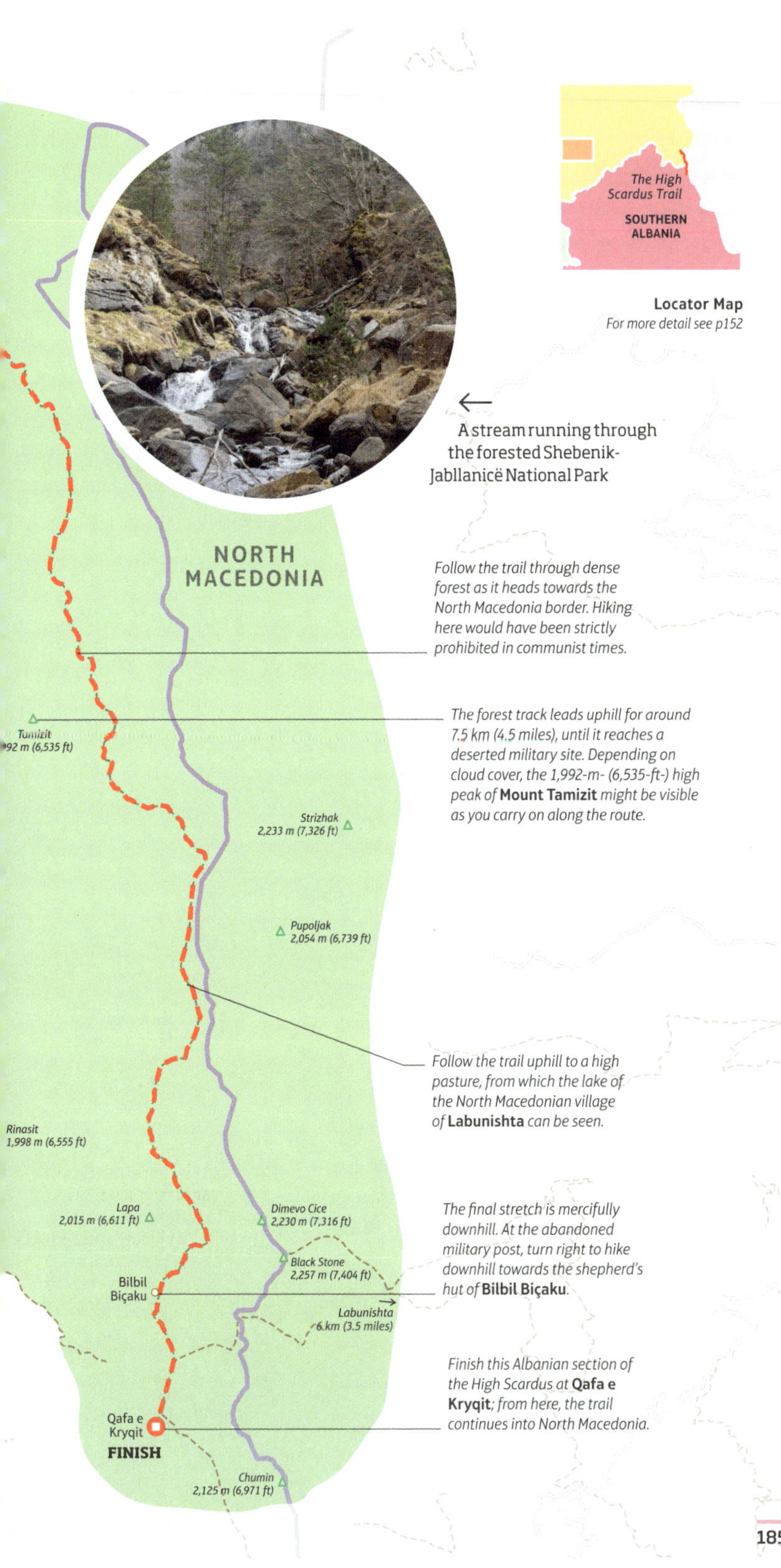

Locator Map

For more detail see p152

A stream running through the forested Shebenik-Jabllanicë National Park

Follow the trail through dense forest as it heads towards the North Macedonia border. Hiking here would have been strictly prohibited in communist times.

The forest track leads uphill for around 7.5 km (4.5 miles), until it reaches a deserted military site. Depending on cloud cover, the 1,992-m- (6,535-ft-) high peak of ***Mount Tamizit*** *might be visible as you carry on along the route.*

Follow the trail uphill to a high pasture, from which the lake of the North Macedonian village of ***Labunishta*** *can be seen.*

The final stretch is mercifully downhill. At the abandoned military post, turn right to hike downhill towards the shepherd's hut of ***Bilbil Biçaku****.*

Finish this Albanian section of the High Scardus at ***Qafa e Kryqit****; from here, the trail continues into North Macedonia.*

NEED TO KNOW

Driving to Hidrovor Beach, near Vlorë

BEFORE YOU GO

Things change, so plan ahead to make the most of your trip. Be prepared for all eventualities by considering the following points before you travel.

Passports and Visas

For entry requirements, including visas, consult your nearest Albanian embassy or check on the **Albanian Ministry of Foreign Affairs** website. Passports must have an expiry date of at least three months after the day you plan to depart Albania. Citizens of the United Kingdom, United States, Canada, Australia, New Zealand and the European Union can enter Albania for up to 90 days within a 180-day period.

Albanian Ministry of Foreign Affairs
W punetejashtme.gov.al

Government Advice

Now more than ever, it is important to consult both your foreign office and the Albanian government's advice before travelling. The **UK Foreign, Commonwealth and Development Office (FCDO)**, the **US Department of State**, the **Australian Department of Foreign Affairs and Trade** and the Albanian Ministry of Foreign Affairs offer the latest information on security, health and local regulations.

Australian Department of Foreign Affairs and Trade
W smartraveller.gov.au

UK Foreign, Commonwealth and Development Office (FCDO)
W gov.uk/foreign-travel-advice

US Department of State
W travel.state.gov

Customs Information

You can find information on laws relating to goods and currency taken in or out of Albania on the **Albanian General Directorate of Customs** website.

Albanian General Directorate of Customs
W dogana.gov.al

Insurance

We recommend taking out a comprehensive insurance policy covering medical care, theft, loss of belongings, cancellations and delays, and

reading the small print carefully. UK citizens are not eligible for free emergency medical care in Albania, and visitors must arrange private medical insurance. Be aware that outside of Tirana, medical facilities can be found lacking.

Vaccinations

No inoculations are required to visit Albania.

Booking Accommodation

Albania offers a wide range of accommodation, from luxurious five-star hotels to traditional mountain lodges, as well as short-term rentals. Rooms around the coastal resorts tend to book up quickly, especially in summer, so it's worth arranging accommodation in advance.

Money

Albania's currency is the Albanian Lek (ALL). Major credit and debit cards are accepted by most larger businesses, while prepaid currency cards and American Express are accepted less widely. Contactless payments are increasingly common across the region. For small purchases and in rural areas, cash is preferred. Some larger purchases, like car hire payments, may be priced in euros instead.

Cash machines (ATMs) and currency exchange booths (which often offer better exchange rates compared to ATMs) can be found in most places. It's customary to tip waiting staff 10 per cent of the bill, and to round up taxi fares to the nearest 100Lek.

Travellers with Specific Requirements

Albania still has some way to go to adapt to travellers with specific requirements. Few hotels and restaurants are adequately equipped, although things are improving. There are low floors and sound signals on some buses, while major transport hubs have toilets equipped for travellers with reduced mobility.

Language

The official language is Albanian. Although not official languages, English is widely spoken and Italian is more commonly known among older generations.

Opening Hours

Situations can change quickly and unexpectedly. Always check before visiting attractions and hospitality venues for up-to-date opening hours and booking requirements.

Opening hours in Albania can sometimes vary from what is advertised, depending on the day, season and location of the site or venue in question. Often, opening hours only offer an indication of when the site can be visited.

Although the opening times given in this book have been checked at the time of going to print, it's advisable to use them as a rough guideline only and check locally for up-to-date opening hours and booking requirements before visiting a point of interest.

Sunday Most shops are closed and public transport services are reduced.

Public holidays Schools, post offices and banks are closed.

PUBLIC HOLIDAYS

1-2 Jan	New Year's Day
14 March	Dita e Verës (Summer Day)
22 March	Dita e Nevruzit (Nevruz Day)
Mar/Apr	Eid al-Fitr
Mar/Apr	Catholic and Orthodox Easter Sundays and Mondays
27 Apr	Resistance Day
1 May	Labour Day
May/Jun	Eid al-Adha
5 Sep	Mother Teresa Day
22 Nov	Alphabet Day
28 Nov	Independence Day
29 Nov	Liberation Day
8 Dec	National Youth Day
25 Dec	Christmas Day

GETTING AROUND

Whether you're visiting for a short city break in Tirana or a rural Albanian retreat, discover how best to reach your destination and travel like a pro.

AT A GLANCE

PUBLIC TRANSPORT COSTS

TIRANA (CITY BUSES)

45L

Single journey by bus

TIRANA TO SHKODËR

500L

Single journey by bus

BERAT TO GJIROKASTËR

1,100L

Single journey by bus

SPEED LIMIT

MOTORWAY

110 km/h (68 mph)

INTER-URBAN ROADS

90 km/h (55 mph)

URBAN AREAS

50 km/h (31 mph)

Arriving by Air

All international air passengers will land at Tirana's modern **Mother Teresa International Airport**. The airport is located just over 15 km (9 miles) from the city and can be easily accessed via taxi or a 24-hour shuttle bus service; both options take 20–30 minutes to reach the city centre. There is also a bus service available from the airport to the cities of Durrës, Fier, Vlorë and Shkodër.

Currently, it is Albania's only international airport; however, airports in Vlorë and Kukës are anticipated.

Mother Teresa International Airport
W tirana-airport.com

Long-Distance Bus Travel

With few airports and no existing passenger railways, bus services are the mainstay of inter-city and international travel in, and from, Albania. Coaches are the best way to get between major cities like Tirana and Shkodër, which have regular services. In the absence of major service stations, many long-distance buses make rest stops at rural inns, where home-cooked food is often served.

It is also possible to travel beyond the Albanian border to neighbouring regions, including Montenegro, Croatia, North Macedonia, Kosovo and Greece; there are also some lines connecting Albania to Turkey and Germany. Travel documents are necessary for any international journeys.

Bus prices are often reasonable, and services are generally frequent. For a detailed list of routes, prices and timetables, visit the **Albanian National Tourism Agency** website.

Albanian National Tourism Agency
W albania.al/traveling-information

Tickets

Online bus ticketing is still being established, so passengers are advised to buy tickets at the bus station. Tirana has multiple coach stations; check the Albanian National Tourism Agency website for more information based on your destination.

GETTING TO AND FROM THE AIRPORT

Transport	Destination	Fare	Journey time
Bus (LU-NA shpk)	Central Tirana	400L	30 mins
Taxi	Central Tirana	2,500L	20 mins

LONG-DISTANCE BUS JOURNEY PLANNER

Buses are one of the best ways to travel through Albania. Plotting the main long-distance bus routes according to journey time, this map is a handy reference for travelling between Albania's towns and cities. The times given reflect the fastest and most direct routes available.

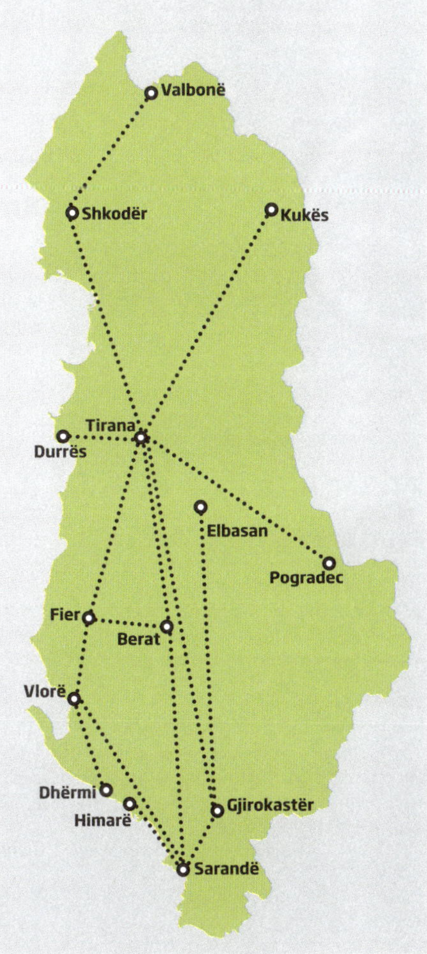

Tirana to Durrës	30 mins
Tirana to Berat	2.5 hrs
Tirana to Vlorë	3 hrs
Tirana to Pogradec	3 hrs
Tirana to Kukës	3.5 hrs
Tirana to Gjirokastër	4 hrs
Tirana to Sarandë	4.5 hrs
Shkodër to Tirana	2 hrs
Shkodër to Valbonë	6 hrs
Vlorë to Dhërmi	1.5 hrs
Vlorë to Sarandë	3 hrs
Fier to Berat	1 hr
Sarandë to Himarë	1 hr
Berat to Sarandë	4 hrs
Gjirokastër to Sarandë	1 hr
Elbasan to Gjirokastër	4 hrs
Berat to Durrës	2 hrs

Train Travel

For a short period in the 20th century, Albania had a small railway system in place. Much of this historic line has fallen into disrepair since the 1990s and is no longer in use for passenger services. There is, however, a railway line in the works, which will connect Durrës, Tirana and the Mother Teresa International Airport once opened.

Public Transport

The main cities and towns of Albania have public transport options, which mainly consist of bus services. In the capital Tirana, there are over 20 bus lines that connect key sights and areas of the city with its suburbs.

Many stops can be found in central Tirana, including near the Cultural Palace and behind the National Museum. Check the **Visit Tirana** tourism website for more information on all bus routes and stops throughout the city. Services run from 6am to 11pm most days; times may vary on weekends and public holidays.

Visit Tirana
W visit-tirana.com/explore-tirana/tirana-transport/tirana-city-transport

Tickets

It's not possible to buy city bus tickets in advance; instead, these should be purchased on the bus when boarding. The bus fare is 45L for a one-way journey.

Taxis

Metered taxis are ubiquitous across Albania and can be identified by their distinctive yellow colour in most cities and towns. Taxis can be hailed on the street and at transport junctions; in Tirana, there are also a number of taxi stands.

Boats and Ferries

With a wealth of lakes and a sweeping coastline that stretches for over 440 km (270 miles), Albania has no shortage of travel options on its picturesque waters.

International Routes

Travelling from one of the ports along Albania's lengthy coast is a great way to set out to other shores: some of the most popular destinations are other coastal towns in neighbouring countries, like Italy and Greece.

Albania has a number of established ports in Durrës, Vlorë, Shëngjin and Sarandë, and tourist services from these are growing. Some of the ferry companies that run international services from these ports include **Grandi Navi Veloci**, **Ventouris Ferries**, **Adria Ferries** and **Finikas Lines**.

For a day trip, it's easy to make the short journey from the city of Sarandë to the Greek island of Corfu. For longer ferry journeys, routes take passengers to the Italian ports of Bari, Brindisi and Ancona; most of these Italy-bound services depart from the ports of Vlorë and Durrës. Many of the long-distance ferries also offer some comfortable accommodation options.

Adria Ferries
W adriaferries.com/en
Finikas Lines
W finikas-lines.com
Grandi Navi Veloci
W gnv.it/en
Ventouris Ferries
W ventourisferries.com/en

Domestic Routes

Boat trips can be made in a few spots across Albania, but the **Komani Lake Ferry** is an especially lovely option. It takes passengers across the lake before disembarking close to mountain hiking trails.

Komani Lake Ferry
W komanilakeferry.com

Driving

Travelling around Albania by car is a good option for those short on time, especially when looking to visit its rural towns, remote archaeological sites or natural attractions. Petrol stations and rural food stops are plentiful along most of the main roads, although it can often be hard to find services that remain open late into the night. Keep in mind that street addresses often include only the street name and no building number.

Driving to Albania

Albania has around five road border crossings with neighbouring Montenegro, Kosovo, North Macedonia and Greece. It's relatively quick and straightforward to cross these borders outside the summer months, when they tend to get busier. Be aware that some border controls are open 24 hours a day, while others close at night; check the **Albanian National Tourism Agency** website for more information on opening hours. Travel documents are required when crossing international borders.

Albanian National Tourism Agency
W albania.al/traveling-information

Driving in Albania

Driving in Albania can be erratic at times and road traffic accident numbers in the country are high. Driving styles can often be aggressive, with honking and sudden stops a common occurrence.

Roads are not always in the best condition and some of the signage can be poor, especially on roads that pass through more rural areas. While on the road, take care to look out for uneven surfaces, roadworks and unmarked potholes, as well as vehicles driving past without any lights.

Traffic can be particularly bad in the centre of Tirana, but is generally minimal outside of the capital. Albania's modern highways and tunnels, like the Llogara Tunnel near Vlorë, have also done much to make it easier to navigate the region by road.

Car Rental

There are plenty of car rental options in Albania, and many local companies will arrange car hires on the spot with no advance booking required. The usual car hire caveats apply: check your hire car thoroughly and make sure that you read the insurance documents carefully before setting off. Age restrictions may apply to certain vehicle rentals, with some types requiring drivers to be at least 23 years old.

Rules of the Road

Driving regulations in Albania are similar to other European countries, and cars are driven on the right side of the road. To drive in Albania, you must: be over 18 years old; hold a valid, full driving licence; have a V5 registration document or hire car paperwork; and carry headlamp converters, a warning triangle, a first-aid kit and a reflective jacket. If driving in the winter months (between 1 November and 30 April), you must also have snow chains in the car with you. To drive your own vehicle in Albania, you may need to register the car in advance; the car must also bear a sticker indicating the country of residence.

Drink-driving limits are strict: the drink-drive limit is set at 0.01 mg/ml. Wearing a seatbelt is a must for both the driver and any passengers. Any children under the age of 12 years old sitting in the front seat require a child restraint, as do any children under the age of 4 years old sitting in the back seats.

In case of an emergency, call either the emergency services or the rescue police *(p194)*. If you are involved in a road traffic accident, you must wait for the police to arrive on the scene.

Parking

Well-signed parking zones and car parks are widely available throughout Albania. Parking spots usually fill up quickly near key driving destinations, especially close to the more popular beach areas and within busy cities. Currently electric vehicle (EV) charging points are few; if needed, check for charging locations in advance.

Hitchhiking

Hitchhiking is regarded as a legitimate mode of transport in rural areas throughout the country. Some drivers may expect a contribution towards fuel.

Cycling

With its lush nature and stunning cycle routes, Albania is a beautiful destination to explore by bike. Although you shouldn't expect much in terms of cycle lanes or urban cycle networks within the cities and towns, there are many routes throughout the region that make it easy to enjoy a countryside escape on two wheels.

In rural areas, paved roads and gravel tracks form part of official cycle routes through Albania. The most dramatic trails circle stunning lakes, like Komani Lake, and cross the epic Albanian Alps. The arrival of the Trans Dinarica cycle network in 2024 *(p182)* has improved the local cycle scene dramatically; for more information on this route, visit the **Trans Dinarica** website.

Bike hire is available from travel agencies in most tourist centres. Specialist agencies like **Cycle Albania** and **Beyond Albania** can provide everything from quality mountain bikes or e-bikes to organized cycle tours, complete with cycle hire, vehicle support and accommodation.

Cycle Albania
W cyclealbania.com
Beyond Albania
W beyondalbania.com
Trans Dinarica
W transdinarica.com

Cycle Safety

Bikes are still a rare sight on Albanian roads. Motorists don't always know how to treat their fellow road users, although the introduction of cycle routes means that this attitude is slowly changing. Most rural roads remain blissfully empty, but it's still essential to wear a helmet and cycle cautiously. Be aware that bike repair shops are few outside of Tirana.

Walking

Albania is rich with ancient cities, varied topography and national parks that make it ideal for hiking. The most historic cities – including Berat, Shkodër, Pogradec and Gjirokastër – are comfortably walkable, as is the busy capital, Tirana. Well-marked walking trails have sprung up across the country over the last decade. These include the **High Scardus Trail** *(p184)* and the **Peaks of the Balkans** trail.

High Scardus Trail
W high-scardus-trail.com/en
Peaks of the Balkans
W peaksofthebalkans.com

PRACTICAL INFORMATION

A little local know-how goes a long way in Albania. Here you can find all the essential advice and information you will need during your stay.

AT A GLANCE

EMERGENCY NUMBERS

POLICE	AMBULANCE
112	**127**

FIRE SERVICE	RESCUE POLICE
128	**129**

TIME ZONE

CET/CEST. Central European Summer Time (CEST) runs from the last Sunday in March to the last Sunday in October.

TAP WATER

Locals drink bottled water and use tap water only for washing, bathing and cleaning teeth; travellers are advised to do the same. In rural areas, mountain springs are usually a safe and delicious source from which to fill water bottles.

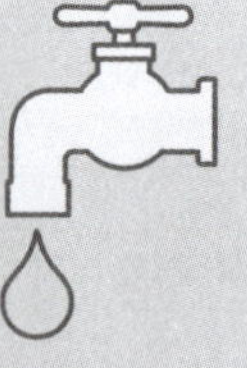

WEBSITES

Visit Albania

The official website of the National Tourism Agency offers an inspiring overview *(www.albania.al)*.

Personal Security

Albania is generally safe, but petty crime does take place. Pickpockets sometimes target known tourist areas and busy streets. Use your common sense and be alert to your surroundings. If you have anything stolen, report the crime as soon as possible at the nearest police station. Make sure to get a copy of the crime report in order to make a claim on your insurance. Contact your embassy or consulate immediately if your passport is stolen or in the event of a serious crime or accident.

Although same-sex relationships were legalized in Albania in 1995, same-sex marriages are still not recognized. It remains a conservative country in which LGBTQ+ communities are relatively rare. Tirana and the Riviera beaches feature a growing number of hotels, bars and clubs that welcome the LGBTQ+ community.

In the northern regions that border with Kosovo, some unexploded landmines may be present. Take care when hiking through this area and follow instructions on any signage indicating that landmines might be present. If in doubt, consult local tourist information points.

Health

Healthcare in Albania is adequate, although underfunded and understaffed health services remain an issue throughout the region and especially outside the capital. Currently, Albania does not have a reciprocal health treatment agreement for citizens of the UK, EU or US. For visitors to the country, payment of medical expenses is the patient's responsibility. For this reason, it's important to make sure that you have arranged comprehensive medical insurance before travelling.

At pharmacies, which can be found in most towns and cities, it's possible to purchase over-the-counter medication and remedies with ease. For more specific medications, a prescription authorized by a local doctor will be needed. Many minor health problems can usually be dealt with in a pharmacy, where trained staff can often provide professional advice.

For more serious injuries or illnesses, head to the emergency department of the nearest hospital. Most hospitals have English-speaking staff who can help with translations. There are also private hospitals available in larger cities like Tirana and Durrës.

Smoking, Alcohol and Drugs

Smoking remains popular in Albania, and puffing on a cigarette or vaping on outdoor terraces and at bus stations is commonplace. Although smoking is not permitted inside restaurants and bars, the rule is not always observed, especially in more rural areas.

The legal age for drinking alcohol is 18 years old. While many Albanians will enjoy a beer with friends or pair their dinner with a glass of raki, heavy drinking is uncommon. Alcohol is available to purchase almost everywhere, with little restriction on opening hours. However, drink-driving laws are extremely strict and the maximum blood alcohol level legally allowed when getting behind the wheel is set at 0.01 mg/ml *(p193)*.

Importing, supplying or possessing recreational drugs in Albania is a criminal offence. It's possible to receive a prison sentence of 5 to 10 years for drug possession offences and up to 15 years for drug supplying. In 2023, the Albanian parliament voted overwhelmingly to legalize the medical use of cannabis; recreational use of the drug, however, remains illegal.

ID

All Albanians are required to carry a biometric identification card at all times. It is therefore wise to carry some documents or at least a copy of your passport at all times while exploring Albania. Identification is also sometimes requested when purchasing a bus ticket.

Visiting Places of Worship

Albania is home to a number of historic places of worship, including mosques and churches, as well as remains of earlier synagogues and Roman temples. Many have a donation box, and it is polite to ask before taking photos.

Always dress respectfully when visiting places of worship: cover your torso and upper arms, and ensure that shorts and skirts cover your knees. Leave shoes at the entrance when visiting mosques. Try to keep noise to a minimum.

Responsible Travel

The ongoing climate crisis is having a big impact on Albania. Heatwaves and forest fires are becoming increasingly frequent, usually occurring from late June onwards. Ensure that you carefully dispose of cigarette butts and any flammable litter; starting a forest fire, even accidentally, is deemed a criminal offence in Albanian law.

Although the impact of overtourism is not immediately apparent at the vast majority of sights, it is a growing issue at some of the busiest tourist destinations, like Butrint and Gjirokastër. With this in mind, time your trip accordingly and consider travelling to the more popular sights during shoulder seasons instead. When staying in Albanian hotels, support water conservation efforts by reducing shower times and reusing towels when possible.

Mobile Phones and Wi-Fi

Free Wi-Fi hotspots are widely available in most city centres. Cafés and restaurants will usually give you their Wi-Fi password on the condition that you make a purchase. Pay-as-you-go SIM cards are available at Albania's ubiquitous mobile phone stores.

Avoid relying on mobile phones or other devices for navigation or emergency communications, especially when travelling in remote areas where mobile reception can be intermittent.

Post

Post offices are usually prominently located in city centres and town squares. Allow up to seven days when sending post to the UK, and up to 15 days for the US, Asia or Australia.

Street Addresses

Across Albania, addresses often include the street name but no building number.

INDEX

Page numbers in **bold** type refer to main entries

N

PHRASE BOOK

Albanian is a language from the Indo-European family. It's also the only surviving language of the Albanoid tongue, once related to Thracian, Dacian and Illyrian, that bears little relation to any nearby languages. A long history of trade and occupation introduced loan words from Latin, Slavic, Turkish and Italian.

The first written Albanian dates back to the 15th century but, as the language was scorned under Ottoman rule, printed books in Albanian only became widespread in the 20th century. There are two main types of Albanian: Gheg, spoken in the north, and Tosk, spoken in the south. Both dialects are mutually intelligible. The version of Albanian used today is based on the Tosk dialect.

GUIDELINES ON PRONUNCIATION

Stress: Stress usually falls on the second-to-last syllable of words.
Silent letters: The letter "ë" might be silent or sound very weak.
Double consonants: Double letters like "ll", "rr" are pronounced with extra emphasis.

The Albanian vowels are **a, e, i, o, u, ë**, and they are almost always pronounced the same way:

a	as in "father"
e	as in "bed"
i	as in "machine"
o	as in "more"
u	as in "moon"
ë	is usually silent or very weak

Pronounce consonants in Albanian like these English words:

ç	is like "ch" in "check"
dh	sounds like the "th" in "this"
gj	is similar to "j" in "juice", but softer
xh	sounds like the "j" in "jungle"
zh	like the "s" in "measure"
sh	like the "sh" in "shop"
ll	like the "ll" in "skill"
nj	like the "ny" in "canyon"
th	like the "th" in "think"
j	like the "y" in "yes"

COMMUNICATION ESSENTIALS

Yes	**Po**	poh
No	**Jo**	yoh
Please	**Të Lutem**	tuh **loo**tem
Thank you	**Faleminderit**	fahlehmin**deh**reet
Excuse me	**Më falni**	muh **fal**nee
Hello	**Përshëndetje**	puhrshen**deh**tyeh
Goodbye	**Mirupafshim**	meeroo**pahf**sheem
Goodnight	**Natën e mirë**	**na**ten eh meer
Morning	**Mëngjes**	**mun**jess
Afternoon	**Pasdite**	pas**dee**teh
Evening	**Mbrëmje**	**mbreh**myeh
Yesterday	**Dje**	dyeh
Today	**Sot**	sot
Tomorrow	**Nesër**	**neh**suhr
Here	**Këtu**	kuh**too**
There	**Atje**	aht**yeh**
What?	**Çfarë?**	**chfah**ruh
When?	**Kur?**	koor
Why?	**Përse?**	**puhr**seh
Where?	**Ku?**	koo
Which?	**cili/cila?**	**see**lee/**see**lah

USEFUL PHRASES

How are you?	**Si jeni?**	see **yeh**nee
Very well, thank you	**Shumë mirë, faleminderit**	**shoo**muh meer, fahlehmin**deh**reet
Pleased to meet you	**Kënaqësi që u njohëm**	kuhnah**chees**see chuh oo **nyoh**em
See you soon	**Shihemi së shpejti**	shee**heh**mee suh **shpay**tee
That's fine	**Kjo është në rregull**	**kyoh** usht ne **reh**gool
Where is/are...?	**Ku është/janë...?**	koo usht/**yah**nuh
How far is it to...?	**Sa larg është deri tek...?**	sah lahrg usht **deh**ree tek
How can I get to...?	**Si mundet të shkoj në...?**	see **moon**det tuh shkoy nuh
Do you speak English?	**A flisni Anglisht?**	ah **flees**nee ahn**gleesht**
I don't understand	**Nuk e kuptoj**	nook eh koop**toy**
Could you speak more slowly please?	**Mund të flisni më ngadalë ju lutem?**	moond tuh **flees**nee muh nuh**dah**leh, yoo **loo**tem
I'm sorry	**Më vjen keq**	muh vyen **keh**ch
How do you use this?	**Si e përdorni këtë?**	see eh pur**doh**nee **kuh**tuh
Could I possibly have ... (very polite)?	**A mundem të të kem ...?**	ah **moon**dem tuh kem
Is there ... here?	**A ka ... këtu?**	ah kah ... **kuh**too
Where can I get ...?	**Ku mund të marr ...?**	koo moond tuh mahr
How much is it?	**Sa kushton?**	sah koo**shton**
What time is ...?	**Në çorë është ...?**	nuh chor **ehsh**tuh
Cheers! (toast)	**Gëzuar!**	guh**zoo**ar
Where is the restroom/toilet?	**Ku është tualeti?**	koo **ehsh**tuh tooah**leh**tee

USEFUL WORDS

big	**madh**	mahth
small	**vogël**	**voh**gul
hot	**nxehtë**	**hndz**eht
cold	**ftohtë**	ftoht
Good	**mirë**	meer
bad	**keq**	kehch
enough	**mjaft**	myaft
well	**mirë**	meer
free (no charge)	**falas**	**fah**lahs
here	**këtu**	**kuh**too
there	**atje**	**ah**tyeh
this	**kjo**	kyo
that	**ajo**	**ah**yo
that (far away)	**atje larg**	**ah**tyeh larg
open	**hapur**	**hah**poor
closed	**mbyllur**	**mbee**loor
left	**majtas**	**my**tahs
right	**djathtas**	**dja**thtahs
straight on	**drejt**	drayt
near	**afër**	**ah**fur
far	**larg**	lahrg
up	**sipër**	**see**pur
down	**poshtë**	**posh**tuh
early	**herët**	**heh**ret
late	**vonë**	**voh**nuh
entrance	**hyrja**	**hyr**yah
exit	**dalja**	**dah**lyah
toilet	**tualet**	**too**ahlet
more	**më shumë**	muh **shoo**meh
less	**më pak**	muh pahk

MONEY

I'd like to cash these travellers' cheques	**Do të doja të ktheja këto çeqe udhëtarësh**	doh tuh **doh**yah tuh **ktheh**yah kuh**toh** **cheh**keh oothuh**tah**resh

Do you take credit cards/ travellers' cheques?	**A pranoni kartë krediti/ çeqe udhëtarësh çeqe?**	ah prah**noh**nee kahr**tah** kreh**dee**tee **cheh**keh oothuh**tah**resh
cheques?	**çeqe?**	**cheh**keh
bank	**bankë**	bahnk
cash	**para në dorë**	pah**rah** nuh **doh**ruh
credit card	**kartë krediti**	kahrt kreh**dee**tee
currency	**monedhë**	moh**neh**duh
exchange office	**zyrë këmbimi**	zyr kuhm**bee**mee
dollars	**dollarë**	doh**lahr**
pounds	**paundë**	**pah**oond
Albanian lek	**lek**	lek

SHOPPING

How much does this cost?	**Sa shumë kushton kjo?**	sah **shoo**meh **koosh**ton kyoh
I would like...	**Do të doja...**	doh tuh **doh**yah
Do you have...?	**A keni...?**	ah **keh**nee
I'm just looking	**Thjesht po shikoj**	**thye**st poh **shee**koy
Do you take credit cards?	**Mund të paguaj me kartë krediti?**	moond tuh **pah**goo yah meh kart kreh**dee**tee
What time do you open?	**Çfarë ore hapeni?**	**chfah**ruh **oh**reh **hah**pehnee
What time do you close?	**Çfarë ore mbylleni?**	**chfah**ruh **oh**reh **mbee**lehnee
This one	**këtë**	**kuh**tuh
That one	**atë**	**ah**tuh
expensive	**shtrenjtë**	**shtreh**nyt
cheap	**lirë**	**lee**ruh
size (clothes)	**masa**	**mah**sah
size (shoes)	**numri**	**noom**ree
white	**e bardhë**	eh **bar**duh
black	**e zezë**	eh **zeh**zuh
red	**e kuqe**	eh **koo**cheh
yellow	**e verdhë**	eh **ver**duh
green	**jeshile**	yeh**shee**leh
blue	**blu**	bloo

TYPES OF SHOP

bakery	**furrë buke**	**foo**ruh **boo**keh
bank	**bankë**	bahnk
bike hire	**qira biçikletash**	**chee**rah beechee**kle**tash
bookshop	**librari**	leebrah**ree**
butcher's	**kasap**	**kah**sap
cakes	**tortë/ëmbëlsira**	tort/uhmbuhl**see**rah
chemist's	**farmaci**	farmah**see**
fishmonger's	**dyqan peshku**	duh**chan** **pesh**koo
market	**dyqan/pazar**	**duhchan**/pah**zar**
hairdresser's	**parukier/e**	pahrookee**air**/ pahrookee**ehr** (male/female)
newsagent's	**dyqan gazetash**	duh**chan** gah**zeh**tash
tobacconist	**duhanxhi**	doo**chahn**jee
post office	**postë / zyrë postare**	**poh**stuh/**zy**ruh **poh**stahreh
shoe shop	**dyqan këpucësh**	duh**chan** kuh**poo**tsesh
supermarket	**supermarket**	sooper**mar**ket
travel agent	**agjent udhëtimi**	ah**jent** oothuh**tee**mee

SIGHTSEEING

archaeological site	**zona arkeologjike**	**zoh**nah ar**keh**ohloh**gee**keh
art gallery	**galeri arti**	gahleh**ree** ar**tee**
bicycle	**biçikletë**	beechee**kleh**tuh
bunker	**bunker**	**boon**kehr
bus station	**stacion autobuzi**	stat**see**on owtoh**boo**zee
cathedral	**katedrale**	kahteh**drah**leh
church	**kishë**	**kee**shuh
closed for holiday	**mbyllur për festa**	**mbee**loor per **fes**tah
library	**bibliotekë**	beebleeoh**teh**kuh
mosque	**xhami**	**jah**mee
museum	**muze**	**moo**zeh
national park	**park nacional**	park nahtseeoh**nahl**
rafting	**rafting**	**rah**fteeng
railway station	**stacioni i trenit**	stat**see**ohnee ee **treh**neet
tourist information centre	**qendër informacioni për turistët**	**chen**der eenformah**tsyoh**nee per tooree**s**tet
town hall	**bashki**	**bahsh**kee
vineyard	**vresht**	vrehsht

GETTING AROUND

baggage room	**dhoma e bagazheve**	**dhoh**ma eh baga**zhe**ve
bicycle	**biçikletë**	bichi**kle**të
bus	**autobus**	owto**bus**
car	**makina**	ma**kee**na
motorcycle	**motoçikletë**	motochi**kle**tuh
one-way ticket	**biletë njëanshme**	bi**le**tuh nja**ansh**me
return ticket	**biletë kthimi**	bi**le**tuh kthi mi
taxi	**taksi**	tak**see**
ticket	**biletë**	bi**le**tuh
ticket office	**zyra e biletave**	**zy**ra eh bee**le**tave

STAYING IN A HOTEL

Do you have a vacant room?	**A keni një dhomë të lirë?**	ah **keh**nee nyuh dhom tuh **lee**ruh
I have a reservation	**Kam një rezervim**	kahm nyuh rehzer**veem**
I'd like a room with a bathroom	**Do të doja një dhomë me një banjo**	doh teh **doh**yah nyeh **dhom**uh meh nyeh **bah**nyoh
What is the charge per night?	**Sa është tarifa për natë?**	sah ësht teh tah**ree**fah purr **nah**teh
Is tax included in the price?	**A është taksa e përfshirë në çmim?**	ah ësht taksah eh **purr**feershee ruh nuh chmim
Can I leave my luggage here for a little while?	**Mund të lë bagazhin këtu për një kohë të shkurtër?**	mund tuh luh ba**gazh**een kuh**too** pur nyeh **koh**tuh tuh **shkur**ter
double room	**dhomë dopio**	**dhom**uh **doh**peeoh
single room	**dhomë teke**	**dhom**uh **teh**keh
room with a bath	**dhomë me banjë**	**dhom**uh meh **ban**yuh
disabled access room	**dhomë me akses për personat me aftësi të kufizuara**	**dhom**uh meh **ak**ses puhr **pehr**sonat meh af**tsee** tuh koo**fee**zooarah
internet	**internet**	**een**ternet
shower	**dush**	doosh
porter	**roje**	**roh**yeh
key	**çelës**	**cheh**luhs
Wi-Fi	**wifi**	**vee**fee

EATING OUT

Have you got a table for...?	**keni një tavolinë për...?**	**keh**nee nyuh tahvoh**lee**nuh pur
I want to reserve a table	**dua të rezervoj një tavolinë**	**doo**ah tuh rehzer**voy** nyuh tahvoh**lee**nuh
The bill please	**faturën ju lutem**	fah**too**ruhn yoo **loo**tehm
I am a vegetarian	**jam vegjetarian**	yahm **veh**jehtahreeahn
waiter/waitress	**kamarier/e**	kahmahree**eer**/ kahmahree**ehr**
menu	**menu**	meh**noo**
wine list	**lista e verave**	**lee**stah eh **veh**rahveh
glass	**gotë**	**goh**tuh
bottle	**shishe**	**shee**sheh
knife	**thikë**	**thee**kah
fork	**pirun**	**pee**ron
spoon	**lugë**	**loo**guh
breakfast	**mëngjes**	**mhen**jess
lunch	**drekë**	**dreh**kay
dinner	**darkë**	**dah**rkay
main course	**pjatë kryesore**	**pyah**tuh kreeeh**soh**reh
starters	**aperitivë ose meze**	ahpehree**tee**vuh **oh**seh **meh**zeh
cafeteria	**kafene**	kafe**h**neh
canteen	**menzë**	**men**zuh
Chinese restaurant	**restorant kinez**	res**toh**rant **kee**nez
coffee shop	**kafene**	kafe**h**neh
café	**kafe**	**kaf**eh
local bar	**bar lokal**	bar loh**kal**
restaurant	**restorant**	res**toh**rant
sushi on a conveyor belt	**sushi mbi një rrip transporti**	**soo**shee mbee nyeh reep trans**por**tee
upscale	**i nivelit të lartë**	ee nee**veh**leet tuh **lar**teh
vegetarian	**vegjetarian**	veje**ter**ian

MENU DECODER

peshk	peshk	fish
supë peshku	**soo**puh **pesh**koo	fish stew
qofte	**choh**feh	meatballs
rizoto	ree**zoh**toh	risotto
ëmbëlsirë	umbuhl**see**reh	dessert
pjatë kryesore	**pyah**tuh kreeeh-**soh**reh	main course
fasule/grosh	fah**soo**leh/grosh	beans
gulash	goo**lahsh**	goulash
supë	**soo**puh	soup
vaj ulliri	vie oo**lee**ree	olive oil
mish zgare miks	mish **zgah**reh micks	mixed grilled meats
uthull	**oo**thool	vinegar
petulla	peh**too**lah	pancakes
piper	**pee**per	pepper
djath dele	**djahth deh**leh	sheep's cheese
pulë	**poo**luh	chicken
qengji	**chen**gee	lamb
pjate dytesore	**pya**teh **doo**teh soreh	side dish
proshutë e tymosur	proh**shoot**uh eh tee**moh**soor	smoked ham
kallamar i skuqur	kahlahmar ee skoo**qur**	fried squid
biftek	**beef**tek	steak
sufllaqe	soo**flah**cheh	souvlaki
peshk zgare	peshk **zgah**reh	grilled fish
sallatë	sah**lah**tuh	salad
sallatë oktapodi	sah**lah**tuh oktah**poh**dee	octopus salad
akullore	ah**kool**lohreh	ice cream
sardele të kripura	sahr**deh**leh tuh **kree**poorah	salted sardines
spageti me fruta deti	spah**geh**tee meh **froo**tah **deh**tee	spaghetti with seafood
perime	**peh**reemeh	vegetables
byrek	**bee**rehk	pie
tavë kosi	**tah**veh **koh**see	sour cream casserole
pastiçe	**pah**steetseh	pasta bake
fërgesë	**fur**gehseh	cheese and tomato dish
flia	**flee**ah	layered pancake dish
pispili	**pee**speelee	cornbread with leeks
tarator	**tah**rahtor	yoghurt, garlic and cucumber dip
lakror	**lahk**rohr	traditonal pie
syltjash	**seel**tyahsh	traditional rice pudding
hashure	**hah**shooreh	barley pudding

DRINKS

verë e bardhë	**veh**reh eh bardh	white wine
verë e kuqe	**veh**reh eh **koo**cheh	red wine
konjak	**kon**yak	brandy
çaj	**chah**ee	tea
ujë mineral me gaz	**oo**yeh meene**h**ral meh gaz	sparkling mineral water
kafe	**kah**feh	coffee
ujë mineral pa gaz	**oo**yeh meene**h**ral pa gaz	still mineral water
birrë	**bee**reh	beer
raki	ra**kee**	raki (alcoholic spirit)
ujë	**oo**yeh	water
bozë	**boh**zeh	bozë
dhallë	**thah**lleh	Aryan (yogurt drink)

HEALTH

I don't feel well.	**Muk ndihem mirë**	kook **ndee**hem meer
I have a pain in ...	**Kam dhimbje në ...**	kam **dheem**byeh neh
I'm allergic to ...	**Jam alergjik ndaj ...**	yam alerg**jeek** ndaj
asthma	**astmë**	**ast**muh
cough	**kollë**	**koh**lluh
dentist	**dentist**	den**teest**
diabetes	**diabet**	**diah**bet
diarrhoea	**diarre**	**diah**reh
doctor	**doktor**	dok**tor**
fever	**temperaturë**	tempehrah-**too**rah
headache	**dhimbje koke**	**dheem**byeh **koh**keh
hospital	**spital**	**spee**tahl
medicine	**medikament**	mehdeekah**ment**
pharmacy	**farmaci**	farmah**tsee**
prescription	**recetë**	reht**seh**teh
stomach ache	**dhimbje stomaku**	**dheem**byeh stom**ah**koo
toothache	**dhimbje dhëmbi**	**dheem**byeh **dheh**mbee

NUMBERS

0	**zero**	**zeh**roh
1	**një**	nyeh
2	**dy**	dee
3	**tre**	treh
4	**katër**	**kah**tur
5	**pesë**	**peh**seh

6	**gjashtë**	jahsht
7	**shtatë**	**shtah**tuh
8	**tetë**	**teh***teh*
9	**nentë**	**nen***tuh*
10	**dhjetë**	**djee***teh*
11	**njëmbëdhjetë**	**ny**ehm**beh**-dhyehteh
12	**dymbëdhjetë**	**deembeh**-dhyehteh
13	**trembëdhjetë**	**trehmbeh**-dhyehteh
14	**katërmbëdhjetë**	**kah**turm**beh**-dhyehteh
15	**pesëmbëdhjetë**	**peh**su*mbeh*-dhyehteh
16	**gjashtëmbëdhjetë**	**jah**shtu**mbeh**-dhyehteh
17	**shtatëmbëdhjetë**	**shtah**tu**mbeh**-dhyehteh
18	**tetëmbëdhjetë**	**teh**tu**mbeh**-dhyehteh
19	**nentëmbëdhjetë**	**nen**tu**mbeh**-dhyehteh
20	**njëzet**	**nyeh**zet
21	**njëzet e një**	**nyeh**zet eh nyeh
22	**njëzet e dy**	**nyeh**zet eh dee
30	**tridhjetë**	**tree**dhyehtuh
31	**tridhjetë e një**	**tree**dhyehtuh eh nyeh
40	**dyzet**	**dee**zet
50	**pesëdhjetë**	**peh**seh**dhyeh**tuh
60	**gjashtëdhjetë**	**jah**sht**dhyeh**-tuh
70	**shtatëdhjetë**	**shtah**tuh-**dhyeh**tuh
80	**tetëdhjetë**	**teh**tuh**dhyeh**tuh
90	**nëntëdhjetë**	**nen**tuh**dhyeh**tuh
100	**njëqind**	nyeh**cheend**
101	**njëqind e një**	nyeh**cheend** eh nyeh
102	**njëqind e dy**	nyeh**cheend** eh dee
200	**dyqind**	dee**cheend**
500	**pesëqind**	pehseh**cheend**
700	**shtatëqind**	shtahtuh**cheend**
900	**nentëqind**	nentuh**cheend**
1,000	**njëmijë**	nyeh**mee**yeh
1,001	**njëmijë e një**	nyeh**mee**yeh eh nyeh

TIME

one minute	**një minutë**	nyeh mee**noo**-tuh
one hour	**një orë**	nyeh **o**reh
half an hour	**gjysmë ore**	**gyee**smuh **o**reh
Monday	**e hënë**	eh **heh**nuh
Tuesday	**e martë**	eh **mahr**tuh
Wednesday	**e mërkurë**	eh muhr**koo**reh
Thursday	**e enjte**	eh **ehn**teh
Friday	**e premte**	eh **prehm**teh
Saturday	**e shtunë**	eh **shtoo**nuh
Sunday	**e dielë**	eh **dee**ehluh

ACKNOWLEDGMENTS

Contributors Suzy Pope, Tristan Rutherford
Senior Editor Keith Drew
Senior Designers Laura O'Brien, Stuti Tiwari Bhatia
Proofreader Kathryn Glendenning
Indexer Hilary Bird
Picture Research Kate Hockenhull
Publishing Assistant Simona Velikova
Illustrator Peter Bull
Jacket Designers Laura O'Brien, Stuti Tiwari Bhatia
Jacket Picture Researcher Lisa Zammit
Senior Cartographer Mohammad Hassan
Senior Executive Cartographic Editor James Macdonald
Cartography Manager Suresh Kumar
Pre Production Designer Rohit Rojal
Pre Production Coordinator Tanveer Zaidi
Pre-Production Manager Balwant Singh
Image Retouching Syed Md Farhan
Production Controller Kariss Ainsworth
Managing Editor Beverly Smart
Managing Art Editor Gemma Doyle
Senior Managing Art Editor Priyanka Thakur
Editorial Director Hollie Teague
Art Director Maxine Pedliham
Publishing Director Georgina Dee

The publisher would like to thank the following for their kind permission to reproduce their photographs:

Key: a-above; b-below/bottom; c-centre; f-far; l-left; r-right; t-top

123RF.com: Allasimacheva 20bl.

4Corners: Lucie Debelkova 141; Olimpio Fantuz 13br, 22tc; Chantal Reed 4.

Alamy Stock Photo: Album 56bl; Leonid Andronov 124–125bc; ArabianEye FZ LLC 59tr; Prisma Archivo 53tr; Associated Press 50cr, 57cl, 126br; Dennis Beetlestone 35br; Grazyna Bonati 73tr; Ian Bottle 102tl, 110; Neil Bussey 36bl; Chad Case 24br; Tim Chong 76br; Chronicle 55br; Cola images 57bl; Matjaz Corel 26tl, 29br, 148, 179tc; Roberto Cornacchia 26–27cb; Luis Dafos 51tl; Ian Dagnall 10–11bc; Vladimir Dimitrov 177tc; DPA picture alliance 20br; Dragoncello 71br; Pavel Dudek 13cr, 69, 82; Dynamoland 133tr, 177cr; Peter Eastland 42tc; Jackie Ellis 54–55tc, 159; Everst 101; Peter Forsberg 76tc; Mariano Garcia 12bl; Geogphotos 134bl; Godong 37cl; Narda Gongora 97tr; Gryf 178tl, 179br; Dmitriy Gura 167, 179; Damian Hadjiyvanov 144cl; Hemis 16c, 31tr, 32br, 33br, 34tc, 34cb, 58tl, 62, 66–67bc, 75tr, 78bl, 138–139, 140, 147, 158bl, 167tl, 181tr; Historic Collection 52tl; History docu photo 173tr; imageBROKER.com GmbH & Co. KG 42br, 53tl, 99bl, 106tc, 133cr, 145tr, 164, 165, 174, 176, 180cr; Ivy Close Images 55; Kamila Kozio 29tr; Lebrecht Music & Arts 54bl; Simon Leigh 67cr; Mauritius images GmbH 130br, 132–133, 178bc; Andrew Mayovskyy 119cr; Aliaksandr Mazurkevich 26tc; Tuul and Bruno Morandi 47cl; Alexander Mychko 109tr; Bardhok Ndoji 98–99tc; Ollirg 46tl; Maciej Olszewski 167tr; Panther Media GmbH 47tc, 74–75bc, 77; Photomecan 8, 38bl; Greek photonews 31cl; Edward Reeves 41, 184; Daniel Reiner 36–37; Panu Ruangjan 99c; Arda Savaşcoullar 8cl; 48tl; Alla Simacheva 45tr, 45br; Witold Skrypczak 157cl; The History Collection 35cl; The Picture Art Collection 159br; The Picture Pantry Ltd 43cl; Manfred Thürig 71cr; Jan Wlodarczyk 14c, 18c, 24bl, 24cr, 84, 112; Xinhua 50br; ZUMA Press, Inc. 67tc.

AWL Images: Walter Bibikow 156; Christian Kober 136.

Bridgeman Images: Julian Chichester 53br.
Cobo Winery: Cobo Winery 175bc, 175cr.

Richard Collett: Richard Collett 33cl.

Dreamstime.com: Andrew Angelov 142–143tc, 144–145tc; Esin Deniz 122cl; Digistockpix 169br; Evis Disha 10bl; Dudlajzov 68cl; Dynamoland 161bl; Gabweal 135tl; Dmitriy Gura 8–9cr; Jojjik 10tc, 101cr, 101br, 143br; Leonidtit 109bc; Aliaksandr Mazurkevich 49br, 56br; Milosk50 53cl; Christopher Moswitzer 22br; Alexander Mychko 109cr; Marketa Novakova 49; Photoschmidt 13tc; Saxanad 128bl; Alla Simacheva 43br; 161br; Spamd5 173bc; Aleksandar Todorovic 122; Valentinbutaru 158c; Elena Vlasova 20cr; Whpics 54br; Zatletic 55bl.

Getty Images: Ioanna Alexa 90; Anadolu 50tl, 51bl; Leonid Andronov 116–117; AscentXmedia 39, 31br, 39cl, 106, 168; Krzysztof Baranowski 169bc; Adnan Beci 168–169tc; Bettmann 57tl; Bloodua 12tl; CCat82 126tl; De Agostini Picture Library 56tl; DEA / ICAS94 55tr; Dmitriymoroz 52bl; Dynamoland 135br; EyeEm Mobile GmbH 38–39tc; Thomas Faull 20tc, 67tr, 118–119bc; Gestur Gislason 137; Nejc Gostincar 6–7c, 60–61c; Joanne Hedger 96cl; Hulton Archive / Stringer 54tl;

imageBROKER / Unai Huizi 149; Fani Kurti 51br, 52br, 58–59cb, 72–3bc, 129tc, 146bl, 162, 170; Ferdi Limani / Stringer 37br; Kateryna Mashkevych 125tc; Mlenny 32tl, Nastasic 141tc; Bardhok Ndoji 104–105; Ozbalci 48bl, 134cr; George Pachantouris 169; Resulmuslu 50cl; Thomas Roche 12–13bc; Marius Roman 57tr; RossHelen 11tr, 30bl; Chiara Salvadori 29cl, 172; Gent Shkullaku 57br; Martin Siepmann 96–97bc; Simon Skafar 186–187; Pintai Suchachaisri 46br; Unaihuizi Photography 30tl; Universal Images Group 125tr; ViliamM 88; Adonis Villanueva 108; Westend61 2–3c, 97tl, 111; Elton Xhafkollari 60–61, 185.

Hysen Belliu Group: Hysen Belliu Group 51cr.

MVRDV: Ossip van 78cl.

Robert Harding Picture Library: Goupi Christian 22cr, 27tr, 142bl; Unai Huizi 22bl, 93tl; ProCip 8tl, 47.

Shutterstock.com: Ajstudio Photography 91br; Elena Alex Ferns 26cl; Ioanna Alexa 74cr; Ungvari Attila 129br; Brilliant Eye 49cl; Darkdriver84 28tl; Dynamoland 40; Iurii Dzivinskyi 119tr; Everst 19c, 150; Tom Korcak 95; Leopictures 45; Lindasky76 122–123bc; Dedo Luka 91tr; Marketa1982 102bl; Andrew Mayovskyy 107, 130, 120–121, 180–181bc; Martin Mecnarowski 166–167bc; Mitzo 24tc; Doriana Musaj 157tr; Posztos 68; Nicola Pulham 70–71tc; Matthew Storer 28bl; Trabantos 79tr, 80, 154; Mazur Travel 92–93bc; German Vizulis 53bl; Zedspider 161cr.

Taproom by Pans Microbrewery: Taproom by Pan's Microbrewery 44tl.

Tirana Ekspres: Tirana Ekspres 51tr.

Tirana Film Institute: Tirana Film Institute 50.

Trans Dinarica: Matevž Hribar / Trans Dinarica 182, 183.

Uka Farm : Uka Farm 44.

Visit Berat: Visit Berat 51.

Visit Shkoder: Visit Shkoder 50tr.

Front flap images:
Alamy Stock Photo: Dmitriy Gura cra; Daniel Reiner cla; **Getty Images:** AscentXmedia bl, Simon Skafar c; **Shutterstock.com:** Nicolas Decorte br, Andrew Mayovskyy tc.

Cover images:
Front and Spine: **Dreamstime.com:** Aleksandar Todorovic c, bc, t; *Back*: **Alamy Stock Photo:** Everst cl; Aliaksandr Mazurkevich tr; **Dreamstime.com:** Marketa Novakova c.

For further information see: www.dkimages.com

Cartographic Data:
Maps/data sourced from OpenStreetMap and its contributors, available under the Open Database License (ODbL).

Contributors

Suzy Pope is a freelance food and travel writer for *Wanderlust* travel magazine, *The Independent* and *The Guardian*. She first visited Albania on a day trip from Corfu and immediately fell in love with the jagged mountains and fierce sense of hospitality. Numerous trips later, her favourite place in Albania is the shambling heart of Gjirokastër and she has a dangerous penchant for Albanian raki.

Tristan Rutherford has won seven journalism awards for his work in *The Times* and *The Daily Telegraph*. He has reported from 75 countries and written about Albania for *The Guardian*, *The Sunday Times* and the BBC. Tristan first visited Albania in 2002 and was beguiled by the friendly welcome and amazing food, which includes his beloved *pispili* (spinach and onion pie). His favourite Albanian destination is Butrint.

The contributors would like to thank the following for their help while researching and writing this guide:

Suzy Pope: Linda Alia; Elizabeth Gowing; Ana Koka; Bledar Kola; Alan Packer; Fabio Shkelqimi; Flori Uka; and her daughter Maeve, who was the size of a walnut on research trips to Albania.

Tristan Rutherford: Bledar Kola; Nikola Kola; Jorida Labaj; Mirela Kumbaro; His Excellency Qirjako Qirko; I Professor Vasil S Tole; Iir Tsouko; Erjon Uka; Flori Uka; and Edlira Zyfi.

First edition 2025

Published in Great Britain by
Dorling Kindersley Limited,
20 Vauxhall Bridge Road, London SW1V 2SA

The authorised representative in the EEA is
Dorling Kindersley Verlag GmbH. Arnulfstr.
124, 80636 Munich, Germany

Published in the United States by DK Publishing,
1745 Broadway, 20th Floor, New York, NY 10019, USA

Copyright © 2025 Dorling Kindersley Limited
A Penguin Random House Company

25 26 27 28 10 9 8 7 6 5 4 3 2 1

All rights reserved.

No part of this publication may be reproduced, stored in or introduced into a retrieval system, or transmitted, in any form, or by any means (electronic, mechanical, photocopying, recording, or otherwise), without the prior written permission of the copyright owner.

DK values and supports copyright. Thank you for respecting intellectual property laws by not reproducing, scanning or distributing any part of this publication by any means without permission. By purchasing an authorised edition, you are supporting writers and artists and enabling DK to continue to publish books that inform and inspire readers. No part of this publication may be used or reproduced in any manner for the purpose of training artificial intelligence technologies or systems. In accordance with Article 4(3) of the DSM Directive 2019/790, DK expressly reserves this work from the text and data mining exception.

The publishers cannot accept responsibility for any consequences arising from the use of this book, nor for any material on third party websites, and cannot guarantee that any website address in this book will be a suitable source of travel information.

A CIP catalog record for this book
is available from the British Library.

A catalog record for this book is available
from the Library of Congress.

ISSN: 1542 1554
ISBN: 978 0 2417 3322 6

Printed and bound in China.

www.dk.com

This book was made with Forest Stewardship Council™ certified paper – one small step in DK's commitment to a sustainable future.

Learn more at **www.dk.com/uk/information/sustainability**

A NOTE FROM DK

The rate at which the world is changing is constantly keeping the DK travel team on our toes. While we've worked hard to ensure that this edition of Albania is accurate and up-to-date, we know that opening hours alter, standards shift, prices fluctuate, places close and new ones pop up in their stead. So, if you notice we've got something wrong or left something out, we want to hear about it. Please get in touch at travelguides@dk.com